This book is dedicated to the friends and family who have supported and loved me through some hard times. You know who you are.

Special thanks are due to Caitlin Morrison who has given generously of her time and talent, and also to Rob Davies, Clark Lloyd and Andrew Gransden who have kindly contributed their pictures to this book.

recipes by Karen Davies

design & principal photography by John McMaster

I would love to hear from readers,
contact me at info@savourcookbook.com
or take a look at www.savourcookbook.com

1st Edition June 2017

Kickstarter sponsors

The initial production costs of this book have been raised by running a Kickstarter campaign. Below are some of the people to whom I owe particular thanks for helping me to get this book into physical form.

Their kindness, and faith in me, mean a tremendous amount.

In addition, the fact that so many old friends with whom I had lost touch have supported me has meant that this campaign has not only helped to make my project a reality, but greatly enriched my life.

Robert Davies & Laura Jones, England
Tanya Davies, England
Nicholas & Caitlin Finlay, N Ireland
Tony Green, England
Steve Hudson, England
Steve Klein, USA
Lani McGregor, USA
John McMaster, Scotland
Sophie Morgan, Scotland
Michael Morrice, England
Caitlin Morrison, Scotland
Brodie Nairn & Nicky Burns, Scotland
Martie Negri, USA
Philip Overton & Sonya Paul, Scotland
Matthew Pemble, Scotland
Pitzcalzean House, Scotland
Valeta Roach, Canada
Anthony Scala, England
Jo & Robbie Scott, Scotland
Cathryn Shilling, England
Dave Smith, England
Gary Walker, England

contents

Whaligoe Steps - seen from the sea side

Born in London, I spent my early years in Malta, a small island in the Mediterranean. After returning to London, then working in many countries, I now live in the far north highlands of Scotland - where I run a small restaurant at the top of a cliff, and bring a bit of mid-med flavour to the county.

For someone who has spent the majority of their life loving cooking, from the simplest of dishes to technical nightmares, it is ironic that my two earliest memories associated with food both involve no cooking whatsoever.

My mother was a terrific gardener, and had a wonderful orchard behind our villa. My favourite place to be was in the far corner, sitting on a cushion with a book, under the shade and fragrance of a large lemon tree. If I could also have a gnarly tomato, freshly picked that morning and chilled in the fridge, I was in heaven.

It does perhaps speak to my respect for fresh seasonal ingredients, and the recognition that sometimes, all you have to do is combine some wonderful flavours and textures, and put them on a plate.

When we lived in Valletta, before my father built our house in Attard, we attended a church in the city. Before church started, many people would bring their trays to the baker next door, covered with a tea towel, and they would be slid into the large oven to roast while the family attended the mass. On days when a sermon was appearing to drag on, you could see the 'mammas' fidgeting, as they thought of their dinner cooling next door. The smell when you left the church, as everyone collected their roasted dinner and rushed it home was amazing.

My early food history is all about Malta. We moved back there when I was about four years old, so really they are my first memories.

Food is very important on the Island. One reason for this is that the Maltese Islands are situated in what was a highly strategic place - in effect a staging post between Africa and what is now Europe. Sicily, Tunis and Libya are close.

It was settled originally by the early Phoenicians who were prolific traders and voyagers, and the language has the same basis as modern Arabic. Malta was under Roman rule in Antiquity, had an Arab period in the Middle Ages, was occupied by France between 1798 and 1800 (*they didn't like the French much*) and was part of the British Empire. The position of the Maltese Islands has meant that they can be a prize for other more militant nations, and for the vast majority of its history it has been under the sometimes less than benign rule of others.

In that context, food becomes a statement of identity. However, the Maltese are nothing if not pragmatic - if a nation is going to annex the Islands, they feel free to annex their food. So the influence of Arabic, Roman, French, and British cooking has been assimilated. A typical surname in Malta is Borg - surely not a coincidence - someone in the Star Trek writing team has a sense of humour, resistance is indeed futile.

Don't be fooled however into seeing Maltese food as individual components from other cuisines. Maltese dishes - even when they appear at first glance to be blatant copies of other dishes, have a character uniquely their own.

Another consideration is that the Maltese have suffered through many sieges. While most people who know anything of the Islands' history are aware of the immense suffering and devastation from the Second World War, previous wars have also been very bad news for the Maltese, and there is undoubtedly a 'race memory' of hunger which can perhaps explain why generally when food is available, it's served in GIGANTIC portions.

Over the years, I have done many things, travelled and worked in several countries and had friends with many different origins, but an abiding interest has always been cooking and learning about other people's food and culture. This book is therefore not limited to a specific cuisine, although it is heavily influenced by my most fond early food memories of eating in Malta, and of the dishes that my grandmother made.

For some reason, there is a relative paucity of Maltese cookbooks available, and many of those that are available, concentrate upon the post-war frugal version of Maltese food. While absolutely, corned beef, margarine and lots of semolina as a filler have their place where necessary, this doesn't always provide you with an authentic or delicious version of a dish.

My grandmother (*nanna*) was a great cook, and would encourage me to 'take the taste, and make it better'. She's right of course, we should keep the spirit of a dish, but if it can be improved upon with modern techniques and ingredients, where's the loss?

Having spent some years living out of suitcases in hotels, and eating too many overly sauced and rich dishes, it has always been the craving for a simple meal that wins through. During one particularly onerous contract in Poland, I was the only person left staying in the hotel over the Christmas holiday, and the staff who had got to know me quite well by that point (*as I ended up living in the hotel for 13 months*), presented me with a key to the kitchen area, and told me I was welcome to help myself to whatever I fancied cooking, and just to note it on their whiteboard.

That was undoubtedly the best Christmas present I could have had.

Time moves on, and I am now living in the far north of Scotland, in the county of Caithness. I love the coast, and have a small restaurant in part of my house, perched on the edge of a cliff and looking out to the North Sea.

Oddly, the coastline is in some ways quite similar to that in Malta (*albeit much cooler*). After five years of running my small restaurant, and giving hundreds of customers my recipes, either on the back of a waitress pad, or via email, I have finally decided to put together a book of my favourite dishes.

This book covers recipes I frequently serve in the Whaligoe Steps Café, both from my childhood and my travels around the world.

The reason for choosing to call this book **savour**, is that it entirely sums up my attitude to food, both preparing and eating.

The act of preparing food should be as much a source of enjoyment as the eventual eating of it. If this can be accomplished with friends and loved ones, great, but the solitary enjoyment of both should not be underestimated.

Take the time to enjoy the process.

You may notice that I do not include small quantities of olive oil or butter in the ingredients lists. It is after all expected that you would have something of that nature available. It is only specified where nothing else will do, and it is critical to the success of the recipe.

In the same vein, I have not specified salt & pepper, you should expect to be tasting and seasoning each dish to your personal taste.

I hope that you enjoy the recipes in this book, and even if at first some seem more challenging, they are generally straightforward and rewarding both to make and eat.

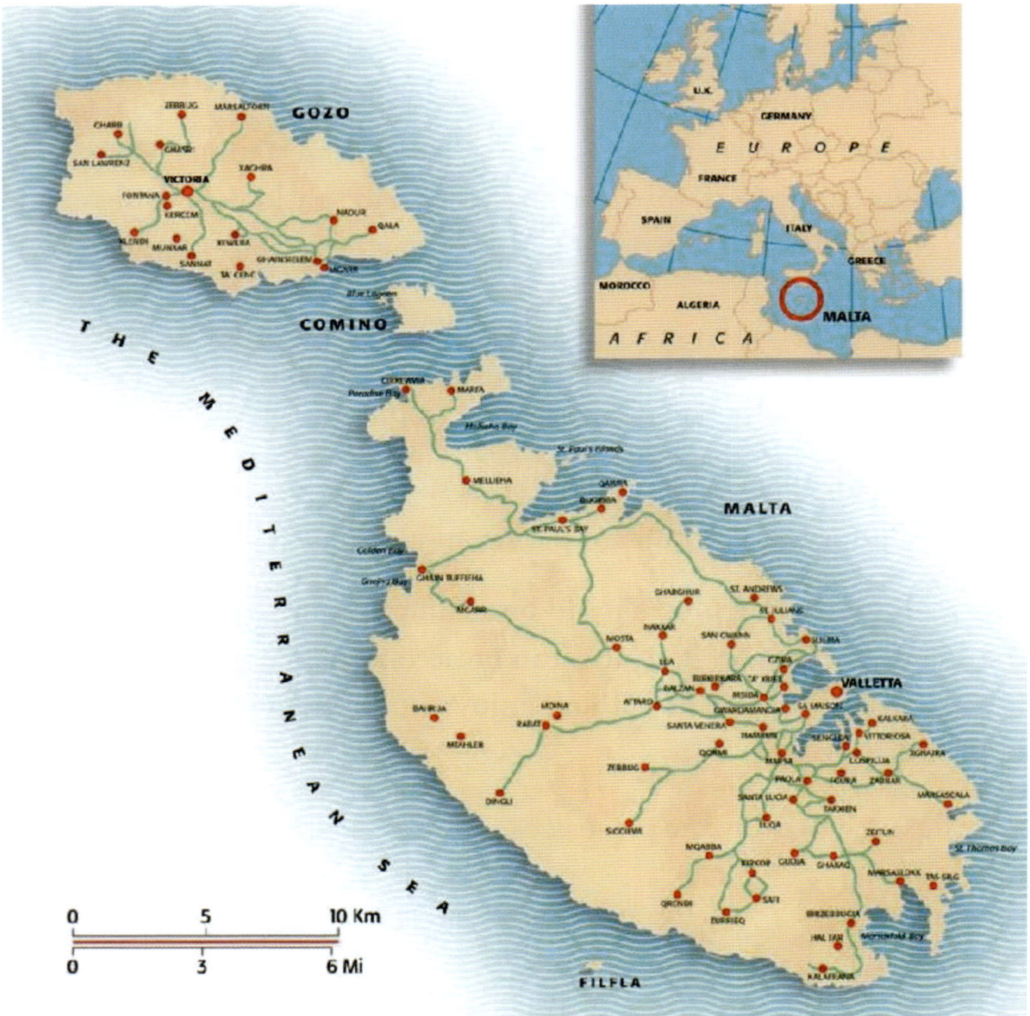

how to use this book

I very rarely tend to sit down to a formal 'meat & two veg' style meal these days. That's partly down to the fact that I am often working unsocial hours, so frequently end up eating alone.

That's pretty much a pattern of modern life for many people, whether they live alone, or as part of a larger family unit.

It's also down to the fact that I tend to eat less meat and fish, using them as a 'treat', and spending the extra for ethically sourced premium products. If you are working on a tight budget, to be honest, large quantities of meat and fish are not the best choice for protein anyway. Far better to use them as a texture and flavouring ingredient, rather than a bulk protein ingredient.

I'm not advocating giving up meat or fish, I love them both. By all means, you can choose to avoid them if you wish, but I think that taking a middle ground, of enjoying the produce that you do purchase, but making sure that you use every scrap that you have is a way that suits me better.

It shows a huge disrespect for the animal whose life has been taken, to toss away it's flesh because you haven't taken the time to treat it properly.

This book is therefore laid out in a similar vein to the way I offer food in my restaurant. Soups are a starting point (*and often, a finishing point for me*). I love a good soup with a hunk of fresh bread, hard to beat and it can range from a light tasty snack to a full meal in a bowl.

Then there are small dishes - these are things which may be served as part of a larger meal, offering some variety for you to choose from. They may also be very successfully used as individual dishes for one or more people.

One of the advantages of eating and cooking in a Mediterranean way, is that it is generally the case that when sitting down at a large gathering, it is common to have multiple smaller dishes, offering a greater variety of taste and texture. Of course many larger dishes can be made up from an assemblage of smaller ones, allowing you to create a more elaborate meal while still having the advantage of an easily understood and staged process.

The bread chapter is very close to my heart, as anyone who has ever eaten my food will know. I love bread, and I love making bread. However, for many years I stuck rigidly to recipes, as I didn't have the confidence (*or understanding)* of how bread really works. After many thousands of hours of practical experience, and experimentation, I have tried to give you an easy to understand but thorough description of the joys of bread making.

That chapter then segues into dough based products; pizza, pasta, dumplings and other such delights. From there, it seemed natural to move to sauces, and pastry.

This leads to cakes and other sweet things. Biscuits, both sweet and savoury are a natural progression.

I finish with a section on extras; seaweed, sauces, flavour boosts, and other useful items which can lift a dish.

You will see that there is a full index for the entire book, together with a vegan index, vegetarian index & gluten free index. In these indices, I have listed both recipes which fit directly into that category, or those which require very little modification to do so.

I hope that you find this book both useful and enjoyable, and would welcome feedback from you.

the 3 t’s

It is often said that the most important things to consider when choosing or creating a dish are the '3 T's'.

Taste, texture and temperature are all critical elements that contribute to our enjoyment of any food. This is especially true of soup making, where all too often thin vegetable purées are offered up as 'soup'.

A good soup should be a joy, a comfort. Either hearty and warming, or light and refreshing. Comfort in a bowl, or a kick in the palate.

It should never be boring.

Achieving this involves producing complex layers of flavour in your soup - and while I will be giving you some fantastic quick and easy soups, for others, you have to just bite the bullet.

Time and effort will often yield spectacular results.

I tend not to use the word 'stock', as that has been so de-valued by the nasty salty cubes that masquerade as flavour providers. Instead, you need to consider the flavour base, or profile of your soup, and then work within that to produce something interesting, and delicious.

Part of that process involves considering the flavour possibilities of scraps. Too much food is wasted, when it is not only perfectly edible, but a positive reservoir of additional flavour. The answer is, in my opinion, to consider what might be a useful flavour enhancer for a future meal, when cooking other things.

After sitting down to a roast dinner, few of us want to leap up and make a soup base with the bones and dripping - but what a terrible waste to put it in the bin. Get yourself some decent sized containers, and designate them as 'beef scraps', ' fish scraps’, 'chicken scraps' and so on.

Don't throw out parsley stalks - they may be too tough to chop into your finished dish, but they contain much more parsley flavour then the leaves - tossing them into your flavour base can never be a bad thing.

In the same way, we often end up buying a bunch or pack of herbs that is more than needed for a specific use - again, put them in the freezer, and use them in your next pot of bubbling goodness.

One thing to avoid though, and I speak from bitter experience, is putting small individual scraps into bags in your freezer. They invariably fall to the bottom in a chest freezer, never to be seen again, or end up frozen to a lump in the back of a crowded shelf.

Eschew small bags, go for just a few decent sized boxes and be judicious about what you keep. This is not an excuse to keep rubbish - if it doesn't look good enough to eat, you won't eat it - so don't clutter up your freezer with it.

One extremely handy tip if you are going to be using lots of whole spices, or bones in your bases, is to invest a a dozen or so fine mesh nylon jelly bags. They're not expensive, and you can place your bones, spices etc. in them, tie the top with a bit of string, and when you are ready to take out the bits, there's no mess and no unpleasant chewy bits for your diners to find in their meal later.

Bear in mind that often when a specific cut is required, such as an oblique cut *(which is frequently used to showcase a particular aesthetic quality of your vegetable)*, there can be significantly more waste. These scraps should wherever possible be utilised in your stock and vegetable purées.

Frugality is a state of mind - in a professional kitchen, your scraps are your profit margin being tossed in the bin, and you quickly learn to be creative with what you have paid good money for.

Why should your home kitchen be any different?

It shows respect to the product, and the people who produce it, to utilise everything you can wherever possible.

Texture, or 'mouth feel' is all important too.

However fine something might taste, if it feels unpleasant, you won't enjoy it. Soups can be 'thin' as a clear broth or brodo, or a hearty broth cooked with pearl barley which releases starch into your mix, giving you some thickening, and an entirely different (*but equally good*) experience.

'Mouth feel' is a term used by distillers in the whisky trade up here, and it generally refers to whether or not a whisky has been filtered before bottling or not. Filtered whisky has greater clarity, but unfiltered whisky has a better 'mouth feel'. This is because there is a tiny amount of fat within the spirit from the grain used, and even this small an amount will impact how the whisky affects the palate.

It's worth noting that this holds true for us with food too. Our palate loves fat, and sometimes a dish can taste a little flat. Often the merest sprinkle of a flavoured *(or even neutral)* oil can lift the dish and make it sing.

Another common misconception is that a cream soup is the same as a puréed soup. Not at all; you may certainly add cream to a puréed soup, and you may in some instances add some puréed vegetable to a cream soup, but the two remain quite distinct dishes.

Puréed soups tend to be quite thick but beware of making them too thick. A good test is to dip a wooden spoon into your soup - remove it, and use a *(clean)* finger to run a stripe down the back of the spoon. If the stripe remains clear for about 20 seconds, then your soup has a good thickness. If a clear ridge is able to be seen, it may be too thick, and if a stripe is not evident, it's not thick enough.

With a cream soup, it is quite possible that it might be reasonably thick, but that is usually a result of the other ingredients breaking down in the soup, rather than the cream itself.

In the past, this style of soup was frequently thickened with a roux *(a cooked mixture of butter and flour),* however this has fallen out of favour and tends to be used in sauce making (*where it originated and is relevant*), rather than in soup making, where it is a rather lazy way of adding thickness without taste, which I personally consider a waste of both time and calories.

If you wish to add texture, think about American chowders - they are often served with a small pack of salty crackers which are crumbled into the soup, or in Italy, a small dish of crunchy breadcrumbs, frequently fried with a little garlic & hot pepper may be offered to your table. Croutons are of course another welcome way of adding some texture.

It is also worth considering adding extra texture by using additional cooking styles with the same *(or a complementary)* vegetable or protein being used. In my cauliflower soup, I add beautifully tender and nutty florets which have been sautéed gently in butter and finish with a sprinkle of toasted almonds. If I have some available, some succulent pea tendrils add a little crunch and colour too.

Another point to bear in mind is that that when you have cooked a vegetable for a long time, to extract the maximum flavour from them into your flavour base, what remains can be a rather soft and unattractive vegetable. When making soups or broths which involve a long simmer I will therefore often have 'sacrificial' vegetables. They will give up their heart and soul to the soup and then be discarded. *(Although actually, my Scottie loves these, and knows to hang around when I am straining soup, as they are a welcome addition to her diet).*

Towards the end of the cooking time, the soup should be strained into a large basin and the base broth returned to a clean pan. The contents of your strainer can then be picked through to remove the bones, skin, gristle, spices, soft vegetables etc. All you want is lovely clean flesh returned to the pot, and a carefully prepared selection of fresh vegetables placed in the pot to simmer until just tender, therefore retaining flavour and freshness.

To this end, you should learn to cut your vegetables correctly - if you want to cook, you must learn how to handle the basic cuts. I'm not advocating some kind of Ninja knife skills here *(it might be fun, but it's completely unnecessary).*

There are three aspects to a professional cut, the first is that by keeping vegetables of a similar type a similar size and shape you enhance the attractiveness of the finished dish. The second is that it also ensures that your vegetables are cooked consistently.

The third reason so much emphasis is placed by chefs on the correct use of a knife, is fatigue. If you have ever had to peel and dice a sack of carrots, or a couple of sackfuls of potatoes, or produce a 'soffrito' for a dish to feed 200 people, you will know that after a couple of hours *(or usually, much less)* your hands cramp up. You can easily pinch nerves, and the chance of slicing some part of your own hand rather then the vegetables becomes ever more likely.

asparagus, pea tendril & cavolo nero salad
oblique cuts on the asparagus stems offer additional visual interest

We all like to keep our fingers if possible. So, learning good knife skills if you are working in that way is essential. *(Oh, and it looks cool too).*

If all you're doing is cutting up a few vegetables for a family soup - by all means hold the knife however you want, but please still cut them in the correct shapes if it is specified in the recipe.

Often you may be asked to just 'roughly chop' something. Use your head though - you may cut these to whatever style or size you find most convenient at the time, but still bear in mind that if you have a large variation in size you will have a large variation in the quality of what you cook.

If you're bothering to read this, I can only assume that it is not what you want.

The reason to specify a cut is therefore important to the finished product. Of course this holds true for any recipe, but in this case I am referring particularly to soup.

It can be unpleasant for people to have overly large chunks of meat or vegetable which can slip from the spoon, splash in their face, or just be awkward to eat. You want anyone who eats your soup to enjoy the entire experience, and the right vegetable *(or meat)* cut can enhance or destroy your soup.

knives top to bottom:
medium chefs knife
bakers dough knife
usuba style knife
small paring knife
filleting / boning knife
large chefs knife

Finally, we come to Temperature.

Again, a make or break situation.

Luke-warm soups are no good to anyone.

Serve a clear soup close to boiling at around 95°C , a cream or puréed soup should be served in the temperature range of 88°C to 93°C.

A chilled soup should be properly cold, I work on a range of 2°C to 8°C.

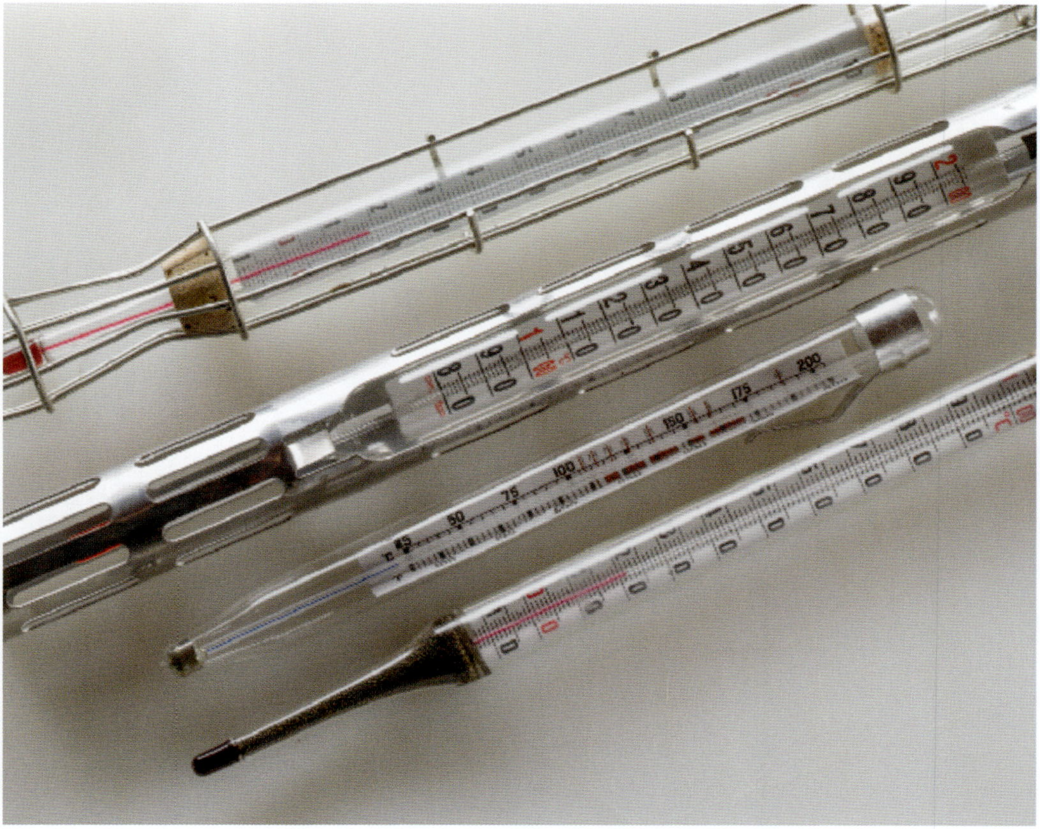

Range of thermometers top to bottom:
cage thermometer -10°C to 110°C
candy cage thermometer 80°C to 205°C
candy / deep fry thermometer 25°C to 205°C
floating cheesemakers thermometer -10°C to 110°C

common knife cuts

cooks (should) love knives - use them well

There are a number of regular knife cuts that are used in many recipes, each produces a standardised cut for a piece of food.

The two basic shapes for these cuts are the strip and the cube.

Strips are generally defined by width, from thickest to thinnest as "batonnet", "allumette", "julienne", and "fine julienne". The cube shapes, in order from largest to smallest, are the large, medium, and small dice, the brunoise, and the fine brunoise.

When dealing with vegetables of an appropriate shape, you should also consider the "plank', which can be the preliminary stage to a strip cut, or may be used as is, particularly for potatoes.

batonnet; translated literally from French, batonnet means "little stick". The batonnet measures approximately 6 mm x 6 mm x 5 cm to 6 cm.

It is also the starting point for the small dice.

julienne / allumette / matchstick; referred to as the allumette when dealing with potatoes, and sometimes also called the "matchstick cut" *(which is the translation of "allumette" from French)*, the julienne measures approximately 3 mm × 3 mm × 3 cm to 5 cm in length.

It is also the starting point for the brunoise cut.

fine julienne; the fine julienne measures approximately 1.5 mm × 1.5 mm × 3 cm to 5 cm in length.

It is also the starting point for the fine brunoise cut.

cube cuts - cuts with six even sides include:

large dice / carré; sides measuring approximately 2 cm.

medium dice / parmentier; sides measuring approximately 1.25 cm.

small dice / macédoine; sides measuring approximately 6 mm.

brunoise; sides measuring approximately 3 mm.

It is often used as a garnish for soup, or the base of a soffrito, typical vegetables used are carrot, onion, turnip and celery.

fine brunoise; sides measuring approximately 1.5 mm.

other cuts

paysanne; 1 cm x 1 cm x 3 mm. This cut may be either squares, triangles, circles or half rounds. In order to cut economically, the shape of the vegetable will decide which shape to use. All are cut thinly, about 1-2 mm thick.

lozenge; diamond shape, 1 cm x 1 cm x 3 mm.

fermière; cut lengthwise and then sliced to desired thickness, 3 mm to 1 cm.

rondelle; cut to desired thickness, 3 mm to 1 cm.

tourné; 5 cm long with seven faces.

chiffonade; finely sliced or shredded green leafy vegetables or herbs, which are used as a base, garnish or in soups.

savour

antonyms:

bland

dull

insipid

Roget's 21st Century Thesaurus, Third Edition Copyright © 2013

soup

Soup can take anything from 20 minutes to several days to prepare, but whichever route you choose, remember that your soup will only ever be as good as the ingredients and the thought that you put into it.

Soup is not an excuse to use soggy poor quality produce, however it is a great way to use up scraps that you have carefully stashed in your freezer, and once you are in the habit you will never throw out fish scraps, bones and herbs again.

Take a look at the recipes in this section, make them, enjoy them, and then use them as inspiration to create your own 'house' soups.

Phil Overton's borscht

This recipe is dedicated to Phil, a good friend and talented chef.

His chosen ingredients were duck, venison or sashimi, so I hope that he enjoys this recipe.

This soup is loaded with venison and beetroot. It's ideally paired with a good dollop of sour cream and a large glass of iced vodka.

Note: This recipe can be made very successfully using a pressure cooker.

ingredients:
1 kg venison *(shoulder is good for this - if bone in, use 1.5 kg)*
500g raw beetroot, coarsely grated
500g raw beetroot, finely diced
300g onion, finely diced
300g finely sliced potatoes
200g carrot, brunoise cut
3 bay leaves
few fronds of dill
2 tsp caraway seed
400g tin of chopped tomato
3 tbsp tomato purée
4 tbsp red wine vinegar
to finish:
sour cream
toasted caraway seed fresh dill
(**optional**) vodka *(I prefer bison grass vodka with this)*

method:

1) If you are using a whole shoulder of venison, break it down into small enough chunks to fit easily in your chosen pot. Otherwise, leave your meat in reasonably large pieces.

2) Using a heavy based pan brown your meat well and set it aside. Now fry your onion in the residue from browning your meat, scraping the pan well to ensure you get all the sticky goodness into your onions.

3) Once your onions are browned return your meat to the pot, and add your sliced potatoes, grated beetroot, carrot, bay leaves and caraway seed.

4) Pour in your chopped tomato, add the dill, and top up with enough water to submerge your ingredients.

5) Cover the pan with a close fitting lid, and simmer for 1.5 to 2 hours, checking occasionally to make sure sufficient liquid is in the pot and nothing is catching on the bottom.

6) When the meat is tender - lift it out of your pot and set it aside to cool enough to handle. Add your chopped beetroot and shredded cabbage to your soup, together with the tomato purée.

7) Simmer for 15 minutes.

8) If you've used a whole shoulder, shred and chop your cooked venison before returning it to your soup, together with the red wine vinegar.

9) Season to taste with salt and pepper, and adjust the balance as necessary to give you a rich but slightly acidic broth.

10) Finish with a generous spoonful of sour cream, a sprinkle of freshly toasted caraway seeds and a few dill fronds.

brown your onions well, taking care not to scorch them

red beet, golden beet and candied beet add visual interest

serve piping hot with sour cream & dill, together with a glass of vodka

sweetcorn & coconut soup

makes approx. 1.75 litres of soup

This soup is quick to make, and keeps well for several days if refrigerated. Always give it a good whisk before re-heating, as it can sometimes separate - this does not affect it in any way other than cosmetic.

This soup is best when fresh sweetcorn cobs are used to add flavour to the base - so when cooking sweetcorn at other times, save the cobs in your freezer and put them in the pot for this soup, it's well worth doing.

ingredients:

4 sweetcorn cobs *(or 400g frozen sweetcorn kernels)*
1 litre coconut milk
500ml water
2 medium potatoes *(peeled & chopped)*
2 medium onions *(peeled & chopped)*
¼ head of celery *(sliced)*
2 (or more) fresh chillies *(stalk removed & sliced lengthwise)*

to finish:

fresh padron chillies

method:

1) If using fresh sweetcorn, start by removing any husk and silk, then strip the kernels from the cob. Make sure that you retain the cob.

2) This soup is ultimately blended to give a smooth consistency, so don't worry over-much about the size & shape of your chopped vegetables - but do bear in mind that cutting them smaller will mean your soup cooks more quickly, which is great for retaining a fresh flavour.

3) Place the onions, potato, celery and chilli into your soup pot, together with the coconut milk. If you have prepared fresh sweetcorn, then you should place the cobs into the pot also.

4) Bring gently to the boil, and simmer until the potatoes are tender *(about 20 mins)*. If you have time, leave the soup aside to infuse for an additional 30 minutes. After this, you should remove the cobs from the soup, and discard them, they've done their job, and added a wonderful nutty corn flavour to the soup.

5) Now add most of the sweetcorn, either frozen or fresh *(but take care to hold back approx. 100g of your kernels)*. Bring the soup back to a gentle simmer for 5 minutes.

6) In a separate pan, cook the remaining sweetcorn until tender.

7) Blend your soup until it is smooth, and check for seasoning - at this point you may decide to add more chilli, but if so, add a little at a time, blend it into the soup and whisk that batch back into the main pot of soup before checking the flavour balance again.

8) Add the reserved *(cooked)* sweetcorn to your blended soup for some additional texture, and finally, add a few finely sliced padron chillies before serving.

pistachio soup with mint & leeks

this makes approx. 2 litres of soup.

A tremendously versatile soup, this may be served hot, or cold.

When hot, it is comforting and when cold, refreshing.

The pistachio nuts offer a creamy goodness and the large amount of fresh mint gives a fantastic counterpoint.

Do try it both ways, you won't be disappointed.

ingredients:
500g prepared leeks - green and white parts coarsely chopped
300g shelled pistachio nuts
1 clove of crushed garlic
½ tsp ground cumin
1.75 litres of chicken stock or if preferred, vegetable stock
120g fresh mint
juice of 2 lemons
to finish:
chopped pistachio nuts
chiffonade of mint
fresh lemon wedges

method:

1) Sauté the chopped leeks with a small amount of oil, in a heavy based soup pot. Cook until the leeks are tender, then add the crushed garlic, cumin, 1 tsp salt and the pistachio nuts - keeping a few back to use as garnish.

2) Cook for another couple of minutes, until the 'raw' flavour is gone from the garlic and cumin. Add your stock, either chicken or vegetable whichever you are using, and bring to the boil.

3) Simmer uncovered for 15 minutes, then remove from the heat and add your mint leaves (*again, keeping some back to use as a garnish*) and lemon juice.

4) Pour the mixture into a blender, and process until smooth. This will take a few minutes, be patient, you don't want a gritty soup.

5) Season to taste, then either serve hot, or refrigerate to serve chilled.

6) Before serving, check for seasoning development, and adjust if necessary.

7) Finally, make a fine chiffonade with the reserved mint leaves, and roughly chop the pistachio nuts, sprinkle a bit of both over each portion of soup before serving.

8) It can also be nice to offer a wedge of fresh lemon on the side.

cauliflower soup with buttery florets

makes approx. 2 litres of soup.

This is a subtle and creamy soup, and the final addition of the browned florets and toasted almonds gives a textural dimension which greatly enhances the whole dish.

ingredients:
approx. 1 kg cauliflower
200g onion,
100g celery
100g potato
freshly grated nutmeg,
approx 400ml double cream
to finish:
50g flaked almonds
125g unsalted butter

method:

1) Prepare your cauliflower as follows: strip away any green leaves, and discard them - everything else should be used. Break up the cauliflower into small florets, stripping them away from the main stalks. Chop the larger stalks into smaller pieces. Set aside 200g of the most even florets in a separate basin to use as your garnish.

2) Place the rest of the cauliflower in a heavy based soup pot, together with the sliced onion, celery & potato. Pour in enough water to just cover your vegetables, and bring to a simmer. Simmer for about 20 minutes, until the vegetables are tender.

3) Meanwhile, toast your flaked almonds until golden, either in a dry pan, or in the oven. They tend to go from slightly brown to black in a flash - you're aiming for a warm honey colour.

4) Gently melt the butter for cooking your reserved florets. Once fully melted, pour off the upper clarified layer, and pour the remaining milk solids into your soup pot to add some extra richness to the soup. *(Working with clarified butter will help to avoid you scorching your cauliflower).*

clarify your butter to avoid scorching your cauliflower,
but save the milk solids for the pot - frugality & decadence in one spoonful

5) Next, heat the clarified butter in a deep sauté pan, and toss in the reserved florets. Keep turning them in the butter, and continue to cook until they are tender. You should continue until they are gently golden all over, then remove from the pan with a slotted spoon and allow to drain in a sieve until needed.

6) Blend your soup until it is really smooth, then pass it through a fine sieve. Return it to a clean pan, and add the cream and some freshly grated nutmeg.

7) Whisk gently and heat again, seasoning with salt & pepper to taste.

8) Check the soup for thickness - you may want to add a little water to thin it down, or conversely, you may need to reduce it for some time. When you are happy with the flavour & texture of your soup, you are ready to go.

9) Serve in a shallow bowl with your cauliflower florets in the centre, pour the soup around the florets, and scatter with toasted almonds.

Lewis's zingy tomato soup

This soup was inspired by a young lad at a cookery class I ran in a local school. Lewis Gill was really keen to add lemon *(lots and lots of lemon)* to the soup he was making.

In truth, it was a bit too much, but even though the lemon flavour dominated, it was still pretty good. So I've developed the idea, and softened the citrus flavour, but it's still pretty zingy.

It makes a great change from a more conventional creamy tomato soup, thank you Lewis for the inspiration.

ingredients:
1.5 litres chopped tomatoes (*tinned are fine*)
3 tbsp tomato paste
1 large onion, finely diced
3 celery stalks, finely diced
1 medium carrot, brunoise cut
1 clove of garlic, crushed
2 oranges *(if you have blood oranges, use these)*
1 lemon
2 tbsp pomegranate molasses (*optional*)
to finish:
orange & rosemary oil (*see Valeta Roach's panna cotta recipe)*

method:

1) Using a small amount of olive oil in the bottom of your soup pot, gently sauté the onion and garlic until translucent, but not coloured. Add the chopped carrot and celery, and cook for a further minute or two to soften them slightly.

2) Add your chopped tomatoes and their juice into your pan, together with the tomato paste, and gently simmer for 10 minutes.

3) While the vegetables are simmering, remove the zest from your two oranges and your lemon using a potato peeler. Place the peels in a small pan together with the juice from your zested fruit, and bring it to the boil.

4) Simmer for 5 minutes until the peel has softened.

5) Put the mixture into a blender with a couple of ladles of the tomato and vegetable mixture. (*The aim is to have a textured soup, rather than a smooth uniform one, so don't blend the whole pot*). Blitz until smooth.

6) Return the mixture to your soup pan and stir well.

7) Taste, and season with salt and pepper as needed.

8) Check the balance of sweet and sour flavours - you should have a residual sweetness from the tomato and orange, and a zing from the lemon. If desired, add pomegranate molasses to taste. This will increase the sweet & sour note.

9) Serve hot or cold, with a drizzle of orange and rosemary oil over the top for additional flavour.

Maltese vegetable soup (ministra tal-haxix)

makes a (very) large potful.

This is similar to an Italian minestrone, but traditionally has a greater variety of vegetables - maybe because it was being made with whatever came to hand during the winter months.

In any case, this is a hearty and warming soup, and should always be served with fresh crusty bread if possible.

ingredients:
300g onions in small dice
200g carrots in small dice
200g celery paysanne cut
1 kohlrabi in small dice
1 turnip in small dice
2 large potatoes - thinly sliced
1 large or 2 small courgettes - in large dice
400g pumpkin *(or other squash)* diced
½ cauliflower in small florets
500g fresh spinach
200g shredded greens
4 tbsp tomato purée
450g tin of chopped tomatoes
small bunch of flat leaf parsley
2 bay leaves
1 small stick of cinnamon
to finish:
200g soup pasta
freshly grated Parmesan

method:

1) Make your soffrito by sautéing the onion, carrots and celery until tender. Add the tomato purée, and stir well to combine.
2) Now add 4 litres of water *(or vegetable stock)* to your pot, together with the tinned tomatoes, cinnamon stick, bay leaves, kohlrabi, turnip, potato and pumpkin.
3) Simmer for 10 minutes, then add the courgette and cauliflower.
4) Simmer for a further 10 minutes, and check the vegetables - they should be tender, but not mushy.
5) If they are ready remove the pot from the heat, and discard the cinnamon stick and bay leaves.
6) Set the soup aside and prepare the soup pasta. This should be cooked in plenty of boiling salted water, and drained when just cooked - rinse well with hot water to remove excess starch, and add a drop of olive oil to stir through and avoid the pasta sticking together. **Do not add to the soup at this stage**.
7) When you are almost ready to serve, re-heat the soup, and add the shredded greens, spinach, and finely chopped parsley. Serve in a shallow bowl over a generous portion of the cooked soup pasta, with a sprinkle of grated parmesan over the top.

leek, potato & celeriac soup

makes approx. 3 litres of soup

This is a truly delicious variation on a classic leek and potato soup, which has now become my preferred recipe.

It has wonderful texture, is not over-rich but is as comforting as a hug. This soup will become your friend, I guarantee it.

This soup keeps extremely well and I think is better on the second day, so it's great to prepare ahead and re-heat when needed.

However, make sure that when you are heating this soup that you don't go above a simmer, as otherwise you will run the risk of splitting the cream out of the soup.

It wouldn't affect the taste, but would spoil the look of the soup.

ingredients:
2 medium onions - chopped into small dice
2 large leeks - paysanne cut
4 sticks of celery - paysanne cut
4 large potatoes - chopped into small dice
1 celeriac bulb - roughly chopped
400ml double cream
100g unsalted butter - split into two equal portions
nutmeg to taste
to finish:
finely chopped flat leaf parsley
to finish (*optional*):
crispy bacon lardons

method:

1) Sauté your onions and chopped leeks in one portion of your butter, making sure that you only cook them at a gentle heat. You want to achieve a translucent state but definitely not brown them.

2) Stir in the chopped celery and potatoes, and mix well.

3) Add 2.5 litres of water to your pot, and bring up to the boil.

4) Simmer gently for about 10 minutes until your potatoes are tender, then remove from the heat.

5) Meanwhile, in a separate pan, boil the celeriac in just enough water to cover, together with the final portion of butter. Once the celeriac is soft, tip the entire pot (*including the water and melted butter*) into a blender, and blend until smooth.

6) Add this mixture to your pot of soup, together with the double cream and season with nutmeg, salt and pepper to taste.

7) Stir well, and check the texture. You should be aiming for a soup that has plenty of body from the chopped vegetables, but is not over thick. If it appears to be a little thin, you can thicken it slightly by blending a ladle of the entire mixture, and returning it to your pot. Don't do too much at once as the texture will change quite quickly.

8) When you are happy with the thickness of your soup, serve with plenty of fresh bread and a sprinkle of parsley.

9) If you must, add some crispy bacon lardons to the finished soup just before serving - it doesn't really need it, but for some people, pig is an essential part of this soup.

spiced fava bean soup

makes enough for 4 hungry people.

With a chunk of bread, this soup is more then enough for a meal and is a textural treat - add a fresh salad and you are truly spoilt.

This soup also freezes really well, and can be reheated to provide a quick and filling supper.

ingredients:
400g dried fava beans - soaked overnight
150g diced red onion
3 cloves of garlic, sliced
1 litre of chopped tomatoes
4 stalks celery - paysanne cut
2 medium carrots - brunoise cut
2 tbsp tomato concentrate
3 tbsp pomegranate molasses
2 fresh red chillies *(or more if you wish)*
2 tsp cumin seed
1 tsp coriander seed
½ tsp ground cinnamon
¼ tsp ground cloves
to finish:
finely chopped flat leaf parsley

method:

1) First, toast your spices - place the cumin and coriander seed in a dry pan, and heat until fragrant - mix with the ground cinnamon and cloves, and the finely chopped chilli and set aside.

2) Next, pick through the drained soaked beans and ensure that there are no small bits of grit or stone. Place the beans in a large pot with enough cold water to cover, and bring to the boil.

3) Boil for 10 minutes, then reduce to a simmer and add your spice mixture. Cook until the beans are tender - it varies, but usually takes about 30 minutes.

4) Meanwhile, gently sauté the onion, garlic, celery and carrots in a little olive oil, until lightly browned.

5) Add the tomato pulp, tomato purée and pomegranate molasses and set aside to infuse while the beans finish cooking. If the water level in the bean pot appears low, then add some of the tomato mixture to the pot to keep the level up.

6) Once the beans are tender, combine the two pots and stir well.

7) Set aside for at least 1 hour for the flavours to amalgamate and develop. It can also be left overnight in a fridge at this stage if you wish.

8) To finish, re-heat the mixture and gently mash some of the beans in the pot to thicken it slightly if you wish. You should have a soupy stew with a slight kick. If necessary, add a little more chopped tomato (*or chilli*) and adjust the seasoning to taste.

9) Sprinkle with a little chopped flat leaf parsley before serving.

Nanna's chicken broth

makes approx. 4 litres of broth

This broth is my son's favourite.

It takes some time, so allow at least a couple of hours for a really good result - although this can be done much quicker if you carry out the first stage in a pressure cooker. In either case, the second stage should be done in an open pot, to allow you to taste and adjust seasoning as you go.

The flavour is worth the wait.

ingredients for flavour base:
1 kg chicken thighs & 1 kg chicken wings
2 large onions
2 large carrots
4 sticks celery
3cm piece of cinnamon
2 bay leaves
¼ small lemon
2 tbsp tomato purée
small bunch of flat leaf parsley or bundle of parsley stalks
ingredients for finished broth:
200g pearl barley or 150g soup pasta
250g finely chopped onions
200g finely chopped carrots
200g finely chopped celery
200g finely chopped red peppers
finely chopped flat leaf parsley

method:

1) This broth is all about flavour so start by segmenting the chicken wings - each wing should give you 3 pieces; the tip, the wing blade and the drummet. It is worth spending the time at this stage, as it allows the wings to release more flavour, and also makes de-boning the soup later easier. For this recipe I tend to only use the wing tips and blades, the drummets may be set aside (*or frozen)* for later use. *(They are perfect as little fried chicken morsels, see fried chicken wings later in the book).*

2) Now place the chicken wing pieces into a tray and roast them at 200°C until they have picked up a good colour - this caramelisation has a large impact on the flavour and colour of your finished broth.

3) While they are roasting you may prepare the finely chopped vegetables, placing them in separate bowls for later use.

4) You will notice that there are also some whole vegetables specified and these simply need to be peeled and roughly chopped - they are used for flavour, and will be removed from the broth after the first stage.

5) When peeling the onion, try to retain the inner brown skin (*discarding the outer papery skin*), these can be added to your broth for a natural golden colour.

6) You can now start working on the broth - place the roughly chopped onion in a deep stockpot with a little olive oil, and cook at a moderate heat until browned but not burnt.

7) Add the chicken thighs and brown them lightly, then add the roughly chopped celery and carrot, together with the bayleaves, lemon, cinnamon stick and brown onion skin if it's being used.

8) Take your parsley, chop off the stalks and any tough looking sprigs, and add those to the pot also. Finally add 4 litres of water and bring to the boil.

9) Turn down to a slow simmer and as soon as the chicken wing pieces are a golden brown, add them to your stockpot. Continue to simmer the broth for at least 1 hour, and up to 2 hours if you have the time. During this time keep tasting your broth and when it is at a pleasing level, remove and discard the cinnamon stick and lemon. The broth will gradually reduce slightly and become beautifully fragrant.

10) During this time cook your pearl barley or soup pasta, whichever you prefer, in plenty of salted boiling water. Once tender, remove from the heat, drain and rinse well to remove excess starch. Stir through a small amount of olive oil and set aside.

11) Once you are happy that your base broth is tasty, you may now carefully lift out your chicken thighs and set them aside.

12) Strain the rest of your stock into a large colander, making sure to catch all the liquid in a large basin. Return the stock to your pan, together with the finely chopped vegetables you prepared earlier, and gently simmer until they are tender *(approx. 10 - 15 minutes).*

13) Meanwhile, carefully remove the flesh from your chicken wing portions, making sure that all skin, gristle and bone is removed.

14) Add the finely picked chicken flesh to your soup, together with the tomato purée and finely chopped parsley.

15) If you want a super chunky chicken broth, then shred in the meat from your chicken thighs, alternatively do as my Nanna did and serve them as the main meal with some boiled potatoes and green beans.

chicken soup with a stiff breeze

widows' soup (soppa tal-armla)

makes enough for 1 widow and her friend

This is a very tasty and hearty soup, and another Maltese speciality.

Many people assumed that because it is called 'Widow's soup', it must be a frugal meal. My grandmother said, not a bit of it - it's Widow's soup because you can't afford to cook it for the whole family.

Choose your reason, but I give you here a recipe for one very generous portion, or for two to share. *(After all, many widows have friends).*

ingredients:
1.5 litres good chicken stock
100g shredded cooked chicken
1 diced onion
2 stalks of celery diced
1 large carrot diced
½ kohlrabi sliced
1 small potato sliced
2 cloves of crushed garlic
¼ head of cauliflower in small florets
100g peas
100g broad beans
2 tbsp tomato purée
to finish:
2 x Maltese ġbejniet *(or other small semi-soft cheese)*
2 x soft boiled eggs *(see method for instructions)*
finely chopped flat leaf parsley

method:

1) First, prepare your eggs by placing them in a small pan of cold water and using a moderate heat, bring the pan to the boil. As soon as you reach a boil switch off the heat, and leave the pan covered for 1 minute. Remove the eggs from the pan and place them in a bowl of cold water to stop them from cooking further, and to make peeling them easier.

2) This method will give you a soft boiled egg with a white firm enough to allow you to peel it with care, and a liquid yolk.

3) Using a soup pot with a little olive oil, cook your onion, celery, garlic and carrot until tender but not coloured. Stir in the tomato purée and allow it to cook for a minute or two longer.

4) Add the chicken stock, kohlrabi, potato and cauliflower, then simmer for 10 minutes.

5) Add the shredded chicken, peas and broad beans, then simmer again for a further 5 minutes. While this is simmering, peel your eggs carefully - you don't want to break the white.

6) Place a ġbejniet and soft boiled egg in each soup plate, ladle over a generous helping of the soup and sprinkle with a little chopped parsley.

beef brodo

makes approx. 3 litres of broth

This soup is best made with either shin, or ox cheek. You ideally should have the collagen in these cuts to give the correct melting shredded texture to your cooked meat.

Sometimes, when I make this, I pre-smoke my bones - it's a great way of banging in a bit more flavour. I love the hint of burning wood in the finished broth.

If you have time, do try it - you may either hot or cold smoke them, using a smoker if you have one or by burning tea in a covered pot if you don't. It all works.

The malt extract is optional, but it does add a lovely background sweet and savoury note to the broth.

If you have any seaweed tucked away this is a good time to use some.

ingredients:
1 kg beef shin (*if not available you may use ox cheek to good effect*)
3 kg beef bones (*if possible*)
500g finely chopped onions
200g finely chopped carrots
200g finely chopped celery
50g double concentrate tomato paste
1 star anise pod
2 bay leaves
(***optional***) 2 tbsp malt extract
(***optional***) 20cm blade of frozen or dried kelp
small bunch of flat leaf parsley

method:

1) This is a light and flavoursome broth, perfect with a chunk of home baked bread. The idea when making any broth is to pack in flavour, and layer in some complexity if possible. This takes time. (*Of course, if you have some pre-cooked beef bones in your freezer, now's a great time to dig them out*).

2) Otherwise, start by caramelising your beef bones, either in a hot oven or on the stove-top with some olive oil. If they are in large pieces, chop them into smaller chunks with a cleaver - more surface area to brown means more flavour.

3) While that is happening, in a large soup pot gently brown your onions in a small amount of olive oil. It is very important that you don't burn them as this would ruin your broth - if they do catch, ditch them and start again.

4) When you have a toasty golden colour on your onions, remove them from the pot, and turn up the heat to brown off your beef shin (*or whichever cut of beef you have chosen to use*). There is no need to cut the beef as it will be shredded at the end of the cooking time, and it's easier to do that to larger chunks than smaller.

5) Make sure that you brown the meat in small batches, as if you over-crowd your pan, you will end up 'boiling' the meat, rather then searing it. What you want is a nice tasty crust. As pieces are ready, just remove them from the pot and continue with the rest of the meat. It may be necessary to add extra olive oil to keep the meat caramelising, don't worry about it as any extra will be tipped away. (*Remember, you are not trying to cook the meat at this stage, just sear the outside to pack in some more flavour*).

6) Once the meat and onion are browned, drain off any excess oil from the bottom of your soup pot but keep any nice crusty looking residue - this will dissolve into the soup.

7) Return the beef and onions to the pot and add the beef bones, star anise, bay leaves, and tomato paste. Chop the stalks from your bunch of parsley and add only the stalks to your pot too. If you are using them, this is a good time to add the malt extract and seaweed to your pot.

8) Pour in 3 litres of cold water *(or more if necessary - you should ensure the bones are covered by water)*, and bring to the boil, then turn down to a simmer, and keep at a low bubble for 1 hour.

9) After the first hour, check for flavour and at this stage you may choose to remove the star anise pod from the broth. Star anise has a wonderful affinity with beef, but you can have too much of a good thing - you should be aiming for a balance of flavours. Check the liquid level during this time, it may be necessary to top up with some more water as the broth reduces.

10) Simmer very gently for another hour, then turn off the heat and leave to cool for about 30 minutes.

11) Strain the broth into a large basin, be careful as it will be very hot and could splash and scald you.

12) It's usually best to use a large ladle or spoon to scoop out the solid elements. Lift out your beef, and set aside to cool slightly before shredding. Discard the beef bones and aromats.

13) Check the broth for flavour and season as necessary. Put the finely chopped carrots and celery into the hot broth, and simmer gently for 10 mins to soften and meld the flavours.

14) Finally, return the shredded beef to the pot, check seasoning again, and add a small amount of finely chopped parsley for a little freshness and colour.

beef & barley soup

makes approx. 2.5 litres of broth

This is a rich and warming soup both hearty and tasty. It's also an ideal recipe to use a pressure cooker if you have one, as it cuts down the preparation time dramatically. However, don't be tempted to cut out the essential browning of meat and bones - this is what gives you a full flavour profile.

Make sure you use a collagen-rich cut of beef - ideal cuts are shin, beef cheek or short ribs - these would ensure tasty beef that stays tender even after being cooked at high heat. When you brown your meat, keep it in larger pieces, it helps to keep it from toughening and also makes it easier to shred later.

Thai fish sauce, anchovies or seaweed will add additional umami flavour, and increase the savoury quality of the soup.

ingredients for base stock:

1 kg beef shin or cheek & 1 kg beef bones (*marrowbones are ideal*)
or if using short ribs, use 2 kg to allow for the bone weight
1 large carrot, roughly chopped
2 celery stalks, roughly chopped
1 large onion, inner skin retained, halved
2 garlic cloves
1 litre dark bitter beer *(or porter)*
1 litre good beef stock
few sprigs fresh thyme & 2 bay leaves
either a 20cm piece of kelp, 20g anchovies or 2 tbsp Thai fish sauce

to finish:

2 large carrots, chopped into fine dice
2 celery stalks, chopped into fine dice
1 large onion, chopped into fine dice
200g frozen peas
200g pearl barley

method:

1) Heat a large heavy based pan (*or your pressure cooker if you are using one*) with a little oil, or if you have it some beef dripping.

2) Sear your meat and bones well, making sure you have a rich brown crust without burning them. Sear in small batches, as you want the meat to fry rather than boil, removing as soon as appropriate. (*Overloading your pan would bring down the temperature*).

3) Once all your meat and bones are browned, scrape any sticky residue to release it from the bottom of your pan, and add the stockpot veg (*roughly chopped*) to this mixture. Sauté gently for a few minutes until the onions, garlic and vegetables start to gain a little colour, then return your seared meat and bones to the pot.

4) At this stage, you may add either the anchovy, fish sauce or seaweed to your pot. I harvest kelp from the beach at the bottom of my garden as I know the water quality is excellent. If you don't have a reliable source you may buy dried seaweed from many stores these days.

5) Place the thyme and bay leaves into your pot, together with the beef stock and dark beer. If your meat and bones are not submerged, add just sufficient water to do so.

6) If using a pressure cooker, fasten it now and bring to steam pressure - cook for 45 minutes, then allow to cool naturally until the pressure is released. If cooking conventionally, then you should bring to the boil, turn down to a simmer, and simmer for at least 2 hours until the meat is spoon tender, and falling off any bones.

7) While the base is cooking, you should rinse your pearl barley and bring it to the boil. Simmer gently for 25 minutes, then test - it should be tender but not mushy. Keep a close eye on it, and stop cooking as soon as you achieve the desired stage. Remember, it will be added to your hot soup, so a little underdone is better than a little overdone.

8) Once it is ready, rinse the barley with fresh water and set aside to cool.

9) Strain your broth through a fine sieve (*a chinois is ideal*), or a colander lined with a muslin cloth, into a clean large pan.

10) Pick out the meat and set it on a plate to cool a little before handling. If you have used marrowbones, keep those too, and discard the other flavouring ingredients. As soon as the meat is cool enough to handle, chop it into small pieces. Remember it will be eaten from a spoon, together with some of the other ingredients.

11) If you have cooked marrowbone, use a chopstick or other such implement to poke all the marrow out of the bone and add it to your pot. It will melt into the soup and provide wonderful flavour. Once you have done this you may discard the marrowbones, (*or give them to a grateful dog*) together with your other aromats.

12) Bring your broth up to the boil, and turn down to a gentle simmer. Add your chopped vegetables, and cook for 10 minutes, until the vegetables are almost tender. Now add your frozen peas and chopped meats.

13) To serve, place a generous spoonful of the cooked pearl barley in a deep soup plate and ladle over your broth.

14) Serve piping hot.

smoked haddock chowder

makes approx. 2 litres of chowder

Chowder should be served in a shallow bowl, with heaps of tasty flaked haddock, tender potato and creamy liquid.

If you happen to make some corn fritters and oatcakes to go alongside, all the better.

ingredients for fish stock: (*optional*)
500g fish scraps, bones, heads, prawn shells etc.
splash of vermouth or white wine
parsley stalks
lemon zest
main ingredients:
1 kg undyed smoked haddock
250g coarsely grated potato
500g sliced potatoes, approx ½ cm thick
250g finely chopped onions
200g finely sliced leeks
200g finely chopped carrots
200g finely chopped celery
3 bay leaves
400g frozen sweetcorn kernels
(or 4 fresh cobs, prepared as per the Sweetcorn & Coconut Soup with Chilli recipe in this section)
to finish:
250g smoked bacon lardons
600ml double cream
flat leaf parsley

method:

1) Like any other soup or broth, flavour is king. Ideally therefore you would start by making your fish stock, which will become the base of your chowder. If you have some fish scraps, prawn shells etc., get them bubbling in a pot with a little butter, and fry off until you achieve a little colour.

2) Add water to cover, together with a small splash of vermouth or white wine if some is available. If you are using fresh sweetcorn in the chowder, put the stripped cobs into this pot to add extra flavour to the stock. Add a curl of lemon zest, and the parsley stalks and let the stock bubble *(but not boil)* for about 20 mins. Allow the stock to cool slightly, then strain over a fine sieve or a muslin cloth ensuring that you have a clear and flavoursome stock.

3) Now, you are ready to start.

4) Measure the fish stock that you have prepared, and if there is not enough add sufficient water to achieve 1.5 litres of liquid - add this to your pot, together with the bay leaves.

5) Add your haddock to the pot and simmer gently for about 10 minutes, before lifting it from the pot. Don't worry about breaking it up at this point, it will be done later.

6) Add the sliced potatoes, leeks, carrots and celery to your pot.

7) Meanwhile, sauté the onion and grated potato in a little butter, until softened but not coloured. Then add that to your soup pot.

8) Once it has cooled slightly flake the fish with your fingers, or a pair of forks, trying to keep nice large flakes of fish. Some parts will appear slightly stringy or tough, and these should be set aside.

9) Place a ladle full of the chowder into a blender together with 350g of the frozen *(or fresh)* sweetcorn, and add the tough or stringy bits of haddock (*these will have the most smoke flavour, so once blended they will add to the flavour profile of the soup)*. Blend until smooth, and if necessary strain, before returning to your pot.

10) Place the flaked fish back into your pot and add the double cream together with the final 50g sweetcorn. Simmer gently for a few minutes and add a little finely chopped parsley.

11) Meanwhile, fry the bacon lardons until the fat is rendered and they are crisp and golden, drain them on kitchen paper and reserve them to scatter on the surface of the soup when it is served.

12) When ready to serve, ensure the chowder is served in warm bowls with plenty of crusty bread, or salty crackers. Garnish each bowl with some crispy bacon lardons and a sprinkle of flat leaf parsley.

lettuce soup with crispy bacon

makes approx. 2 litres of soup.

Lettuce is a natural soporific, (*as the Flopsy Bunnies discovered, almost to their cost*), so this is an ideal late supper dish.

ingredients:
500g well flavoured lettuce (*cos or baby gem is ideal*)
150g sliced onion
1 garlic clove
200g chopped celery
400g sliced potato
parsley stalks
to finish:
grated nutmeg
200g bacon lardons - fat rendered, and slightly crispy

method:

1) Gently sauté the onions in a little butter, taking care not to brown them. Add the garlic clove and potato, then cook for a few minutes more.

2) Add 2 litres of water, the celery and parsley stalks, and simmer until the potato is tender (*approx. 15 minutes*).

3) Add the chopped lettuce to the pan, and as soon as it wilts, blend to a smooth consistency. You may wish to add some more liquid if it is a little thick - some cream would work well too.

(Don't be tempted to add the lettuce to the pan too early, if you cook it for too long, it becomes bitter and unpalatable).

4) Season to taste with plenty of grated nutmeg, and some salt and pepper.

5) Garnish with crispy bacon lardons.

parsnip & pear soup

makes approx 2 litres of soup.

This is a pale creamy soup, with a subtle sweetness, which is both quick to make and delicious.

It may also be made very successfully without the addition of the cream, making it a very healthy (*and vegan*) option.

ingredients:
(***optional***) 2 litres vegetable stock
1 kg parsnips
400g onions
200g celery
500g pears
(***optional***) approx 400ml double cream
small bunch of parsley stalks (*possibly from your freezer)*
freshly grated nutmeg
4 blades mace
to finish:
1 additional parsnip to make fried parsnip chips

method:

1) First, prepare your vegetables by peeling and roughly chopping them. Do make sure that you set aside one parsnip for the garnish later.

2) The pears should also be peeled, and placed in a bowl of water with a splash of vinegar (*or lemon juice*), to stop them from oxidising.

3) To maintain the soups delicate colour it is important not to brown any of the vegetables. Therefore the parsnips, onion and celery are not fried first, but all roughly chopped then added to your soup pot with approx 2 litres of vegetable stock, or if not available, cold water.

4) Add the blades of mace, and a small bunch of parsley stalks to the pot. Bring to the boil, then simmer for about 20 minutes until the parsnips are tender - then add the pears and cook for a scant 5 minutes.

5) Purée the soup before adding the double cream *(if using)* and taste and adjust the seasoning. If the cream is not being used, it may be necessary to thin the soup slightly - simply add additional stock or water until the desired consistency is achieved.

6) Using a potato peeler *(or mandolin if you have one)*, slice fine shreds of the remaining parsnip and deep fry until they are crisp and golden brown. Drain well on kitchen paper.

7) Finish the soup with a good grating of fresh nutmeg and sprinkle over a generous heap of crisp parsnip chips.

green chilli soup

makes approx. 1.5 litres of soup.

I love this soup, it's served cool, but it's hot.

Team it up with a cold beer and a dish of tortilla chips.

Fantastic on a summers day.

ingredients:
500g padron chillies or 500g green bell peppers
50g green *(hot)* chillies
300g sliced onion
200g sliced potato
2 tsp cumin seed
1 large bunch of flat leaf parsley
1 large bunch of coriander
200g fresh spinach
to finish:
100g finely sliced padron chillies or fresh green pepper in small dice
coarsely chopped mixture of parsley & coriander
olive oil
(**optional**) sour cream or yogurt

method:

1) Slice your green peppers into rough chunks, and sauté gently in your soup pot with the onion & garlic until soft.

2) Add 1.5 litres of water, together with your chilli, potato & cumin seed. Bring to the boil, and simmer for 10 minutes until the potatoes are tender.

3) Set aside some of the parsley and coriander to chop for garnish, and put the rest into your pot together with the spinach. Cook for a scant 2 minutes, until the greens are wilted, and remove from the heat.

4) Blend the soup well until it is super smooth, then chill well.

5) Once the soup is chilled, taste and adjust seasoning, add the finely diced green or padron pepper and chopped herbs. Drizzle with a little olive oil and enjoy.

6) If you wish, a dollop of sour cream or yogurt will mitigate the heat, and give you something extra to dip your tortilla chips in.

Maltese fish broth (aljotta)

makes approx. 2 litres of broth.

Aljotta is a fish broth, laden with garlic and herbs.

Any larger pieces of fish that are poached in the broth would usually be removed, kept warm and served as the main meal with vegetables or salad. Two meals from one pot - a very Maltese process.

ingredients for fish broth flavour base:

Raid your freezer (*or speak nicely to your fishmonger*). You should have at least 1 kg of fish scraps, bones, heads, lobster shells - whatever you have saved.

1 large onion
1 carrot
3 stalks of celery - all roughly chopped.
2 bay leaves
the peeled zest of ½ lemon
1 tsp dried marjoram
1 tbsp coriander seeds parsley stalks
1 bottle white wine

ingredients for finishing fish broth:

3 small squid - sliced thinly
100g prawns - chopped
(hopefully you have put their shells into the 1st stage broth)
1 tbsp tomato paste
125g short grain rice (*soaked in water for at least 30 minutes*)
1 large carrot - brunoise cut
2 medium onions - fine dice cut
6 cloves of garlic peeled and the cloves finely sliced
2 large ripe tomatoes - skinned and chopped into small dice
3 tbsp finely chopped parsley
2 tbsp finely chopped mint

method:

1) In a large heavy based pan *(you want a good bit of surface area to brown your fish bits in)* pour a splash of olive oil, bring up to heat and fry the fish scraps and shells until they have gained some colour for caramelisation, but make sure you don't scorch them.

2) Next, pour over the bottle of white wine together with enough water to cover if necessary. Add the onion, celery, carrot and bay leaves from the first stage - just chop them into rough chunks as they will ultimately be discarded. Add the marjoram and parsley stalks together with the coriander seeds.

3) Simmer for about 30 minutes, while the broth is simmering you can prepare the vegetables, herbs and fish for the next stage.

4) Strain your broth through a muslin cloth to ensure that no small bones remain in the broth. Measure the amount of broth which you have remaining, and if it is less then 2 litres make it up with some water.

5) In a separate pan, cook the rice in plenty of boiling water until just tender - it will absorb some liquid from the broth, so do make sure you don't overcook it at this stage. Rinse the rice and set aside to cool.

6) In a clean pan with a small amount of olive oil, fry the onions until they are translucent. Add the tomato paste, diced fresh tomatoes, sliced garlic, brunoise carrots and your measured 2 litres of fish stock mixture. Simmer for 10 minutes then add the finely sliced squid, chopped prawns and finely chopped herbs. Cook for a scant 2 minutes until the squid and prawns have just lost their translucency, and remove from the heat.

7) To serve, place a scoop of rice in a shallow soup bowl, ladle over the fish broth and add a final squeeze of lemon.

spiced tomato soup with lobster

makes 4 servings as a main course, or 8 servings as a first course soup.

This is certainly a more luxurious and complex soup than many, but for special occasions or just as an indulgent treat it is well worth the effort.

Although similar to a Lobster Bisque, it is less rich and a little less 'fishy' which makes it appealing to a broader audience.

This is a great Boxing Day or celebration lunch, as it is delicious, decadent and can be prepared almost entirely ahead of time. Perfect.

ingredients for flavour base:
4 medium size live lobsters
curl of lemon zest
1 litre white grape juice or white wine if preferred
2 medium sized onions
2 stalks of celery
3cm stick of cinnamon
small bunch of flat leaf parsley
ingredients for spiced tomato soup:
tail, knuckle & claw meat from the 4 prepared lobsters
1 litre tomato passata
4 medium onions finely chopped
2 garlic cloves finely chopped
4 stalks of celery finely chopped
1 fresh red chilli - de-seeded & finely chopped
finely grated zest of 2 oranges
3 tablespoons pomegranate molasses
to finish:
400ml sour cream
500g unsalted butter

to prepare the lobsters

First, you have to deal with your lobsters - if you really can't do this then go ahead and buy cooked ones, if you must, but it will adversely affect the flavour of your soup.

So, assuming that you have gone ahead with buying your live lobsters there are a couple of things to bear in mind - they should not be kept too long before being cooked - the longer you keep them, the more they will metabolise their own fat to sustain themselves and the less tasty they will be.

But, do be kind to your lobster, after all they are going to be a pleasure for you - so, until you are ready to cook them keep them in the fridge wrapped in a damp tea towel or three - also, make sure that they are in a dish they can't get out of easily, some of them can be frisky.

When cooking lobster, to maximise flavour I usually either butter poach or roast the flesh. The initial boiling is done purely to blanch the lobster, and make it easier to remove it from the shell. Therefore, you should only cook it for a couple of minutes, just long enough for the colour of the lobster to change to a strong red hue.

It is worth noting that although roasting your lobster achieves better flavour, it should always be briefly blanched first as if you roast it without doing so, the flesh will stick to the shell, and make it very difficult to remove without damage.

About 1 hour before you are ready to start cooking, take the lobsters out of the fridge and place them into the freezer - this will lower their metabolic rate still further and help send them off to sleep.

1) Bring a very large pot of salted water to the boil, and take the first lobster out of the freezer - get a sharp chefs knife, and holding the lobster feet down on a chopping board, slide the blade into the 1st crease in the carapace at the bottom of the head - and cut downwards. This will sever the main nerve ganglia, and in effect kill the lobster instantly.

Do be aware that due to the extremely primitive nature of the lobster's nervous system, it will continue to display movement in its lower body and claws despite no longer having a direct connection to the brain. It is, nevertheless, effectively dead.

2) It can now be dropped into the boiling pot and cooked for no more than 3-4 minutes. Ideally, you are just waiting for the shells to turn from black or blue to red. Once time is up, remove the lobster with a pair of tongs and place into a sink full of cold water to stop the cooking process. If you were going to eat the lobster without any further cooking you might want to cook it for a little longer, but you will be holding it in warm butter later, so don't risk overcooking it.

Repeat this for each lobster.

Now drain your lobsters, and start to prepare them. For this soup, you will be using the tail and claw meat as your finishing touch - however, little of the rest will go to waste, but will be used to create the flavour base for the broth.

3) Before starting to dis-assemble your lobsters, prepare 4 or 5 basins. One for your shells, two for the sweet claw and tail meat, and the other two for the tomalley and roe should you happen to have a female lobster.

4) Next, twist off each of the large claws, and bring them to the chopping board.

5) With a heavy cleaver, use the flat side of the blade on the flat side of the claw to break the shell - pick away any small pieces, and manipulate the pincers of the claw - you should find that you are able to just pull away the large section of claw meat.

6) If the translucent bit of cartilage in the centre of the claw remains, carefully slice the flesh away with a sharp knife. Don't forget to crack off the large knuckles as they contain more delectable morsels.

7) Then twist off the legs. When you pull them away from the body you will see that they have feathery gills attached. These are sometimes referred to as 'dead mens fingers' and are pretty much the only part of the lobster that is not useful. Once you have discarded the gills, you should use the cleaver to chop the legs into small chunks then put them into the basin that you have reserved for shells.

8) Now you are ready to tackle the head. With a brisk motion, simply twist the head to a 90 degree angle, and you should find that it will pull away easily from the body. When you do so, you will find that there might be something which looks like inky goo - it has a deep and rich flavour. It can be used to make a superb lobster butter, but in this case, will be added to the flavour base

9) Next, you can simply lever up the upper surface of the head and it will pop away from the base - again, it will present you with a slightly challenging sight as it can contain grey or green gloop (*technical term that*), and this is referred to as the tomalley. It has a massive flavour punch, and again, we will be adding it to our base.

10) Using a pair of kitchen scissors, turn the lobster on its back and cut up the belly shell of the lobster. Try to slip the blades just under the shell, as you do not want to damage the flesh if at all possible. It should cut quite easily and you will be able to pluck out the entire tail from the shell.

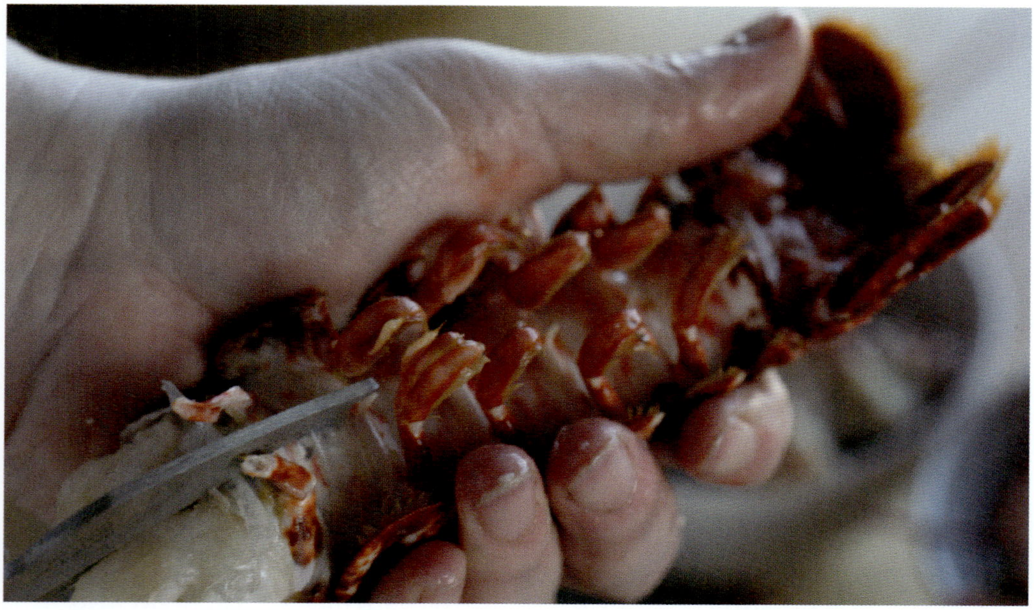

11) Once you have done so, you will see that on the back of the tail there is a dark vein - this is the digestive tract of the lobster and not tasty at all. To easily remove it, start at the tail end and put a skewer or cocktail stick horizontally under the vein, lift upwards and pull down, you should find that the entire vein comes away in a single piece. Discard this.

You should now have your four or five bowls, one filled with assorted shells, and legs (*ideally, you want pieces no large then 10cm, if any larger pieces are in there, now is the time to break them down*). Another with the grey / green goop you have scooped from the head and body junction, one filled with the sweet tail, and a final one with the claw and knuckle meat. *(Plus of course the roe if you had a female lobster).*

It is useful to separate the tail and claw meat, as when you cook it later in the process, they will each take different amounts of time to cook.

Congratulations, you have broken down your lobster, and are ready to start working on your flavour base.

However, I usually take a break at this point to clear everything down, and have a cup of tea, before starting on the broth.

making your flavour base:

1) Put a large heavy based pan on a moderate heat, and add a little sunflower oil, or if you have it Mycryo. Toss your shells in the hot fat, and cook them off for 5 mins or so.

2) Meanwhile, roughly chop 2 onions, and add them to the pan, together with a curl of lemon zest and the chopped celery.

3) Continue to fry these until the onions start to take on some colour, add the litre of white grape juice or wine, and if necessary, enough additional water to cover the shells. Bring to a simmer, add the cinnamon stick and cook for around 30 minutes, then remove it.

4) Once you have a delicious smelling broth, you are half way there - the next thing to do is to extract the maximum flavour from these shells. Carefully strain the broth into a clean pan, and place the cooked shells into a deep tray lined with a chopping board.

5) Pulverise the shells with an appropriate heavy implement - I use a heavy cast iron pan base, it works a treat but a large flat cleaver works too.

6) Return the crushed shells to the pan of broth, and simmer for a further 30 minutes.

7) Strain the broth first through a fine sieve, and then again through a muslin cloth - you don't want any stray bits of shell ruining your hard work. Discard the debris and taste the broth - don't adjust the seasoning at this stage, but start to think about its balance, and how you can improve it.

making your spiced tomato soup:

1) Start by browning your finely chopped onion in a small amount of olive oil - this will take about 15 mins on a gentle heat - don't be tempted to rush it as it is easy to scorch your onions at this stage.

2) Once the onion is browned, add the finely chopped garlic and chilli and stir through to release the flavour.

3) Add the celery, tomato pulp, fish broth, pomegranate molasses and orange zest, and simmer gently for 20 minutes. Taste your soup and adjust the seasoning as required.

4) Now is also the time to consider the soup texture, is it thick enough? If not, reduce by increasing the heat and simmering for a little longer - if it is too thick, add a little water, whisk in and taste again.

5) Once you are happy with the flavour and texture of the soup, set it aside while you finish the lobster meat.

6) Slice your lobster tails into good sized chunks, and set them aside.

7) At this point, you can set aside the lobster and soup until almost ready to serve.

8) 20 minutes before service, bring the soup back up to temperature (*around 85°C is optimum for this soup*).

9) Gently melt the 500g butter in a small pan (*I know, it's a lot, but you are using it as a cooking medium, it won't be in the final dish*). I know, extravagant - but so good. (*After use, don't waste the butter, cool it and use it when you next need to cook some fish, it will add more layers of flavour to your dish*).

10) Once it is melted, gently place the lobster tail chunks in the warm butter. Your lobster should already be almost cooked, you are just using the warm butter to bring up their temperature and finish their cooking without drying them out. When the lobster tail is almost cooked, add the other smaller pieces of lobster flesh to the warm butter.

11) Serve in a warmed shallow bowl with a carefully placed circle of sweet lobster flesh, and a swirl of sour cream. This is a fantastic soup, and with a warm roll, and a crisp green salad it's a complete meal.

I am lucky enough to have access to excellent lobsters from Lybster Harbour

small plates

Starters, appetisers, mezze, tapas, small plates.

There are many ways of describing the tasty dishes that tickle our taste buds, start our mouths watering and give us a pleasurable anticipation of the meal to come.

So it seems a shame to skimp on them - in fact, I often prefer to choose my meal from these dishes, mezze style, rather then commit myself to a single main dish that may after all not be exactly what one would wish for.

They are also perfect dishes to share with a friend over a bottle of wine, or curl up on the sofa with for an evening of quiet indulgence.

I have arranged these small plates by primary ingredient type, starting with dairy and cheese, following on with vegetables, fish and finally meat.

However, in some cases a small amount of fish or meat is included in a vegetable dish - this is because the primary ingredient is still predominantly vegetable, and the meat or fish element may on occasion be omitted.

Valeta Roach's savoury panna cotta

makes enough for 6

I am very pleased to be able to start this section with a special dish, created for Valeta Roach. Valeta visited the restaurant some years ago, and has always kept in touch. She was one of the first people to support my Kickstarter campaign, and was kind enough to sponsor a personal recipe.

Her ingredient choices were dill, rosemary and lamb.

This dish uses dill and rosemary as key ingredients, and is a delicious precursor if you are planning a roast lamb main course.

In an ideal world, I would infuse the oil for a couple of days before straining it out, but if you don't have time a few hours will do.

ingredients for panna cotta:
400ml plain yogurt
300ml double cream
2 thinly sliced shallots
4 leaves gold gelatine
30g fresh dill
finely grated zest of a tangerine
ingredients for rosemary & orange oil:
500ml well flavoured olive oil
30g fresh rosemary sprigs
peeled zest of 2 large oranges
ingredients for crunchy walnuts:
200g walnuts, roughly chopped
splash of olive oil, or sprinkle of Mycryo
Maldon salt
pepper mix

method:

First, prepare your flavoured oil.

1) Pour the olive oil into a heavy based pan, and add the peeled orange zest and the rosemary. Before adding the rosemary, strip the needles from the woody stem, and discard the stem.

2) Heat gently until the oil is bubbling and fragrant, and allow to cool slightly.

3) Blend the warm oil, until a smooth mixture is achieved. If you have time, at this stage, pour into a jar and set aside to infuse for a couple of days. If not, leave for a few hours before continuing.

4) Return the oil mixture to a pan, and heat very gently until bubbling. Remove from the heat and using a fine drum sieve or chinoise, strain the oil. If the strained oil still appears to have some particulates, then strain again, this time lining your sieve with some kitchen paper. Do not press the mixture, allow it to drip through on its own.

5) Set aside until needed.

(This flavoured oil is very fragrant, and will keep for quite some time if kept in an airtight container - out of direct light).

Now prepare your panna cotta.

1) Pour your double cream into a small heavy pan and add the sliced shallots, fresh dill and finely grated tangerine zest, together with a pinch of salt. Gently bring to scalding point, then set aside to cool.

2) Place your leaf gelatine into a bowl *(cutting it to fit if necessary)* and cover with cold water. Leave for at least 5 minutes, but no more than 15 minutes, to 'bloom'.

3) Meanwhile, blend your dill and cream mixture until perfectly smooth, and strain through a coarse sieve to ensure no fibres remain.

4) Re-heat gently, and squeezing out your bloomed gelatine well to remove as much moisture as possible, add it to your pan, and stir until dissolved. As soon as the gelatine has dissolved, remove your mixture from the heat and stir in the yogurt.

5) Whisk gently to ensure that the mix is well blended, and pour into your prepared moulds. Place in the refrigerator to set for at least 30 minutes, and ideally a couple of hours.

Finally, prepare your crunchy walnuts

1) Begin by tossing your walnuts in a small amount of olive oil, or if you have it Mycryo.

2) Spread out on a baking sheet, sprinkle over some Maldon salt crystals and either freshly ground pepper, or some of my pepper mix.

3) Bake in a pre-heated oven set to 170°C until golden brown and fragrant. This will take approx. 10 minutes, but watch them carefully as burnt walnuts are very unpleasant.

4) Once baked, remove from the hot tray and place onto a cool tray. (*If you don't do this, they will continue to cook on the hot tray and may burn despite your care*).

5) Once they are cold, you may store them in an airtight tub until needed.

To serve.

1) About 1 hour before you are ready to serve the panna cotta, remove it from the fridge to allow it to return to room temperature as the chill would deaden the flavours somewhat.

2) Prepare a bowl a little deeper than your mould and fill it with boiling water.

3) Holding your mould by the top rim, plunge it in and out of the boiling water very quickly.

4) Use the tip of a very sharp knife to run around the top edge of the mould, then invert it over your plate, if necessary use the tip of your knife to introduce a small air gap to the side of the panna cotta. It should release easily.

5) Carefully place some of the salt and pepper walnuts around the panna cotta, and place a few on the top.

6) Drizzle with some of the rosemary and orange oil, and serve.

Be aware, this is both light and rich, so make small portions to ensure it is enjoyed to the last mouthful.

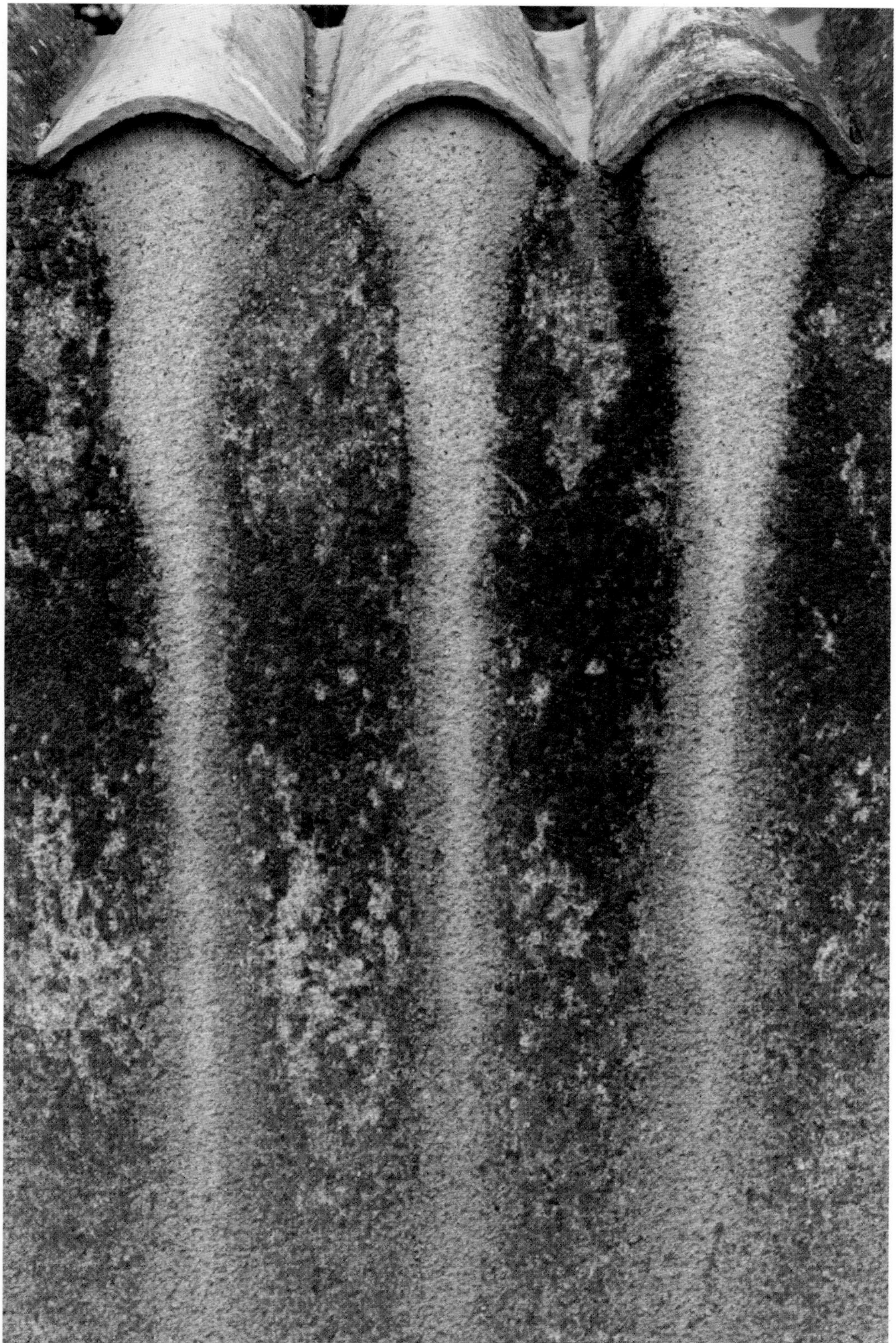

herbed lemon cheese

makes approx. 500g of cheese

This is a fresh and fragrant cheese, which is quick to make and very versatile. I prefer a fairly robust cheese texture, but you may choose to make a smoother and softer version by adding cream and whipping the mixture at the end.

ingredients:
2 litres un-homogenised full cream milk
juice of 3 lemons
10g chopped parsley
10g chopped dill
10g chopped mint
1 tsp fine salt
optional:
25ml double cream

drain your curds and whey

add herbs and seasoning to taste

method:

1) In a large heavy based pot bring your milk up to 80°C, whisking gently to keep the temperature even and avoid the bottom of your pot scorching.

2) As soon as the required temperature is reached, remove from the heat and whisk in the strained lemon juice.

3) Set the pot aside for 20 minutes to allow the curds and whey to separate. If your curds do not separate, warm gently back to temperature and add a little more lemon juice. Then set aside for a further 20 minutes.

4) Line a colander with a fine cheesecloth or muslin, and spoon the curds into it. Alternatively if you make cheese often, invest in a straining bag - it makes life much easier.

5) Allow the curds to drain.

6) If you wish to have a smooth spreading cheese, place the drained curds into a mixing bowl and whisk in sufficient double cream to give a smooth consistency.

7) If you like a slightly firmer cheese, which you can cut, don't add the cream or whisk it.

8) In both cases, add the finely chopped herbs together with sufficient salt to taste, and mix well.

9) You may either leave the cheese in a ceramic dish to serve, or press it into a mould for a more attractive presentation.

10) Chill until needed, but remove from the fridge at least 1 hour before use for maximum flavour.

lemon cheese, bursting with herbs and served with fresh samphire & pea tendrils

fresh Maltese cheese (ġbejniet fresca)

Ġbejniet are a typical Maltese cheese. They can be made from goats milk, sheeps milk, cows milk, or a mixture of all three. Once made, they can be served fresh, preserved in oil, or rolled in crushed peppercorns and left to air dry.

The fresh cheeses are eaten as a snack, often with pickles and olives, while the preserved and dried cheeses may either be used as they are, crumbled into pasta, used as a filling for ravioli, or in more recent times, deep fried.

Making ġbejniet is quite easy, but will take several days with a small amount of intervention each day to check the progress of your cheeses.

Once they have passed the 'fresh' stage, how long you keep them will depend upon the method of preservation you have chosen.

There are a few considerations though, firstly, don't use ultra heat treated or homogenised milk - this will make it impossible for the curds to set properly. If you don't have access to a friendly farmer with lovely Jersey cows *(thank you David, I'm just so lucky!)*, then use Jersey milk from the store.

You will also need some baskets to drain the cheese curds. Traditional Maltese baskets were made of reeds, and called Qwieleb. They are now, more practically, made of plastic. The specific size of the originals was 3" in diameter, and 2 ½" in height, and unlike most cheese baskets, they were cylindrical rather than conical. For some reason, this size is very difficult to find outside Malta - but a No. 18 Ricotta Cheese Basket (110mm x 80mm x 65) is a standard sized mould readily available from cheese making suppliers - and it may be used quite successfully.

Finally, you will need some rennet. You may use either animal or vegetarian rennet, however, be aware that most vegetarian rennet is actually double strength, so for this reason I have not included a specific amount of rennet to use. You should read the instructions on your bottle.

If you make these, and decide that you want to make more to dry for storage, it would be worth making yourself a 'cheese safe'. This is simply a box with slotted shelves, and open sides covered with a fine mesh. The intention is for this to be placed outside (*ideally in a stiff breeze*), allowing air to circulate around the cheeses, but preventing insects from entering.

If you make one large enough to have some hooks in the top, then you also have the perfect drying environment for a Maltese sausage.

ingredients:
2.25 litres un-homogenised Jersey Milk
rennet
(double the amount of rennet you are instructed to use on your specific brand -if using liquid rennet then mix it with 50ml of water before adding the drops to the milk or it will be hard to mix well. For the brand I use, 4 drops is sufficient for this quantity of milk.)
fine sea salt
equipment:
12 to 15 cheese baskets depending upon the size being used
thermometer
large tray with grid over to catch the dripping whey

method:

1) Place milk in a large pot on the stove and warm, whisking gently to ensure that the milk is being evenly heated.

2) Use your thermometer to check when the temperature of the milk reaches 38°C and immediately remove from the heat.

3) Mix your rennet as directed, remembering to use **double** the quantity specified on your bottle and mixing it with 50ml water to aid distribution in the milk. Gently whisk through, then leave at room temperature for 1.5 hours.

4) You should now have a soft mass in your pot *(the curds)* and you need to cut them, in vertical then horizontal lines. Ideally cut the curds in your pot to cubes around 2cm in size (*difficult without a specific curd slicer*). This helps the separation of curds and whey.

5) Leave for another 1.5 hours at room temperature.

6) Prepare dripping tray, and get a basket. Scoop in the curds until the basket is filled, place it on the tray, and continue to fill your baskets.

spoon the curds into your sterilised moulds, and drain on a cheese mat for 12 hours

7) Sprinkle fine salt over the curds, tip away any excess whey from your tray, and place in the fridge overnight. The following morning, turn the cheese over and sprinkle with salt again. Keep in the fridge for another 12 hours.

after the initial draining time, remove from the moulds, salt lightly & drain again

8) Your fresh ġbejniet should now be ready.

9) To store, lightly dress with some olive oil, and pack into ziplock bags which have had as much air expelled from them as possible. If you can vacuum pack the cheeses, they will keep well in the fridge.

10) Alternatively, pack into a preserving jar and fill with a light olive oil, tapping to ensure that no bubbles of air remain. Store out of direct light in a cool place.

dried Maltese cheese (ġbejniet moxxa)

ingredients:
fresh ġbejniet which have been sitting in the fridge for 24 hours
salt
cracked black pepper *(ideally tellicherry)*
chilled light brine solution (*see extras section*)
white wine vinegar
olive oil

You have a number of options here - if you happen to live in a balmy Mediterranean climate, place them in a cheese safe and stick them in the garden - or traditionally, on your rooftop (*which is flat of course*).

Otherwise, they can be dried indoors under a food net, turning them every day to ensure that they dry evenly - that could take anything from a couple of days to a couple of weeks, depending upon the heat and humidity you have present.

Alternatively, I find that they dry very well on the lowest possible setting of my oven (*50°C)*. Be very careful, you're not trying to cook them here - just evaporate the moisture gently. By placing a cooling rack within a tray, and turning the cheeses every ½ hour or so, after 3 or 4 hours you can start to see a difference. From there, it just depends how hard you like your cheese, and what you intend to do with it. If you want to grate it over pasta - then rock hard is the way to go. I like them wizened and chewy, but still tender in the centre. Only you can work out what you like, and how to achieve it in your own situation.

Recently I bought a dehydrator, and this works really well - set it at 35°C and leave for around 8 hours. Depending upon the method of preservation and storage, once made they should keep well for several months at the very least.

method:

1) Prepare a tray which has a draining grid to allow air flow, and choose your preferred option for how to dry your cheese.

2) When you are happy with the level of dehydration of your cheese, you may continue.

flip your cheeses over half way through their dehydration time

3) Place the dried cheeses into a basin, pour over a chilled brine (*see extras section*) and leave for approx 1 hour for every 2.5cm depth of cheese. Your brine solution, if kept chilled, will keep for months (*or years*) so don't throw it away if you intend making these with any regularity.

4) Remove the cheeses from the brine, drain and pat dry with kitchen paper.

5) Crack some fragrant peppercorns (*I love the tellicherry berries*) in a mortar and pestle - you don't want to grind them in this instance as the idea is to have a variation in size, some larger pieces, some smaller. Put a good layer of cracked pepper in a dish, and press the dried Ġbejniet quite firmly into it. Ensure that all parts of the cheeses are coated, and place aside.

6) Once all the cheeses are coated with pepper, make a mix of equal quantities of olive oil and vinegar, and dress the cheeses with it, tossing them gently to ensure they are coated.

7) To preserve them, simply place the cheeses into an airtight jar, with some of the olive oil and vinegar mix, and store at ambient temperature. Should you have a vacuum packing machine, then you are ideally placed to portion up a few cheeses at a time, pack them in a small amount of the oil and vinegar mix, and store them for later use.

spicy red pepper hummus

makes approx 500g of hummus

ingredients:

300g dried chickpeas, soaked overnight & cooked until tender
(or 500g drained tinned chickpeas)
100g sliced onions
6 cloves garlic
2 red peppers cut into strips
zest of 1 lemon
juice of 2 lemons
2 red chillies
250ml olive oil

method:

1) Roast the sliced onions and garlic, red peppers and chilli with the olive oil until tender - this should take about 20 mins in a moderate oven. You don't want to burn them, although a few scorched bits are acceptable, so take them out when they are translucent

2) Put the cooked vegetables and oil into a food processor, together with the lemon zest and juice. Blitz until you have a smooth but quite loose paste.

3) Add salt and pepper, together with your cooked chickpeas, and blitz again - for a smoother hummus, just keep going longer - if it looks a little dry, you may add olive oil to thin it down, but only use a little at a time. (*Adding water to this mix would tend to make it split*).

4) Adjust seasoning, and serve with a wedge of fresh lemon.

roasted onion hummus

makes approx 500g of hummus

I make hummus every week.

Below is the recipe I have developed, which will give you a wonderful hummus in its own right, but can also then be used as a base for additional flavours to make more fabulous variations on this humble dish.

It's considerably lower fat than the original, which is also not a bad thing, *(especially if you are a zaftig Mediterranean type like me).*

ingredients:
300g dried chickpeas, soaked overnight & cooked until tender
(or 500g drained tinned chickpeas)
250g sliced onions
6 cloves garlic
2 tablespoons tahini
finely grated zest of 1 lemon
juice of 2 lemons
20g parsley stalks
250ml olive oil
to finish: *(optional)*
a drizzle of chilli & garlic sauce

method:

1) Roast the sliced onions and garlic with the olive oil until tender - this should take about 20 mins in a moderate oven. You don't want to burn them, although a few scorched bits are acceptable, so take them out when they are translucent.

2) Put the cooked onions, garlic and oil into a food processor, together with the lemon zest and juice, parsley and tahini.

3) Blitz until you have a loose but still slightly textured paste.

4) Add salt and pepper, together with your cooked chickpeas, and blitz again - for a smoother hummus, just keep going longer. If it looks a little dry, you may add some boiling water to thin it down, but only use a little at a time.

5) Adjust seasoning, and enjoy.

drizzle a little chilli & garlic sauce over the hummus for both colour & flavour

green olive tapenade

makes approx 500g of tapenade.

ingredients:

350g pitted green olives
50g capers
50g shallots
3 crushed garlic cloves
100g fresh green pepper
100ml extra virgin olive oil
small bunch of flat leaf parsley

method:

1) Place all ingredients into a food processor, and blitz until you achieve a textured paste. If the mix is too dry, you may add a little more olive oil, but ensure that you don't add too much.

2) Taste and adjust seasoning, and if necessary, blitz for another minute or two.

green olive tapenade, with a garnish of some house dukkah for extra crunch

black olive tapenade

makes approx 500g of tapenade.

ingredients:
350g pitted black olives
100g capers
3 crushed garlic cloves
50g anchovy fillets in oil **or** 50g nori seaweed
100ml extra virgin olive oil
small bunch of flat leaf parsley

method:

Make as per the green olive tapenade.

If a vegetarian / vegan option is desired, replace the anchovy fillets with some crumbled nori seaweed sheets to achieve a similar umami flavour.

how to use this:

While tapenade is traditionally served with bread, it also works well whenever a salty and savoury note would be welcome.

I love this spooned onto crisp slices of cucumber - the burst of freshness complements the salty richness of this tapenade beautifully.

You can also transform this into a wonderful salsa, great for dipping into, by adding diced fresh tomatoes & cucumber to the mix.

Stir well, and leave for at least 30 minutes before scooping up with fresh celery sticks. A great nibble with a drink.

tabbouleh

makes sufficient for 4 to share as a side dish.

Tabbouleh is a dish that is often under appreciated - this is usually due to sloppy execution, and skimpy ingredients.

Take the time to make this a flavour explosion.

ingredients:
150g coarse bulgar wheat
90g flat leaf parsley
90g fresh mint
90g chives
1 small red onion - finely sliced
2 crushed cloves of garlic
500g ripe tomatoes
zest & juice of 2 lemons
olive oil to dress

method:

1) First, soak your bulgar wheat in plenty of cold water and leave it to steep while you prepare the rest of your salad.

2) If using large tomatoes, blanch them and remove the skins *(don't even think about doing this if you are using small tomatoes).*

3) Chop the tomatoes into small dice and place into a large basin, making sure to capture as much of their juice as possible.

4) Zest your lemons directly into the basin, and add the juice to your mix together with the crushed garlic. Stir it around to get the flavours mixing.

5) Strip the leaves from the parsley stalks *(keeping the stalks in a tub to freeze for other uses)*. Strip the leaves from the mint and discard the stalks *(they tend to be bitter)*. Now chop the herbs, including your chives, keeping some texture, but making sure that they are reasonably fine.

6) Add the chopped herbs and very finely sliced red onion to your tomato mix, and stir through again.

7) By now your bulgar wheat should be sufficiently soaked, so drain it in a fine mesh sieve *(or you will lose much of it down the sink),* and press down against it with your hands to squeeze out as much moisture as possible.

8) Add the bulgar to your basin together with a little olive oil, and mix thoroughly.

9) Taste, and season as necessary. Only add more oil if it's absolutely needed, as you want to retain the fresh zing of this refreshing salad.

dukkah or duqua

makes approx. 1 kg of mix

I first encountered this in the wonderful 'A New Book of Middle Eastern Food', by Claudia Roden. As a young cook I worked my way backwards and forwards through this tome, and am now on my second copy, the first one having been retired after over 30 years of use.

I have given you my own personal mixture below, but do feel free to experiment - if you don't like one of the ingredients, don't use it, substitute something else, work to your own palate.

This can be used in a variety of ways; a nutritious snack through the day, eaten with bread dipped in olive oil to help the seeds cling, sprinkled over salads to add flavour and texture, heavily topping some plain thick yoghurt, or scooped up with crisp batons of cucumber.

I am sure that you will enjoy creating your own batch, and will find lots of delicious ways to use it. It also scales really well, so just use this as a guide for the possible ratio you might like to start with.

ingredients:
250g white sesame seed
125g pumpkin seed
125g sunflower seed
125g coriander seed
25g fennel seed
25g cumin seed
15g black peppercorns
125g blanched almonds
125g blanched hazelnuts
25g maldon salt flakes
25g red pepper flakes,

method:

1) All the seeds and nuts should be roasted in a moderate oven until fragrant - this must be done on individual trays, as some will be ready in only minutes, while others will take longer. Once everything is toasted, you are ready to break down your mixture.

2) Prepare a large basin and start by adding the salt and red pepper flakes.

3) Next, you should hand chop your nuts - you don't want to create a 'butter', the idea is to have lovely little nuggets of nut throughout your mixture, so don't chop them too finely. Add the chopped almonds and hazelnuts to your basin and stir well. The toasted sesame seeds may be tipped straight into the basin without any need for further work, and again stirred well.

4) The pumpkin seeds should be blitzed in your food processor (*or hand chopped if you prefer*) again, you don't want to produce 'dust'. Add to the basin, together with the sunflower seeds, and stir well.

5) Put the coriander seed, fennel seed, peppercorns and cumin seed into your food processor, and blitz until you have fine granules. (*Depending upon the power of your food processor, you may find that it is necessary to use a spice mill to grind these final items*).

6) Mix these through the basin, breathe deeply, taste your mix, and decide whether to adjust your seasoning, or mixtures to suit your own tastes.

7) Store in airtight tubs, (*or ideally, vacuum pack*) and use within 3 months.

baba ganoush (aubergine purée)

ingredients:
3 large aubergines
9 or more cloves of garlic
¼ tsp ground cumin
zest & juice of ½ a lemon
few sprigs of flat leaf parsley
optional - to finish:
100g Greek yoghurt or sour cream

method:

1) Wash your aubergines and peel the garlic. Make several deep slits in the flesh of each aubergine, and push a clove of garlic into each slit.

2) Place on a baking tray, and roast at 180°C for 40 minutes.

3) Remove from the oven and allow to cool slightly, just enough to be able to handle them.

4) Remove the skin and discard it. The easiest way to separate the skin from the flesh is to split the aubergine lengthwise, and use a spoon to scoop out the flesh, and scrape the inside of the skin.

5) Place the internal flesh and garlic cloves into a food processor, together with the lemon zest and juice, a few sprigs of flat leaf parsley and your cumin.

6) Blitz to a smooth paste, if you like a creamy finish, fold through the thick yoghurt, and place into a serving bowl - season to taste.

(Don't be tempted to add the yoghurt to the food processor, it will instantly make your mix really runny).

This keeps very well in the fridge, and should be fine for up to a week.

push peeled garlic deep inside your aubergine

split your aubergine to facilitate removing the cooked flesh from the bitter skin

If using yogurt or sour cream, stir in at the end

giardiniera salad (pickled vegetables)

makes lots.

ingredients for pickle:

1 large cauliflower - broken down into small florets
6 - 8 pepperoncini (*or other mild chilli)* - diced or sliced
3 green peppers - large dice
6-8 small carrots - small dice
3 cloves of garlic - thinly sliced
5 celery stalks - paysanne cut
6 scallions or spring onions - thinly sliced
Brine - *(made at a ratio of 1 litre of water to 100g salt - sufficient to cover the chopped vegetables in a glass or ceramic bowl).*

ingredients for finishing:

12 large green olives
few sprigs of fresh thyme
1 tbsp red pepper flakes
1 tsp celery seeds
1 tsp fennel seeds
½ tsp whole black peppercorns
150ml white wine vinegar
250ml extra virgin olive oil

method:

1) Combine all the prepared vegetables in a large glass bowl. Using a measuring jug pour in sufficient water to cover the vegetables, keeping note of exactly how much is needed.

2) Strain the vegetables and put that same quantity of water back into the bowl, together with the appropriate ratio of salt for the liquid needed. Stir until the salt is dissolved, and return the vegetables to the brine. Cover, and refrigerate overnight.

3) The next day, drain and rinse the vegetables and spin dry.

4) In a clean bowl mix the herbs & spices, olives, olive oil and vinegar. Then return the dried vegetables to the bowl, and gently stir to ensure that all the vegetables are coated with this mixture.

5) Allow to marinate in the fridge for at least 48 hours before eating, giving it an occasional stir when you are near.

6) Eat as an antipasto, with sandwiches, or salad.

barley & grape salad

makes enough for 4 - 6

This is a salad that is good served either warm or cold.

It has developed because I love grapes, but cannot eat many of them without affecting my blood sugar adversely. Combining them with the low GI slow release carbohydrate of pearl barley means that overall the salad is OK for me, and it allows me to eat one of my favourite (*but usually forbidden)* fruits.

It keeps for several days in an airtight container in your fridge, and is great standby if you are expecting guests but not sure when they might arrive.

Serve with bread and cheese or sliced hot or cold meats for a great quick supper.

ingredients:
300g dried pearl barley
400g mixed green & red grapes
2 lemons, zest & juice
100g dried cranberries or dried sour cherries
small bunch of flat leaf parsley

method:

1) Rinse your pearl barley to remove excess starch, and place in a moderate sized pan with ample cold water. Bring to the boil, and simmer gently for about 20 minutes, or until the pearl barley is tender. Do taste it frequently after 15 minutes, as you want to retain some bite at the centre of the grain, rather than end up with a mushy mouthful.

2) While the barley is cooking, rinse your grapes. Split them in half and add them to a large mixing bowl.

3) Finely chop your parsley, add that to the bowl, and put the stalks into your freezer for another time.

4) Finely grate the lemon zest into your working bowl and extract the juice. Add the juice to your mixture, together with the dried cranberries or sour cherries. Mix well, and set aside for the flavours to amalgamate until the barley is cooked.

5) Once your barley is cooked, drain, and rinse with warm water. (*You don't want to cool the barley too much, as the warmth will help your mixture to absorb flavours.*)

6) Add the barley to your bowl, season with salt and pepper, and add a glug of olive oil.

7) Now mix well, and taste again. If necessary adjust the seasoning, and cover the bowl with cling film.

8) This salad may be served warm, or at room temperature. If it has been pre-prepared, it may be warmed very successfully in your oven, as long as you cover the surface with foil to avoid it drying out.

Maltese caponata (kapunata)

makes enough for 6.

This is a Maltese classic, and is also claimed by Sicilians. Who knows, who cares, it's great.

It may be served warm or at room temperature. As a side dish, a starter with plenty of crusty bread, or with a couple of fried eggs as a tasty lunch or supper.

However you serve it, remember it is essential that you have a balance of sweet and sour in this dish.

ingredients:
1 kg sweet peppers (*you may use red or green, or a mixture*)
4 large onions - thinly sliced
6 cloves of garlic - thinly sliced
1 aubergine - in large cubes
250g chopped tomatoes
50g capers
50g black olives - halved lengthwise
50g green olives - halved lengthwise
3 tbsp tomato purée
vinegar to taste (*dark if possible*)
honey to taste (*thyme if possible*)
ground cinnamon to taste

method:

1) First, prepare your vegetables as this is a fairly quick cook.

2) The peppers may be cut into medium chunks - it is nice to have good sized pieces, but ideally, not so big that it is necessary to cut them to eat them.

3) Using a large heavy based pan, on a low heat, fry your onions in some olive oil until they are light golden brown and fragrant.

4) Now add the sliced garlic and cook for a further few minutes, add the chopped aubergine, and stirring frequently continue to cook until the aubergine has absorbed most of the oil and is becoming translucent and tender. This can take about 5 - 10 minutes, depending upon how gentle your burner is.

5) Now add your chopped peppers and mix well. Continue to braise gently until the peppers have started to soften, but are not completely cooked. At this stage, you may add the tomatoes and tomato purée.

6) Cook for a further 5 minutes, then add the capers and olives. Now stir through a few tablespoons of honey and vinegar, together with some ground cinnamon. Mix well, and taste, you are looking for an 'agrodolce' sauce - a sweet and sour mix - the sweetness should be your first sensation, with a sour 'pucker' at the finish.

7) There should be sufficient wetness to the dish to give a pleasant sauce, but this is not a 'stew', beware of adding too much liquid. If you do have a very thin sauce, you may either add more tomato purée (*which will thicken it, but also change the flavour)*, or strain off the liquid, boil it down to reduce it, and return it to your dish. (*Definitely the best option in that circumstance*).

cauliflower 'couscous'

makes enough for 6.

This is a useful way of using cauliflower without boiling it. A good winter or springtime salad, it's mainly raw as none of the ingredients (*other than the almonds*) are cooked.

ingredients:
1 medium to large head of cauliflower
4 spring onions, thinly sliced, or 2 shallots
2 large pomegranates
200g flaked almonds
zest & flesh of 2 oranges

method:

1) Remove the florets from your cauliflower, and save the stalks for a crunchy cooks treat. Using a food processor, blitz the florets for just a moment - you want small pieces (*similar in size to cooked couscous)* rather than mush.

2) Place into a large mixing bowl while you prepare the other ingredients. Add the sliced spring onions or shallot, and the coarsely grated zest of your oranges.

3) Then, top and tail your oranges, and pare away the remaining skin. Holding the orange over your mixing bowl, so that any juice is caught, and using a very sharp knife gently slide your blade in between the membrane of your segments. You should be able to separate the flesh from the membrane, and end up with an empty but connected membrane. Give it a final squeeze over the bowl to save any juice, and repeat for the 2nd orange.

4) Using your fingers, gently break up the segments in smaller pieces (*approx. 2cm in size*) and mix the orange flesh, zest and juice into your cauliflower and spring onion mix.

5) To prepare the pomegranates, cut them in quarters to make them easier to handle, and be prepared for a little splash back. (*This is not the time to wear your best whites*). Holding the pomegranate over the bowl, with the cells pointing downwards, use a wooden spoon to bang on the skin side. As if by magic, the pomegranate seeds will leap into your bowl. Check as you go that membrane is not also falling in, and remove it as necessary. This is by far the easiest way of removing the seeds from your pomegranate. Gently stir through your mixture.

6) Finally, spread your flaked almonds on a baking tray, and toast them until they are lightly golden. Do watch them carefully, almonds tend to go from white to black in a flash and a burnt almond is no good to anyone. As soon as they are ready remove them from the hot baking tray onto a cool dish, as otherwise they will continue to cook.

7) Once they are cool (*just a few minutes*), sprinkle them into your mixture. Season to taste, and serve at room temperature.

coconut & chilli potato cakes

makes about 14.

These are great for a party, or just snacking. They can be prepared in advance and finished at the last minute, and may also be successfully frozen - although they will take a little longer to fry if you are cooking from frozen.

ingredients for potato cakes:

500g desiree or red skinned potatoes
200g finely sliced onions
150g desiccated coconut (*unsweetened*)
4 (*or more*) green & red chillies
4 cloves of garlic - crushed
lots of coarsely chopped coriander leaf

ingredients for finishing batter

300g gram (*chickpea*) flour
50ml olive or sunflower oil
1 tsp ground cumin
1 tsp ground turmeric

method:

1) Place your onions in a heavy based frying pan with some olive oil, and gently fry until they are golden brown. This will take approx. 20 minutes. Stir frequently as you want to avoid any blackened edges to your onions. Towards the end of the cooking time, add your crushed garlic and stir, continue cooking until gently fragrant.

2) Meanwhile, wash your potatoes and place them in a pan with enough cold water to cover. Bring to the boil, and simmer until tender - this will take between 15 - 20 minutes depending upon the size of your potatoes, so do check them towards the end of the time.

3) While they are cooking, finely chop your chillies, and mix them with the desiccated coconut and some sea salt.

4) Once the potatoes are cooked, drain them and allow them to cool for only a few minutes. As soon as they are cool enough to handle, carefully peel away the skin and set the potatoes in a large mixing bowl.

5) Using your hands, crush the potatoes squeezing them through your fingers - you want to have a mixture of small pieces of potato and potato purée - don't use a masher or food processor as the texture would be too consistent.

6) Now add your caramelised onions and coconut chilli mixture, and stir well. The mixture blends much better if this is done while the potato is still warm, as the steam from the potatoes will help to bind the coconut and chilli mix.

7) Chill in the fridge until completely cold. The mixture will become quite firm once it is chilled, so you may now shape your mixture. I tend to use 50g per potato cake, as if they become too large they do not heat up sufficiently in the middle when fried.

8) Once you have your measured 50g portions, have a bowl of tepid water on the side and dipping your hands in on a regular basis, roll them in your palms to make balls, then flatten slightly and set them on a tray lined with baking paper.

9) To make your batter, sift your gram flour into a large bowl and add the ground cumin and turmeric. Whisk the mix while adding sufficient hot water to make a batter. You need this to be a thick enough batter to coat your potato cakes, but not too thick. Just sufficient to coat the back of a wooden spoon is great.

10) Preheat your oil to 180ºC, and working in small batches to avoid cooling your oil too much, dip your shaped potato cakes into the batter, and place them into your hot oil. I find that holding them for a moment half submerged in the oil allows a slight crust to form, and avoids them sticking to your frying basket, but do make sure you give the basket a good shake every time you add one to keep them loose.

11) Fry until golden brown, drain well, and eat while hot.

If you wish to make them in advance, you may complete all the stages until the frying - then as soon as a skin has formed, but before they are crisp and golden, remove them from your hot oil and allow to cool.

Freeze until needed, then bake in the oven at 180°C from frozen.

Turkish style poached eggs (cilbir)

makes enough for 2.

This is incredibly simple and quick to make, but so tasty I couldn't leave it out. If you're not confident poaching eggs you can also use a fried egg, as long as the yolk is still runny.

ingredients:
4 eggs
400g Greek or Turkish plain yogurt
3 cloves of garlic
1 small red onion, thinly sliced
2 medium tomatoes, skinned & chopped into large dice
few sprigs of fresh mint
chilli oil

method:

1) Place your thinly sliced red onion into a heatproof bowl, and cover with freshly boiled water. Set aside for 5 minutes, then drain and plunge into cold water.

2) Finely chop your mint leaves, and mix together with your prepared tomato into your onion with a drizzle of olive oil.

3) In a clean bowl, add the crushed garlic and salt to taste to your yogurt and mix well - leave to infuse for 20 - 30 minutes.

4) Poach your eggs (*or if you prefer, fry them*), making sure that the yolks remain soft.

5) Assemble by spreading the yogurt and garlic mix on the plate, topping with the poached or fried eggs, drizzling with chilli oil and setting the onion and tomato mixture on the side.

6) Serve with plenty of fresh bread.

watermelon & feta salad

makes a side dish for 6-8, or a large salad for 4

I've been making this for at least 20 years, and it's simplicity itself - it entirely depends upon the quality of the ingredients.

If watermelons are not at the height of their season, don't make this salad. If they are, you will love it - I guarantee it.

ingredients:
1 medium sized ripe watermelon
150g feta cheese
100g pumpkin seeds

method:

1) Peel, chop and de-seed your watermelon into bite sized pieces.

2) Crumble the feta cheese.

3) Place the watermelon into a large dish, top with the crumbled feta cheese, and sprinkle with the pumpkin seeds.

4) Drizzle with a little olive oil, and grind over some cracked black pepper and sea salt (*or lemon salt if you have it*).

5) Serve at room temperature.

savoury porridge

makes a light lunch for 4.

This dish is dedicated to Fiona Platten, who loved it when she came to the restaurant. She's living far away now but is not forgotten.

Considering how popular salted porridge is in Scotland as a breakfast dish, it's always surprised me that it's not used more in a savoury context.

This a versatile and quick lunch.

I sometimes add some cooked chicken to it too.

ingredients:

50g butter
150g rolled porridge oats
1 large onion, finely chopped
1 large carrot, finely chopped
1 celery stalk, finely chopped
few sprigs of flat leaf parsley, roughly chopped
50g blanched cashew nuts, roughly chopped & toasted
2 cloves of garlic, finely sliced
100g frozen peas
200g chopped mixed mushrooms of your choice
500ml vegetable or chicken stock

method:

1) Using a deep sauté pan, melt most of the butter and gently fry the chopped onion until it is light golden brown. Add the crushed garlic and stir well.

2) While you are doing that, heat your stock in a separate pan as it is best used hot.

3) Now add the carrot, celery and porridge oats to your sauté pan and stir well. The oats should absorb the butter in your pan and start to become fragrant.

4) You can now start to add some stock - don't add it all at once, you may not need it all. Just add sufficient to cover the oats, and stir gently while cooking while it absorbs the liquid. Add more liquid as necessary, and cook for 5 minutes.

5) At this stage, you can add the chopped mushrooms and frozen peas - stir them in well, and if necessary you can add more liquid - if you have no more stock, add a little hot water.

6) As soon as the mushrooms are tender, sprinkle with some chopped parsley and finish with any remaining butter dotted on top.

grilled aubergine with ginger & honey

makes enough for 6

There is no doubt in my mind that this is one of the most delicious ways of eating aubergine I have ever found.

It is usually served at room temperature, but the heat from ginger and chilli will make it seem hot. It may also be served warm, but not hot.

A tingling sensation of a dish.

ingredients:
3 large aubergines
200ml honey
6 garlic cloves
5 hot chillies *(or more)*
8cm piece of ginger zest
juice of 1 lemon
1 tsp ground cumin

method:

1) Slice your aubergines into rounds approx. 1cm thick.

2) Place them into a roasting tin, and pour over some olive oil.

3) Roast at 200°C for about 20 minutes, until the aubergine is becoming translucent, turn it in the pan to coat well with oil, but try to avoid adding much more oil. When tender, remove from the oven.

4) Crush your garlic cloves, and finely mince your chillies and ginger. Mix into a paste with the lemon zest and juice. (*Or use a food processor to blend into a slightly grainy paste*).

5) In a heavy based sauté pan, heat the honey gently until it is liquid, then add your spice paste and the ground cumin. Mix well, and add a little water if necessary to cover the base of your pan.

6) Add the roasted aubergine slices and turn gently in the sauce to ensure that each slice is well coated in the spiced mixture. Don't be tempted to add too much water, you are aiming for the aubergine to be coated with a sticky glaze rather than a runny sauce.

7) Serve warm or at room temperature.

charred broccoli

makes a side dish for 4, or a large salad for 2

This is a great way of giving broccoli some additional interest. I admit it's not one of my favourite vegetables normally, but I love it prepared this way.

ingredients:
500g broccoli florets
a generous few spoonfuls of 'chilli & garlic' sauce *(see sauces)*

method:

1) Bring a large pot of salted water up to a rolling boil.

2) Prepare your broccoli by breaking it into individual moderately sized florets - if your broccoli is tender stem leave with a long stem, should it be the kind with a thicker stem, peel it and slice the stems into rounds of approx ½ cm thickness.

3) Drop your broccoli into the boiling water, and blanch for no more than 1 minute. Drain and plunge into cold water to stop the cooking process.

4) Place the drained broccoli onto a large bowl, and toss in some of the 'chilli & garlic' sauce until the florets and stems are well coated.

5) Transfer to a metal tray.

6) Using a blowtorch sear the broccoli. You can be fairly aggressive with this, you are looking for some charring not to carbonise the whole thing. Ideally, you are looking for blackening on approx 25% of the surface - certainly no more than that.

7) Season with salt and pepper, and serve at room temperature.

caramelised padron chillies

This is a great way to bring out the flavour of a padron chilli. They are mild and quite sweet when raw, but cooking them brings out a gentle warmth and tingle. Combining chilli and caramel is always popular in my house, and adding some Szechuan pepper to the mix is just right.

These chillies are a great way to add texture and flavour to a platter, or they may be used as part of an antipasto. However, be aware, the caramel will slip from the chilli over time, and it will 'weep', so make them just before you need them, to taste them at their best.

ingredients:
handful of padron chillies
1 tsp Szechuan pepper
150g caster sugar

method:

1) Wash and dry your chillies.
2) Using a heavy based cast iron pan, sprinkle the caster sugar and Szechuan pepper over the base.
3) Giving the pan an occasional shake, make a dry caramel.
4) Do not over brown the caramel, as it will continue to cook once the heat is turned off.
5) As soon as the caramel has reached your desired shade, tip the pan to get a 'puddle' of caramel, and holding the chilli by it's stalk, dip it in the caramel.
6) Set it aside to cool slightly on some baking paper, or a silicone mat.
7) Use as desired, either as a garnish or as part of an antipasto platter.

Maltese stuffed artichokes (qaqoċċ mimli)

makes enough for 4

This is another recipe I remember fondly from my childhood. It's a quintessential 'grandmother' dish. Time consuming, a bit fiddly but delicious.

Usually globe artichokes must have the prickly 'choke' removed before cooking, but in this instance you simply eat your way down to it, then discard it and eat the heart.

A great way to enjoy your artichoke this is a dish to eat with friends, it takes time to consume as well as make.

ingredients:
4 large globe artichokes
400g good breadcrumbs
4 garlic cloves
50g drained capers
1 medium bunch of parsley
200g mixed green and black olives
good extra virgin olive oil

method:

1) First, prepare the stuffing.

2) Place the breadcrumbs into a large bowl, and add the finely chopped capers, parsley, garlic and olives. Mix well, then add just enough olive oil to bind - a teaspoon of mixture pinched in your fingers should hold together.

3) Taste, and season as needed with plenty of black pepper and sea salt. Set aside for the flavours to mingle, and prepare your artichokes.

4) Prepare a large basin of acidulated water, as the artichokes will oxidise when cut.

5) Trim the sharp pointed tip of your artichoke if it has one, and if the leaves are particularly spiky use a pair of scissors to snip off the sharp tips.

6) Working from the outside in, gently pull out a leaf, and place a small amount of the filling at the very base of the leaf. Continue to work around the artichoke, until you have reached the centre. Repeat for the remaining artichokes, and place them in a steamer.

7) Steam for between 45 minutes to 1 hour, until a leaf gently pulled from the base of the artichoke comes away easily.

steamed artichokes with hollandaise sauce

makes enough for 4

This recipe is simplicity itself, but a quick and tasty treat if you have unexpected guests *(and some artichokes of course).*

ingredients:

2 large or 4 small globe artichokes

ingredients for hollandaise sauce:

175g butter - softened, cut into small cubes

4 egg yolks

1 tbsp lemon juice

method*:*

1) Prepare a large bowl of acidulated water, and cut each artichoke in half lengthwise.

2) Using a paring knife, carefully remove the hairy 'choke' from the centre of each halved artichoke, quarter the prepared half, and place in the acidulated water while you repeat for the others.

3) Once all the artichokes are prepared, place them in a steamer, and while they are steaming prepare your sauce.

4) In a small pan, lightly whisk the egg yolks with 1 tbsp of lemon juice and heat gently, whisking all the time.

5) Start adding the cubed butter, whisking all the time to avoid the egg mixture from becoming too hot. The heat of the egg mix should be sufficient to allow you to beat in the butter.

6) Once all the butter is incorporated, if the mixture is a little too thick, you may whisk in a little cold water, until the desired consistency is achieved.

7) Serve immediately.

remove the 'choke' to ensure a pleasant dining experience

Maltese spiced bean salad (bigilla)

makes enough for dinner, and a bit left over for tomorrow…

Traditionally, this is served as a fairly smooth paste and treated as a dip, but my grandmother used to make a more coarsely crushed version.

We usually served it with some sliced ripe tomatoes and crusty bread, or galletti.

I prefer my grandmother's method, so I give it to you below.

ingredients:
500g dried broad *(or fava)* beans
1 small bunch of parsley
1 head of garlic *(roasted)*
2 tsp finely chopped mint
½ tsp dried marjoram
½ tsp fresh thyme
1 fresh red chilli
olive oil to mix
zest & juice of 1 small orange
100g Maltese style kunserva *(see recipe in sauces)*

serve the bigilla with crisp slices of kohlrabi for a distinctly Maltese snack

method:

1) Soak your beans overnight, then cook until tender, (*usually approx. 1 hour*). Drain and set aside to cool slightly.

2) Combine the crushed garlic, mint, marjoram, thyme and finely chopped chilli with sufficient olive oil to make a loose paste.

3) Using the back of a fork, lightly mash the tender beans making sure that you retain plenty of texture.

4) Add the garlic and herb paste and the finely chopped parsley, before seasoning with salt and black pepper.

5) Mix well, and leave for at least 5 minutes before tasting. If need be, add a little olive oil to loosen the salad. Adjust the seasoning to suit.

(If you prefer, you can boil the head of garlic with your beans, and then use the cooked garlic in the paste - it creates a more gentle garlic flavour).

Maltese anchovy stuffed olives

makes about 2 kg

I love these, and you just can't get them anywhere near me, they're a terrible fiddle but so delicious. I often make a big batch of them near Christmas time as they make excellent foodie presents. Although that does pre-suppose that you don't just eat them all yourself.

Don't compare them with those anchovy stuffed tinned olives you can get - they're just not the same beast. Once tasted, you'll find it hard to go back to anything else.

A word of warning though, I've specified the type of olive for a reason, they are large, easy to stuff and taste fantastic.

Don't bother making this unless you have at the very least got a queen olive. It will drive you insane.

ingredients:

1 kg pitted Bella di Cerignola Olives or Sicilian Colossal
1 large can of tuna chunks *(ideally albacore tuna)*
50g anchovy fillets in oil
a couple of handfuls of dried breadcrumbs
3 garlic cloves
1 tbsp red pepper flakes
a small handful of flat leaf parsley
50g capers
extra virgin olive oil

method:

1) Put the drained tuna, anchovy fillets (*including their oil*), capers, parsley and garlic into a food processor and blitz until finely minced, but not a purée.

2) Put the mixture into a basin, add the breadcrumbs and red pepper flakes, mix well. Add more olive oil if it is needed, but you are just trying to get the mixture to hold together, not be a sloppy mess.

3) Taste the mixture, and season with salt and pepper.

4) Now, put on some music, sit in a comfy spot, and start to stuff the olives. If you want, you can try to use a piping bag, but truly, it will be a mess. The mixture is quite dense, and trying to squeeze it into a small hole with increasingly slippery hands is not easy.

5) The best way to handle this is to enjoy the process, have your three basins ready; one empty to receive your finished olives, one full of stuffing, and the other full of your pitted olives.

6) Pick up a little bit of stuffing, and poke it in the hole. Yep, and again, until the olive is clearly full. Stuff from both ends to make sure you don't have a void. Put it in your basin, and repeat, and repeat, and repeat.

7) When you eventually finish *(I usually expect it to take about an hour, but some days, it takes longer)* you should ideally have just a little bit of stuffing left. Tip it into the bowl with the finished olives, and pour over a little extra olive oil. Mix with your hands *(they're a mess anyway)* until all the olives are coated with a little bit of extra stuffing and oil.

8) Put into tubs, jars or bags, but don't forget to save a few for yourself later - **after clean up** - with cheese & pickles and a cold beer. Ahhh.

use good quality albacore tuna for the best results in your stuffing mix

once you have stuffed your olives, use a little of the extra stuffing with some olive oil to provide gloss and additional flavour to your treat

Maltese deep fried anchovy balls (sfineg)

this recipe makes 25 - 30 balls - they are great party snacks

ingredients:

400g Whaligoe hearthbread dough
15g roughly chopped flat leaf parsley
50g thinly sliced green olives
100g anchovy fillets in oil

optional:

100g caramelised onion

method:

1) Chop the anchovy fillets coarsely, mix with your other ingredients *(including the caramelised onion if you are using it)*, and knead the mixture into your dough.

2) Allow to rest for 1 hour.

3) Weigh out 20g pieces, and roll into balls.

4) Place on a baking tray, allow to prove until doubled in size.

5) Heat your oil to 180°C, and deep fry the anchovy balls until golden and crisp.

6) Serve with a cold beer.

cut your rested dough into small pieces, approx. 15g in weight

serve with lemon wedges, a drizzle of garlic sauce & a cold beer

clementine scallop ceviche

makes a generous serving for 4 people.

This is a recipe that was developed as part of a dinner for a special customer of mine. Lani McGregor is an amazing woman and wonderful hostess - this dish went down well at her house, and I'm sure you would enjoy it too.

It is simple, quick and subtle. However, care should be taken with it as it is also simple, quick and easy to mess it up.

Pay attention to what you are doing with this one.

ingredients:
12 - 20 scallops depending upon their size
500ml freshly squeezed clementine juice
(if not available, use grapefruit juice, but leave out the lemon juice)
zest & juice of 1 lemon
4 spring onions or 2 small shallots
200g bag of lambs lettuce, mâche, or other mixed leaves
½ cucumber
optional:
few spoonfuls of my 'chilli & garlic' sauce *(see sauces)*

method:

1) Start by preparing your scallops. If your scallop includes the bright orange 'tongue' of roe, detach it carefully and set it aside.

2) Slice the white part of your scallop horizontally into three pieces - each slice should be no thicker than ½ cm. Set them aside.

3) Divide your clementine juice into two, and into one half add the zest and juice of your lemon - mix well.

4) Into the other half, add 1 tbsp of the 'chilli & garlic' sauce and mix that well too.

5) Remove the watery seeds from your cucumber, and chop the remainder into fine dice. Slice the spring onions finely, and mix with the cucumber. Carefully break up your choice of leaves, and mix through the chopped onion and cucumber.

6) Dress with 1 or 2 tbsp of the 'chilli & garlic sauce', and place on half of your plate, making sure that you leave plenty of space for the scallops.

7) No more than 10 minutes before you are due to serve, place your sliced white scallop flesh into the clementine and lemon juice mixture. Stir carefully to ensure that the flesh is not sticking together, but floating freely in the fluid. This will immediately start to 'cook' your scallop meat, and you will see it start to lose it's translucent quality and become more opaque.

8) After 5 minutes taste a piece, it should be soft but still slightly textural - if necessary leave for a few more minutes. Remove from the mixture.

9) Place the scallop flesh into your second bowl containing the clementine juice and 'chilli & garlic' mixture. Stir well, then remove with a slotted spoon and carefully place on your serving plates.

10) At the last minute, bring a heavy based sauté pan up to heat and quickly sear your scallop roe (*you should take no more than 30 seconds for each side*), and add to each plate.

11) Season with sea salt (*or a little of my lemon salt if you have some*), and fresh black pepper, and serve a little of the final soaking liquid in a sauce boat for diners to add more should they wish.

Whaligoe Haven

Glasstorm's seafood platter

makes enough for 4 to share

This recipe is dedicated to my very good friends Nicki Burns and Brodie Nairn, known as Glasstorm. A pair of very talented glassblowers in the north of Scotland. Their chosen ingredients were squid, pepper and chilli. I have used this platter as a way of demonstrating how several small dishes can be combined together to provide an impressive platter.

Not only have they given me some wonderful ingredients to choose from, they also kindly supplied me with some wonderful glass on which to display the food.

sliced stuffed squid served with crispy fried tentacles, blood orange, crispy seaweed, samphire, caramel coated Padron chillies and pickled candied beetroot (you can also eat the limpet if you wish, but I usually just throw them in my fish stocks)

stuffed squid

makes enough for 4 to share as part of a platter

Squid is seen most often as deep fried, bland white rings - this is not an ideal way to be introduced to what can be a tasty and textural treat.

When cleaning fresh squid, it is common in the UK to remove the outer thin grey membrane. I always try and leave it on if at all possible, as it turns a beautiful pale pink colour when cooked and imparts a rosy glow to the cooked flesh. It can cause the squid to develop a more pronounced fishy flavour though, so this is down to personal choice.

If you buy your squid entire, make sure that you remove the chitinous beak from the centre of the tentacles, and that the transparent quill within the squid's body is removed. You should also remove any soft mass from within the body cavity, leaving only an empty tube.

ingredients:
4 x medium sized squid
½ bottle of white wine or Noilly Prat
2 large shallots, finely sliced
10g finely chopped parsley
stuffing ingredients:
100g fresh breadcrumbs
25g finely chopped fresh parsley
2 finely chopped garlic cloves
50g finely chopped olives
sufficient olive oil to moisten stuffing
(optional for stuffing)
30g anchovy fillets
fried tentacle ingredients:
cornflour to dust
1 egg, beaten
50g semolina, mixed with 2 tsp fine salt

method:

1) Place your fresh breadcrumbs into a large mixing bowl, and mix in all of the other stuffing ingredients.

2) Mix until you have a soft but not greasy mass.

3) When a tablespoonful of mix is squeezed in the fingers it should stay together, but not appear oily.

4) Set the stuffing aside to help the flavours to infuse, and prepare your squid.

5) If you have bought entire squid, start by slicing off the tentacles.

6) To ensure that you cut in the right place, gently squeeze the tentacle bundle at the point where it joins the body. You will feel a hard lump under your fingers. Cut just beyond that point, nearer to the body. The tentacle bundle should come away with a central chitinous beak in the centre. Ease this forward with your fingers, and slice it out. You should be left with a starry tentacle cluster with a couple of very long 'feelers' in the centre. Remove these leaving the rest of the cluster intact.

7) Chop the feelers into small pieces, and mix them into the stuffing.

8) Reach inside the squid, and pull out the transparent quill. Discard this, together with any white or grey soft mass which is inside the body.

9) Rinse under a cold tap, if you are removing the thin membrane on the outside of the squid body now is the time to do it. Personally I like the rosy pink tinge it gives to the flesh, but if you wish to maintain it's snow white appearance you should remove the membrane.

10) Set aside, and repeat the process for each squid.

11) To stuff the squid, hold it carefully and gently squeeze in some of the stuffing, using either a piping bag, teaspoon or your fingers. Don't worry if you get some of the stuffing on the outside of the squid, you will be doing that anyway. Ensure that you do not overstuff your squid - the stuffing will expand as it cooks, and the squid flesh will contract as it cooks, so it is important that you do not fill the squid more than ¾, to avoid it splitting and spoiling your dish.

12) Preheat a cast iron griddle, and lightly oil it. Sear the squid bodies, and set them aside in a small pan.

13) Cover the squid with white wine, or Noilly Prat if using it, together with the sliced shallots and parsley.

14) Gently bring the liquid up to a simmer.

15) Simmer for 30 minutes, with a lid tightly on the pan, checking frequently to ensure that the liquid does not boil dry *(it should however, reduce significantly).*

16) You may either serve the stuffed squid dish hot, with extra stuffing sprinkled over the top, or allow it to cool, and serve it whole. It can also be very attractive sliced, as part of a composite plate.

17) While the squid is simmering, you may prepare the tentacles.

18) Gently pat the tentacles dry on kitchen paper and dust them with cornflour.

19) Dip them in the beaten egg and then in your salted semolina mix.

20) Deep fry for a few minutes until crisp, and set aside on kitchen paper to drain.

21) The fried tentacles may be served with some crunchy samphire as a pre-meal nibble with a drink, or used to make up part of a composite platter.

pressed squid with wild garlic

makes enough for 4 as part of a sharing platter

This is a quick and simple way of doing something a little different with your squid. Only use this method if your squid is perfectly fresh as it is cooked for a minimal amount of time, and will be tough and unpleasant if not absolutely fresh.

It's a seasonal treat.

ingredients:
3 large squid tubes
handful of wild garlic leaves, cleaned & spin dried
25g toasted & finely chopped hazelnuts

method:

1) Clean your squid as per the instructions previously given, and in this instance carefully remove the outer membrane.

2) Slice the squid tubes in half lengthwise, and open out carefully.

3) Lightly score the flesh.

4) Heat a ridged cast iron grill pan which can accommodate a heavy press, or if you don't have one of those a flat plate with a heavy can on top.

5) Lightly sear your squid with a weight on top, to ensure that you have maximum contact made with the ridged grill pan. Cook each of your three pieces for no more than 1 minute each.

(If you have a vacuum packer now is an ideal time to use it as it helps to keep everything in place, but you can also achieve similar results by simply keeping everything weighed down well.)

6) Using a foil board or a flat plate as your base, lay out your first piece of squid.

7) Cover the surface with a layer of wild garlic leaves and sprinkle with some toasted hazelnuts.

8) Add another layer and repeat, ending with a top layer of squid.

9) Now, either lay another foil board on top of your pile of squid and vacuum pack, or place a flat board or plate on top of the squid and weigh it down.

10) Chill for at least 6 hours before removing from the fridge and allowing it to come to room temperature.

11) Slice as required and serve with a salad or as part of a composite seafood platter.

fresh pressed squid with a green salad of wild garlic & samphire

braised octopus in red wine

makes enough for 6 to 8

Octopus can be a delight, but must either be cooked for a very short amount of time or a long one - anything in between tends to give you a chewy struggle to eat.

When properly braised, it should cut with the side of your fork while still retaining a pleasant texture.

It does take a while to cook, so I tend to make a large potful and freeze the excess for a quick treat on another day.

ingredients:
2 kg octopus
400g diced onions
150g diced celery
1 litre chopped tomatoes
3 tbsp tomato purée
4 cloves sliced garlic
100g sliced black olives
1 bottle (*good*) red wine
50ml red wine vinegar
1 stick cinnamon
1 star anise pod
3 bay leaves
1 small bunch flat leaf parsley
1 whole lemon

method:

1) In a large heavy pan heat some olive oil and sauté the diced onions until golden brown. Add the sliced garlic and stir until fragrant.

2) Chop your octopus into pieces approx 3 cm long and add to the fried onion.

3) Cook for a few minutes, until the tentacles start to contract and become opaque.

4) Now add all of the other ingredients except the parsley, and simmer.

5) On the lowest heat possible, simmer the octopus for at least 1 ½ hours, and check for tenderness.

6) The octopus should yield to your tooth easily, and the sauce should be well reduced.

7) If necessary, continue to cook the octopus and reduce the sauce further.

8) When the octopus is cooked to your taste add the chopped flat leaf parsley and adjust seasoning.

Serve piping hot with plain boiled potatoes, a side salad and lemon wedges.

tequila sweet & sour hake

makes enough to add to an antipasto platter

This recipe is dedicated to my very good friend Nicholas Finlay, and his lovely wife Caitlin.

Nicholas and I both developed something of a fondness for tequila many years ago, and he and I had too many good evenings to count imbibing an injudicious amount of it.

We've probably now both grown out of that (*mostly*) but this recipe evokes happy memories. While both fun and unusual, this dish makes a great addition to a seafood platter.

It's also just great served on a crisp piece of cucumber, together with an ice cold glass of tequila.

ingredients:
500g piece of hake
200g caster sugar
100g maldon salt
zest & juice of 3 limes
50ml tequila *(use the best quality you have)*

method:

1) If your hake has skin, remove it now to enable the cure to enter the flesh more easily.

2) Mix together the sugar, salt and finely zested skin of your limes.

3) In a ceramic or glass dish *(a metal dish could impart an unpleasant flavour to the fish)*, completely cover the fish fillet with the sugar and salt mixture.

4) Leave in a cool place for at least 2 hours but no more than 8. *(The longer that you leave it, the harder and drier your fish will be)*

5) You will see that a large amount of moisture has been drawn from the fish, remove the fish from the dish and pat dry on kitchen paper.

6) Mix the juice from your zested limes with the tequila, and pour over your fish.

7) Leave in a cool place for at least 30 minutes, but no more than 2 hours. *(The longer you leave it, the more the fish will 'cook' in the tequila).*

8) Remove the fish from your final cure, pat dry on kitchen paper and slice as thinly as you can.

9) Serve as it is, on a crisp piece of cucumber, or with sour cream on a cracker.

there are advantages to living on a clifftop

lampuki with green peppers & tomatoes

enough for a light supper for 4

Lampuki are probably one of the Maltese people's favourite fish.

It is also known as the Mahi Mahi, Dorado or Dolphin Fish.

They migrate past the Maltese Islands from August through to December, and in the late summer lampuki are often served shallow fried with seasonal vegetables.

Swordfish and tuna are also often prepared in the same way across the islands.

A fresh salad would usually be offered alongside any cooked vegetables.

ingredients:
2 small (*1 kg)* lampuki
1 large onion, thinly sliced
500g green peppers (*the thin fleshed crisp kind if possible*)
2 cloves of garlic
200g thickly sliced ripe tomatoes
50g capers
1 small lemon
plain flour to coat the fish

method:

1) Prepare your fish by cleaning it well, and either fillet it or if you wish to cook it on the bone, *(which is preferable in terms of flavour)* just remove the head and tail. Set aside.

2) Prepare your green peppers by slicing them into squares approx 3cm across and thinly slice your garlic.

3) Heat a pan with some olive oil and gently sauté the sliced onion. Once it is translucent, add the garlic and peppers and cook them until they have softened slightly, but still retain some crunch.

4) Finally, add the capers and thickly sliced tomatoes, and stir to combine. (*Note, you should not be cooking the tomatoes, just allow them to soften slightly in the residual heat from your peppers).*

5) Season, then set aside for the flavours to amalgamate.

6) Lightly dust your lampuki with flour, and place in a sizzling hot pan with a little olive oil. Don't overcrowd the pan, you want to fry the fish not boil it.

7) Lampuki cooks very quickly, so as soon as you have a crisp coat on one side turn it over and do the other. Once you have cooked it for a few minutes *(how long will depend upon the size of the fish, and whether you have filleted it or not)*, remove from the heat.

8) Serve with the pepper and tomato mixture, lemon wedges, and some crisply fried potato chips for an authentic experience of 'fish & chips' Maltese style.

Maltese coffee beef

makes enough for 6 as part of a salad

This is amazingly simple and truly unusual. Do try it. If you are feeling extravagant, you may use fillet steak for this, *(it will melt in your mouth)*, however you will be surprised how good it can be with skirt or flank steak.

Although it's great as it is, do try pairing it with my bitter 'chocolate & coffee' sauce (*see sauces*). I think they are wonderful together - but be warned, reactions are mixed, people either love or hate this combination so use it as a dipping sauce rather than pouring it over your beef.

ingredients:

1 kg piece of either skirt, flank or fillet steak - in a single piece,
(*Ideally no more than 6 cm or 7 cm thick, and of a consistent thickness, to allow it to cook evenly. If using flank or skirt, it will be necessary to trim your meat to achieve these dimensions).*
100g of your favourite freshly ground coffee
2 tbsp fine sea salt
¼ tsp ground cloves

method:

1) In a dish large enough to hold your meat flat, mix together the coffee, salt and ground cloves.

2) If necessary trim your meat, you should make sure that any sinew or excess fat is removed.

3) Press the meat firmly into the mixture and turn it around to ensure that every part is covered.

4) Cover with cling film (*or ideally vacuum pack your meat and mixture*) and refrigerate for anything from 2 hours to 2 days.

5) When ready to cook, remove from the mixture and shake off any loose coffee grounds (*but don't try to remove the rest*).

6) Heat a cast iron griddle to smoking point, brush with a little olive oil and sear your meat. It will almost immediately turn black - don't worry, it's the coffee.

7) Once you have an even sear on your beef, place it in a preheated oven at 200°C for approx. 10 minutes.

8) I like my beef to be seared on the outside, and quite rare in the centre - if you prefer it more well cooked, leave it in the oven for longer (*but please don't overdo it*).

9) Remove from the oven, and cover with foil while it rests for at least 30 minutes, then slice thinly to serve.

10) This may be served either warm or cold - it is fantastic with salads, makes a terrific steak sandwich and is very moreish.

Maltese pulpetti

makes approx. 14 pulpetti.

The Maltese love pulpetti. They are small patties - smaller then a small burger, but plumper. (*and much bigger and flatter then a meatball*)

They should be fried to produce a caramelised crust, and may be either served as they are or then simmered, usually in a tomato sauce, to juicy tenderness.

Serve with pasta or potatoes.

ingredients:
250g minced pork
250g minced lamb
500g minced beef
200g finely chopped onion
60g finely chopped parsley
leaves picked from a few sprigs of thyme
½ tsp cinnamon
2 cloves crushed garlic
200g fresh breadcrumbs
zest of 2 oranges
2 beaten eggs
to finish:
2 beaten eggs
100g dried breadcrumbs
a little flour

method:

1) Put all your ingredients into a large mixing bowl, and get in there with your hands. You need to end up with quite a pasty mixture, so mix all the ingredients well. Initially it will be quite clumpy, but after 5 minutes or so it should start to come together.

2) Once a handful that is squeezed together retains it's shape without crumbling, you are there. I normally find that a patty of around 100g is a good size to work with, so weigh out your mixture to that initially. Once you have made these a few times you can do it by eye.

3) Compress the 100g of mixture in your hands, and form into a neat patty. Set aside and repeat the process until you have finished all the mixture.

4) With clean hands, coat each patty in a small amount of flour, then dip it in the beaten egg, and finally in the breadcrumbs. (*The flour helps the egg to stick, the egg helps the breadcrumbs to stick).*

5) Shallow fry until cooked through. If you are intending placing them in some sauce cook until a crust is formed, then add to your pan of bubbling sauce and continue to cook gently for another 10 minutes.

6) Stir very gently, as you don't want to break up the patty.

7) Serve with a sprinkle of chopped parsley, either with pasta, potatoes or a good hunk of bread.

Whaligoe pulpetti & burger mix

makes approx. 14 pulpetti or 6 large burgers.

These are my favourite version of the ever popular pulpetti, they are well flavoured but melt in the mouth tender.

Served with a rich tomato & red wine sauce, and some crisp chips, *(or even better, buttery mash)* they are wonderful comfort food.

ingredients:
250g minced pork
125g chopped streaky bacon
750g minced beef
125g ox heart (*or lamb heart if ox heart not available*)
200g finely chopped onion
100g chopped celery
100g chopped carrot
60g finely chopped parsley
6 cloves crushed garlic
200g fresh breadcrumbs
4 egg yolks
to finish:
2 beaten eggs
100g dried breadcrumbs
a little flour

method:

1) Remove any obvious sinew or tubes from your hearts and chop into 2cm cubes - then add to the bowl of your food processor and blitz until finely chopped, but not a paste.

2) Combine all your ingredients, and mix until very well amalgamated - you may do this in a stand mixer if you have one. Otherwise, spend at least 5 to 10 minutes mixing by hand, until you have a mixture that holds together when squeezed gently.

3) As this is a slightly richer recipe than the original, I tend to use slightly smaller patties, approx. 75g each, which gives you a moderate portion of a couple of pulpetti per person, or three for the more hungry.

4) Compress 75g of mixture in your hands and form into a neat patty, set aside until you have finished all the mixture.

5) With clean hands, coat each patty in a small amount of flour then dip it in the beaten egg, and finally in the breadcrumbs.

6) Shallow fry until almost cooked through, so they are still tender but have a crisp crust.

7) Add to your pan of bubbling sauce, and continue to cook gently for another 10 minutes. Stir very gently, as you don't want to break up the patty.

8) Serve with a sprinkle of chopped parsley, and some very crisp chips.

Alternatively, divide your mixture into 6 equal portions and press into large burgers. Grill or fry as preferred.

Maltese sausages (zalzett)

makes quite a lot

Maltese sausages are similar to Italian in that they are mainly composed of meat and flavouring ingredients, with no rusk or breadcrumbs. They are ideally air dried for a few days before use (*hanging them in your fridge works quite well).*

Historically, they were left to mature in a cool slightly humid place (*frequently hung in a well, to keep them away from predators*) which would allow the meat to cure, and preserve and intensify the flavours.

They could then either be eaten after a few days, in which case due to their high salt content they are traditionally boiled first to remove some of the salt, then fried to crisp up the skin.

Alternatively they would be placed in a meat safe *(a cabinet with open sides covered with fine mesh to keep out insects)* in a cool environment, and left to mature for several months.

They would then be fully cured and able to be eaten without any further cooking. In that case, they are usually served as part of a plate of mixed antipasto.

ingredients:
1.5 kg minced pork with fat
90g sea salt
45g crushed (*not ground*) black peppercorns
45g crushed coriander seeds
30g crushed fennel seeds
5 cloves garlic finely chopped
5 tbsp chopped parsley
2 tbsp chopped fresh thyme
to finish:
hog casings (*obtain from a butchers supply shop*)

method:

1) Mix all the ingredients together until well amalgamated,

2) Rinse your hog casings in several changes of cold water, and stuff them with your mixture, either with a funnel or if you have one a sausage stuffer.

3) These sausages are usually around 10 cm long, so twist and tie with string at around that interval.

4) Prick each sausage in several places as you want to allow the mixture to dehydrate slightly, then hang to dry for 2-3 days in a handy well. (*Oh alright, use the fridge if you must*).

5) To cook, place in a pan with plenty of boiling water and simmer until they float to the surface, drain well and pat dry, then fry in a little olive oil until you have a lovely crispy brown skin.

6) You can serve these with pretty much anything, they slice well on pizza, they work with vegetables, but I love them with mash.

chicken (or rabbit) stew

serves 6

This stew is a nod to a traditional stewed rabbit, which is still a very popular dish in Malta.

These days, in many countries rabbit bred for the table is not so easily available, and many people prefer not to eat it - but the basic sauce works extremely well with chicken.

However, if you have access to some lovely eating rabbit, please do try making this recipe with rabbit rather than chicken.

ingredients:
6 large chicken legs, or 12 chicken thighs
(or if you can get them - 2 large rabbits broken down)
1 bottle red wine
4 thinly sliced onions
6 cloves of garlic, thinly sliced
2 bay leaves
450g tin of chopped tomatoes
3 tbsp tomato purée
3 carrots in small dice
3 stalks of celery paysanne cut
3 large potatoes cut into large dice
small bunch of parsley
100g pitted black olives
50g capers
100g cooked peas

method:

1) Using a little olive oil in a heavy based large pan, sear the chicken or rabbit until you have a golden glow. As they achieve this remove them from the pan until you have seared all the meat.

2) Using the same pan, fry your thinly sliced onion until it is golden. At that point you can add your thinly sliced garlic and sauté it for a few minutes.

3) Return your meat to the pan and add the bottle of red wine, together with the chopped tomatoes, tomato purée and bay leaves. Your meat should be covered by the liquid in the pan. If it is not, add just sufficient water to cover your meat.

4) Simmer gently for 30 minutes.

5) Add the diced potatoes, celery and carrot, together with the olives (*which you should slice into rings*) and capers.

6) Simmer for a further 20 minutes stirring gently occasionally, the stew should be thickening up as it reduces. (*Don't over thicken the sauce, as you want to have plenty to mop up with your bread)*. If the sauce is very thin, lift out the meat and keep it warm, then boil the liquid hard to reduce it further, and return the meat to your reduced sauce.

7) Finally add the peas, and cook for a few minutes.

8) Sprinkle in the parsley to finish.

9) Season to taste, and serve with crusty bread.

fried chicken wings

makes 1 kg wings - enough for 2 to 6 depending upon how hungry they are, and what else is available.

I started making these for my son's friends - but I've found that they are equally popular with adults.

A quick and tasty bite that you can serve this as part of a larger meal, or an indulgent late night snack.

They work. Try them.

ingredients:
1 kg chicken wings
200g gram (*chickpea*) flour
3 eggs, beaten
sunflower oil for deep fat frying
(*optional*) to finish:
toasted sesame seed

method:

1) Prepare your chicken wings by separating out the three sections of each wing. Place the wing tips in a bowl to be added to your freezer box of chicken bones, and separate the blade from the drummet.

2) Preheat your oil to 160°C.

3) Separate out your drummets from your wing blades - the blades will cook more quickly, so the initial cooking is done separately.

4) Dip your chicken into the beaten egg and coat well with the gram flour. Fry the chicken in batches to keep the oil temperature consistent, and cook the drummets for approx 10 minutes and the blades for approx 6 minutes. Check the internal temperature of the chicken with a probe - it should read 75°C. When your chicken has reached this stage, remove it from the oil and drain well.

5) Raise the oil temperature to 180°C.

6) Now take all the chicken cooked to the first stage, and dip it once more into the beaten egg, and gram flour. If you wish, you may add some sesame seed to the gram flour for this final coating.

7) Fry until crisp and golden, it won't take long.

8) Take care not to overcook the chicken at the second frying stage, it should be cooked from your first fry - this second fry is just to make them extra crunchy and pretty.

9) Take them out and drain them on kitchen paper as soon as they are golden and appealing.

Serve with lots of napkins; and if you have it an aïoli to dip them in works well too.

spiced lamb with pine nuts

makes approx 1 kg of lamb mix

ingredients:

500g minced lamb
250g finely chopped onions
4 thinly sliced cloves of garlic
150g finely chopped celery
50g double concentrate tomato purée
3 tablespoons pomegranate molasses
250g baby plum tomatoes - halved
100g pine nuts
small bunch of flat leaf parsley
½ tsp ground cloves
½ tsp ground cinnamon
1 tbsp red pepper flakes
½ tsp fennel seed

method:

1) Sweat your onions gently in a little olive oil until they are translucent. Add your minced lamb and fry until the mixture is well browned.

2) Add the chopped celery, garlic and tomato concentrate together with the cloves, cinnamon, fennel seed and red pepper flakes.

3) Pour over sufficient boiling water to just cover your ingredients, and allow to bubble for 20 mins Stir occasionally to make sure that the mixture does not catch on your pan.

4) Now season, add the pomegranate molasses and the baby plum tomatoes. Cook for a further 20 mins, until the tomatoes are softened and the entire mixture is binding well together.

5) Add the pine nuts and finely chopped parsley, taste, and adjust seasoning as necessary.

hummus with spiced lamb

makes sufficient for two to share as a starter, or one as a light meal.

I put this on the menu several years ago, and I've never been able to take it off - it's probably my single most popular dish.

Not really a recipe, more an assembly. Serve with a crusty hunk of my hearthbread, and savour the texture and flavour combination.

ingredients:
100g roast onion hummus
125g spiced lamb mix

method:

1) Spread the hummus in a shallow layer in a heatproof dish, and top with the spiced lamb mix.
2) Heat in a moderate oven for approx 15 minutes, and serve piping hot with a lovely chunk of crusty bread.

haggis stuffed mushrooms with whisky sauce

makes 6 large stuffed mushrooms.

This is a really nice way of using some haggis, a great treat in the wintertime in Scotland which I've become really partial to.

It can also be made equally successfully with a vegetarian haggis, as these can be very good.

ingredients for mushrooms:
8 large portobello mushrooms
300g haggis (*traditional or vegetarian*)
100g softened butter
1 small onion
¼ tsp dried sage
ingredients for sauce:
100ml (*good*) whisky
300ml double cream
2 egg yolks

method:

1) Peel your mushrooms and remove the central stalk.

2) Place the stalks, two of the mushrooms (*broken up*), the sliced onion, sage and softened butter into a food processor.

3) Blitz until well broken down, then add the chopped haggis and blitz again until well mixed. Season with salt and pepper to taste.

4) Divide the stuffing between your remaining mushrooms and place into a baking tray.

5) At this stage they may be refrigerated until needed.

6) 1 hour before you need to serve them, preheat your oven to 180°C and bake for 20 to 25 minutes until the mushrooms are cooked and the topping has a crisp crust.

7) While they are baking, prepare your sauce.

8) Gently bring the cream up to scalding point with a little salt and pepper.

9) Simmer for 5 minutes. In a separate bowl whisk together the egg yolks and whisky. Add a little of your hot cream to this bowl to temper, then return the whole mixture to your pan and whisking constantly, heat for a few minutes until the sauce is slightly thickened.

10) Don't boil the sauce as you want to keep the whisky flavour, just lose the rawness of the alcohol by simmering it off a little.

11) Taste and season as necessary

Serve your mushroom with the sauce drizzled around and over the top, or in a small sauce dish on the side.

stuffed marrows (qarabaghli mimli)

serves 6

Unlike the marrows commonly found in the UK, which tend to be large and quite bland, in Malta we have smaller, rounded and more intensely flavoured marrows.

These are a very popular dish.

ingredients:
6 small marrows
500g minced pork
500g minced beef
2 large onions
3 cloves garlic
2 tbsp tomato purée
2 eggs
100g fresh breadcrumbs
1 tbsp fennel seeds
3 tbsp chopped flat leaf parsley
100g coarsely grated parmesan cheese
buttered breadcrumbs to finish

method:

1) Prepare your marrows by slicing off the cap, which you should keep.

2) Carefully using a spoon, scoop out most of the inner flesh making sure that you retain a depth of at least 1cm all around the skin, as otherwise your marrow may collapse when you cook it.

3) Set half the white marrow flesh aside for other uses (*great in a vegetable soup*), and dice the remaining flesh.

4) Heat a pan with a little olive oil and sauté the onion, sliced garlic and marrow flesh until soft.

5) Add the minced pork and beef, and fry until crumbly and lightly browned.

6) Stir in the tomato purée, fennel seeds and chopped parsley.

7) Cook for a few minutes stirring occasionally, until the tomato purée has formed a sauce with the liquid which has formed in your pan.

8) Remove from the heat and add the fresh breadcrumbs, beaten eggs and parmesan cheese.

9) Mix well and set aside for the flavours to combine for at least 30 minutes.

10) Fill the marrows with an overflowing amount of the mixture, and top with a 'cap'.

11) Bake at 170°C for 30 to 45 minutes, or until the marrow is tender but not collapsed.

12) Sprinkle with fried buttered breadcrumbs for a bit of extra texture.

Makes an excellent light supper dish, served with a side salad.

beef khoresh

makes enough for a crowd

I love khoresh. It's a type of Persian stew, usually highly spiced and aromatic with strong citrus and herby notes. It's not chilli hot but a complex and melting mouthful.

To make a good khoresh takes time, don't skimp on it. Allow an afternoon to enjoy the process, your kitchen will smell wonderful.

I often include oxtail in my meat based khoresh as I like the earthy richness of the meat, but it's not to everyone's taste. If you prefer, just substitute another cut of meat. Do however use a 'cheap' cut - they are more appropriate for this dish, long slow cooking is the order of the day.

ingredients:
2 kg oxtail *(or 1 kg beef shin)*
2 kg ox cheeks *(or 2 kg of another beef cut of your choice)*
500g roughly chopped onions
300g celery - paysanne cut
400g dates - quartered & pitted
3 tbsp advieh spice mix *(see extras section)*
4 dried limes
large bunch of flat leaf parsley
1 litre chopped tomatoes
zest & juice of 4 fresh limes
4 tbsp verjuice
4 tbsp pomegranate molasses

method:

1) Bring a large heavy pan up to a high heat and sear your meat in batches to achieve a good crust. Don't try to cook the meat at this stage as you are only adding flavour.

2) Once all the meat is seared, set it aside.

3) Loosen any residue in your pan, add a little more oil if necessary.

4) Cook off your chopped onions until they are a rich brown colour, then return the meat to your pot.

5) Now add the celery, dates, spices, dried limes and chopped tomato, together with half of your parsley, roughly chopped.

6) Add just sufficient water to cover the mixture.

7) Simmer gently for at least 2 hours, stirring frequently to ensure that the mixture is well amalgamated.

8) Once your meat is tender, remove it from the pot and chop it into bite sized pieces. If you have used oxtail, you should remove the meat from the bone.

9) Return all of the chopped meat to the pot, and now add the fresh lime zest and juice, verjuice, and pomegranate molasses. Stir well, and taste.

10) Season with salt and pepper, and adjust the mix of sweet and sour by adding more lime juice, verjuice or molasses. (*You are aiming to achieve a balance of sweet at the outset, with a sour, mouth puckering hit in the middle, balanced with a residual spicy sweetness from the rose petals and cinnamon in your advieh*).

11) Finally, add your remaining parsley and serve with some quartered lemon wedges. Rice or bread are an excellent accompaniment to mop up the juices.

Persian dried limes come in regular or black - I like to use both as they have distinctively different flavour profiles.

when the Khoresh is cooked the sauce should remain quite thin, this allows it to be more easily soaked up with your rice or bread.

crispy pork belly

this recipe scales so easily, just buy a piece of pork to suit yourself

While this recipe does scale extremely well there are a couple of words of warning. This is so simply cooked that the flavour of the meat is the star here, use good quality pork or this dish will be a disappointment.

Also, allow twice as much pork per person as you might in normal circumstances, it's astounding how much of this your guests can eat.

ingredients:
a large piece of whole pork belly (*don't try to use strips, it won't work*)
large bag of regular table salt
2 large onions

keeping the size of your roasting dish the same as your pork will help to maintain the formation of the salt crust during the initial cooking time

method:

1) Peel and roughly chop your onion, then blend it into a fine paste.

2) Wash your pork belly, then pat it dry and turn it skin side down on a chopping block. Taking a handful at a time, massage the onion paste into the flesh of the pork. Take care to keep the skin dry.

3) Select a roasting tray that is as close as possible to the size of your pork, and place any remaining onion paste into the bottom of the tray.

4) Place the pork skin side up in the roasting dish, ensure it is clean and dry, and pour over 1 cm thickness of fine salt over the skin. (*Really, don't worry, it all comes off*).

5) Place into an oven preheated to 150°C, and bake for approx. 2 ½ hours.

6) Remove from the oven, and carefully lever away the salt from the skin of your pork - it will have formed a crust, and should come away quite cleanly.

7) Dust off any residual salt from the skin of the pork, and raise the heat of your oven to 200°C.

8) Once your oven has reached this temperature, return your roasting dish to the oven and bake for approx 40 minutes; until the skin is blistered and golden brown.

9) Remove from the oven and allow to rest for 20 minutes, before cutting into chunks and offering pig heaven to your guests.

the pork will shrink beneath the salt crust, which should easily be removed

once the pork is double baked, the crackling will be a thing of joy

the cooked pork belly slices well, and can be chopped into chunks easily, with each piece retaining it's own individual slab of crackling

bread

My kitchen is my 'happy place', but I am always at my happiest when bread is being made.

I remember as a child being sent to collect our loaves, entering the bakery through a dark passageway, into a large square room with roaring wood fired ovens in the far corner. Men (*at the time, it always was men*) were stripped to the waist, portioning dough, sliding the fresh batches into the ovens, and pulling them out on their long peels. Often I would be tossed a warm sweet bun, glazed with honey, and told they were worried I would starve while I waited.

I always loved a loaf with two 'kisses', so would hover until the loaf I preferred was torn apart from the batch and thrust into my waiting hands with a smile, and a gruff 'imshi' (*walk*). I'd put my money in the biscuit tin full of coins on the side, and skip home with my treasure.

Often my nanna would complain about the ‘mouse-hole' in the loaf knowing that I was that little mouse.

The entire experience was loaded with sensation - the cool of the darkened passage into the bakery, the immense heat of the large room, the smell of bread in all it's stages; not only freshly baked, but proving and souring in large tubs, and always the kindness and good humour of the bakers, both young and old.

Do not be frightened of bread, embrace it and fall in love.

grains

For general bread making, the most effective grain is wheat due to it's taste and performance. However, in many cases, a tasty and interesting result can be gained by understanding the different advantages and properties of other grains, which may be added to a loaf.

wheat: Wheat contains starch to give bulk, feed the yeast and turn brown when baked, germ to add essential fats and oils and improve its nutritional value, bran to aid our digestion and gluten which lets the loaf stretch and rise.

spelt: Spelt flour is a form of ancient grain. It has low gluten levels, so although it rises quickly it cannot sustain it's own weight and must be baked quickly once risen, rather then knocked back and allowed to rise again. It is very easily digested, and can often be tolerated by those with a slight intolerance to gluten.

rye: Rye has a fine flavour, and sufficient gluten to rise in the making (*although not as much as wheat*). Rye loaves will be denser then wheaten, and most bakers mix rye with wheat to help with the texture. These used to be referred to as Maslin loaves in the Middle Ages.

barley: Barley makes a tasty bread, but does not have the gluten necessary to make it light. It is an ancient grain and easy to digest.

oats: Like barley, using oats in loaves has almost disappeared, other than as a decorative flourish on the top crust. Oats must be mixed with wheat for a risen loaf, but are an excellent nutritional addition.

maize / cornmeal: Maize is often used for flatbreads, and in the USA for an enriched batter bread which is raised via baking powder rather then yeast. In Italy, a traditional bread is made with a 50% mixture of wheat and maize, giving a golden dense loaf, often used to mop up soups.

leavening your loaf

Most breads, even those referred to as 'flatbreads' usually contain some form of leavening.

Leavening lightens dough by introducing bubbles in your bread. The way that bread is usually lightened is through some sort of fermentation to create those bubbles. (*either a sour-dough or brewers yeast ferment is the most usual*).

Using a natural fermentation, a fresh dough can be worked on by an existing ferment, and this is conditioned by mixing and kneading, then finally set by the heat of the oven.

Early bakers relied on a natural leaven, it gives a more or less sour taste and needs to be renewed from day to day, but this system is what has produced a traditional sour-dough leaven.

types of yeast

Brewers Yeast offers the opportunity to use a reliable source of yeast. While a natural leaven has wild yeasts, brewers yeast is a by- product of brewing and wine making. Bakers found (*as early as the ancient Romans*) that using brewers yeast was a faster and more reliable way of leavening breads.

All of the recipes here specify active or dried yeast - this is because fresh yeast can be hard to find, and it also has a short shelf life - only up to a week or two if kept in your fridge. In contrast, dried yeast keeps for years *(some of the traditional settlers in the wild west would keep a piece of dried yeast, hard as wood, and reconstitute it by shaving off slivers as needed).*

If you wish to use fresh yeast in any of the recipes, just double the weight of dried yeast specified. If you can get hold of fresh yeast use it, I prefer to use it myself, mainly because I associate the smell of fresh yeast with a happy bakery.

Active Dried Yeast comes in large granules, and must be activated in warm liquid before using.

Easyblend Dried Yeast is a fine grain/powder, and may be mixed directly into your ingredients without pre-activation.

Of the two types of dried yeast, I would always prefer to use the easyblend yeast, which mixes easily and has a lighter, less aggressively 'sour yeasty' aroma.

They may however be used interchangeably, but you must always activate the granulated yeast before mixing into your dough.

As there is no advantage to be gained from using the large grained yeast, and a disadvantage in terms of the additional step & time required to activate it, I would usually avoid using it if possible.

pre-ferment

A pre-ferment is a fermentation starter used in bread making, and is referred to as an indirect method. **It may also be called a mother dough**.

Using a pre-ferment and a longer fermentation time in the bread-making process has several benefits.

To create a risen loaf we need to allow the main component, flour, to be modified by the action of the yeast. Depending upon the type of flour used, and the addition of supplementary ingredients such as malt, enzyme activity may also take place.

This can have a significant effect on the staling properties of your baked bread, and can create greater complexity of flavour and a more developed crumb structure.

Though pre-ferments have declined in popularity, as the direct addition of yeast in bread recipes has streamlined the process on a commercial level, pre-ferments of various forms are still widely used in artisanal bread recipes.

types of pre-ferment

In general, there are two main pre-ferment varieties: sponges, based on brewers yeast, and the starters of sourdough, based on wild yeasts and lactic-acid bacteria. There are however several kinds of pre-ferment commonly named and used in bread baking. They all fall on a varying process and time spectrum, from a mature ferment of many generations, to a first-generation sponge based on a fresh batch of baker's yeast:

Biga and poolish are terms used in Italian and French baking, respectively, for sponges made with domestic baker's yeast.

Poolish is a fairly wet sponge (*typically made with a one-part-flour- to-one-part- water ratio by weight*), whereas a biga is usually drier. Biga's can be held longer at their peak than wetter sponges, allowing for a greater intensity of flavour development, while a poolish is a reliable technique to increase a dough's extensibility (*or rise*).

Old dough (*mother dough*) may be made with yeast or sourdough cultures, and in essence consists of a piece of dough reserved from a previous batch, with more flour and water added to feed the remaining flora. Because this is a piece of old dough, it typically contains salt which distinguishes it from other pre-ferments. Once old dough has rested for an additional 10 hours of age, the French refer to it as 'chef'. Frequently the Italian term 'biga' is used interchangeably with the the French 'levain de chef'.

Sourdough starter is generally considered to be the oldest type, being reliant on organisms present in the grain and local environment. In general, these starters have fairly complex microbiological makeups, the most notable including wild yeasts, lactobacillus, and acetobacteria. They are often maintained over long periods of time. The Boudin Bakery in San Francisco for example, claims to have used the same starter dough for over 150 years.

use of pre-ferments

A pre-ferment is easy to make and usually consists of a simple mixture of wheat flour, water, and a leavening agent *(typically yeast).*

When considering the inclusion of salt or sugar, the timing of their inclusion is key. Salt acts to inhibit or slow yeast growth while sugar will assist growth, as determined by time to proof or rise. Therefore they are not usually included in pre-ferments and instead are added to the final dough. Ultimately, the amounts of each ingredient, and when they are added, should depend on your pre-ferment and final-dough formulae.

When expressed as a bakers' percentage, *(see explanation later in this chapter)* 50 parts of flour added to 50 parts of water or 1:1 is 100% hydration, and results in a relatively fluid pre-ferment. Stiffer doughs such as 50% hydration or 2:1, may also be used. After mixing, the pre-ferment should be allowed to ferment before being added to the final dough as a substitute for, or in addition to, more yeast.

Traditionally fermentation has been performed in a warm place, or in a humidity and temperature controlled environment (*a proofing cabinet).*

However, cooler-than-room or refrigeration temperatures can also work. While this will slow fermentation, enzyme activity continues. This allows you a slow rise, with the additional activity giving you better flavour development in your final dough.

Flavour takes time.

Too warm a temperature can also slow growth, while even higher temperatures will kill the yeast. **Death of the yeast cells occurs in the range of 50–60 °C.**

The answer historically has been to suggest that your dough is a delicate beast, and must be kept away from draughts, coddled in a warm airing cupboard or a cosy corner.

As I've found over the years, not a bit of it. Actually, if anything, it responds to a bit of rough treatment (*within limits of course, like us all).*

Italian biga (yeasted starter)

Most traditional Italian loaves specify the use of a biga.

This is simply a piece of dough which is left over from the previous day's baking, and is used to 'seed' the next day's dough. (*It is different from a 'chef' in that it will therefore usually contain salt*). It reduces slightly the amount of yeast which is used in your main mix, and gives a more pronounced slightly sour flavour to your loaf. You may age your biga for up to 4 days, in a fridge, or in cool weather just on your kitchen counter.

To make a biga from scratch; use 225g strong flour, 1 tsp dried yeast and 100ml water. Mix to a stiff dough, and leave for at least a day before use. It should rise and fall back at least once before being used in a traditional recipe. The longer and more times it rises and falls, the more of a 'sour' flavour you will gain in your loaf.

Personally, I like a biga to be at least 3 days old before use.

The percentage of biga used in your new batch of bread will determine the level of 'sourness', fullness of flavour and texture of your finished dough.

However, beware, using more then 50% biga can adversely affect the texture of your dough. It will be more difficult to handle as the gluten has now lost much of it's strength. Your dough might tear and will not rise particularly well. It will taste great though.

understanding gluten

I am indebted to the writing of Guy Crosby *(www.cookingscienceguy.com)*, for his detailed explanation of the science behind how gluten works, and I have provided here a shortened version. I recommend you looking up his website when you have a minute, it's fascinating.

Gluten is a water-insoluble protein that is formed when water is mixed with wheat flour. Proteins are very large molecules composed of amino acids. Two of the naturally occurring proteins in flour are called glutenin and gliadin. When sufficient water is added to dry flour, the two proteins emerge from a "fixed state" and become flexible and able to move about.

The process of wetting the proteins is called hydration. As water and flour are mixed the hydrated proteins are brought together and begin to interact. They literally begin to stick to each other, through the formation of chemical bonds. These new chemical bonds are called cross-links. When this happens with gluten a number of different types of chemical bonds form between the proteins, with some *(disulfide bonds)* being stronger than others *(ionic bonds and hydrogen bonds)*.

Continued mixing causes more cross-links to form between the proteins until a large network of chemically linked proteins is formed. Mixing can be done with a stand mixer, or by hand such as when dough is kneaded.

When dough is mixed or kneaded the hydrated flexible proteins are stretched and aligned in the direction of kneading, providing more opportunities to form cross-links between the proteins.

Kneading also incorporates air, which helps to form strong disulfide bonds. As kneading continues the protein networks combine to form sheets of proteins. Think of this step in the process as being similar to unraveling thread (*proteins*), and weaving the straightened thread into pieces of cloth (*networks*).

The chemical cross-linking of glutenin and gliadin forms gluten, a very elastic substance. Neither protein alone is as elastic and stretchable as gluten.

The gluten becomes stronger and stronger as more bonds form between the proteins. Gluten will be inflated with steam as dough rises and bread is baked in the oven. As the bread bakes, the inflated gluten dries turning into a strong but flexible structure that gives us the holes in chewy bread.

(Note, freshly baked bread still contains about 35% moisture by weight, which is sufficient to keep the starch soft and the gluten elastic).

Many factors affect the development and strength of gluten. If too much gluten develops it can make baked goods, like pie crust, tough rather than tender. However, when you understand this, it is something that can be used to advantage - it is the very strength of gluten that makes a chocolate chip cookie chewy, rather than crumbly, as bread flour rather than plain flour is used.

The extent of gluten development affects how high leavened baked goods will rise, and whether the crumb is tender or chewy. Weaker gluten is more extensible (*stretchable*) and doesn't shrink as much.

Here are some factors that affect gluten development:

Variety of wheat: Soft wheat contains less protein (*6-8%*), less glutenin, smaller proteins, and forms weaker gluten. Hard wheat contains more protein (*10-14%*), more glutenin, larger proteins, and forms stronger, more cohesive, elastic gluten.

Amount of water: Hydration is essential for gluten development. Glutenin and gliadin absorb about twice their weight in water (*hydration*). Less water results in less gluten development (*reduces protein mobility*), but too much water also reduces gluten development by diluting the proteins so much that their interaction is restricted.

Water hardness: Calcium and magnesium in hard water areas strengthen gluten. Adding some calcium to your dough can therefore impact the strength of your dough in soft water areas.

Water pH: (*a figure expressing the acidity or alkalinity of a solution on a logarithmic scale of 0 - 14 in which 7 is neutral, lower values are more acid and higher values more alkaline.*)

The ideal pH for gluten development is 5-6. Above and below pH 5-6 reduces gluten strength producing more extensible (*easier to stretch*) dough. Adding baking powder raises pH (*producing more cookie spread*), and more porous, tender crumb. (*It is easy to buy PH testing strips, and if you are having difficulties it may be worth checking your results*).

Leavening: Expanding bubbles strengthen gluten, increasing cohesiveness and elasticity, producing a higher volume and finer crumb.

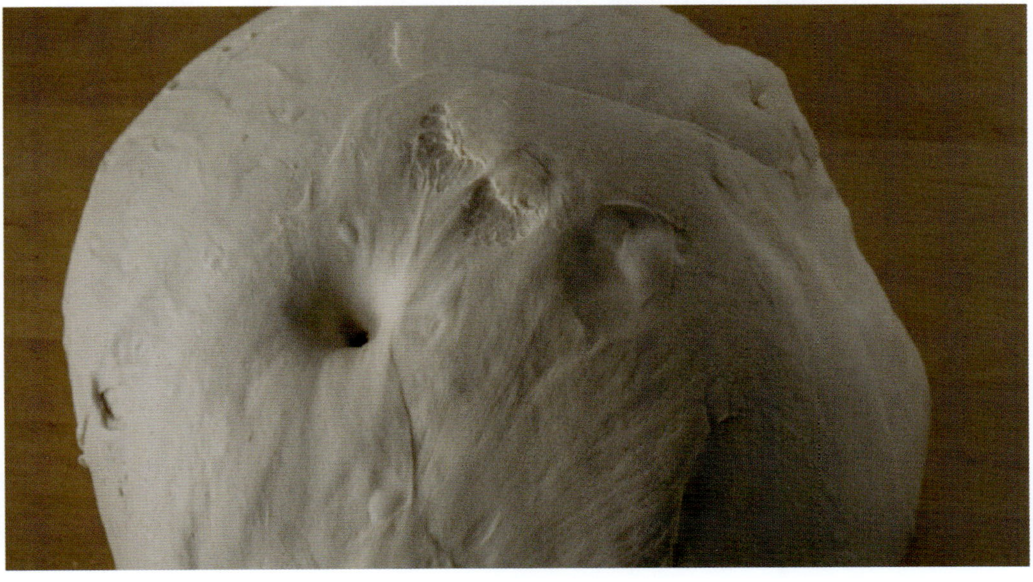

the bakers percentage

The bakers percentage is first and foremost your friend.

This is a baker's notation method indicating the flour-relative proportion of ingredients used when making breads.

It is also sometimes referred to as baker's math.

Baker's percentage expresses each ingredient in parts per hundred as a ratio of the ingredient's mass to the total flour mass *(that is, the unit mass).*

If you are using 1 kg of flour in your dough, then 1,000g is your 100% figure. Anything else you use in the recipe is expressed as a % of that figure.

(*Be aware also that although I am referring to flour within your recipe, you should count as part of the flour % any grain based product that you are using. If you are using 500g of flour, together with 300g of oatmeal, you should consider 800g to be your 100% figure*).

If your recipe calls for 1 kg of flour, and 500ml of water *(500ml =500g)* then the corresponding bakers' percentages will be 100% and 50%.

Because of the way these percentages are stated, as a percent of flour mass rather than of all ingredients, the total will always exceed 100%.

Flour-based recipes are more precisely conceived as baker's percentage, and more accurately measured using weight instead of volume *(cup measurements)*. The uncertainty in using volume measurements follows from the fact that flour settles in storage and therefore does not have a constant density.

hydration percentage

The single most useful part of all this for me, is the fact that you can express the hydration % of your dough easily, and from that, you are able to draw a number of conclusions.

As an example, if a recipe calls for 500g of flour, 100ml of beer, and 200ml of water, then this should be calculated as the following:

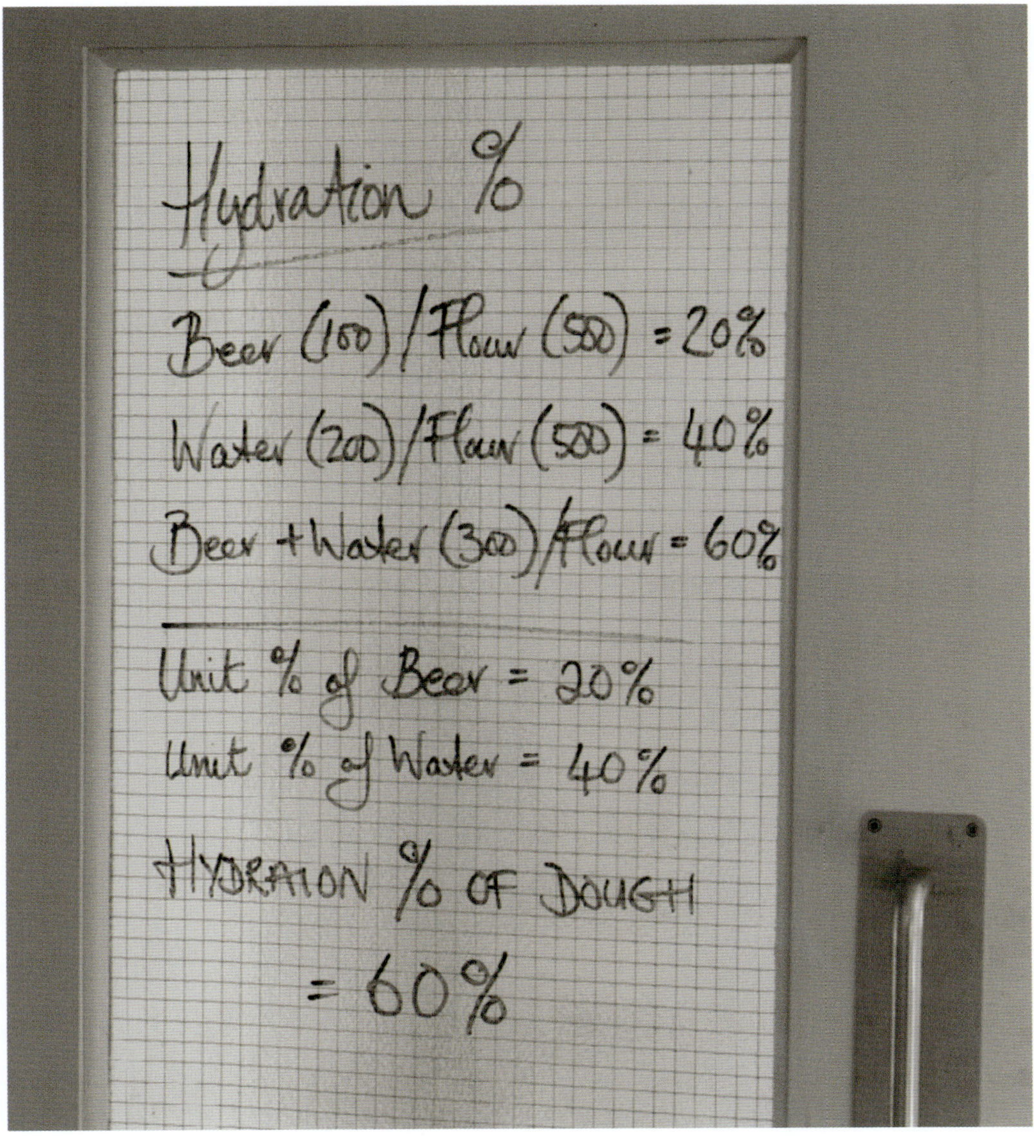

Now what does that mean?

First, you must understand that a hydration % does not only apply to water, but to any fluid added to a dough. Include any oil, egg, beer, yogurt, milk, buttermilk, whatever you are using.

Bread hydration varies widely, "standard" bread using all-purpose (*plain*) flour has a ratio of water to flour weight (*hydration*) in the range of 60-65%. Flour with a higher protein level, labelled as bread, strong, or high-gluten flours, tend to use 65% hydration.

Ciabatta and rustic breads generally use more water than normal. The extra water gives them larger, more uneven holes in the crumb, and can lead sometimes (*depending upon the shaping method used*) to a high-rising bread. These wetter doughs are often referred to as "slack" doughs in baker's terms. They are more challenging for a novice baker, but are well worth mastering.

To complicate matters further, most European strong flours are much softer then American or Canadian strong flours - if you are using an American flour, but trying to replicate a European loaf, you may need to mix through some plain (*soft*) flour, to weaken it.

Bearing that in mind, here are some typical %'s.

You would expect a baguette to be approx. 66% hydration, while a ciabatta would be 73% hydration.

If you consider that, you will see the differences that just 7% hydration can make.

The baguette dough is able to be shaped, and retain it's shape (*the traditional baton)*. It is usually slashed on the top to help the bread rise evenly, and the crumb tends to be close, with even bubbles.

The ciabatta dough is *(in comparison)* very slack.

Although you do shape it before the final prove, it will have a tendency to spread rather then rise. When it does rise (*or spring*) in the oven, the high level of liquid in the dough makes for more steam, and the bubbles will be larger and uncontrolled.

You never slash the top of your ciabatta, as that would only increase it's spreading tendency. Instead, as it rises in the oven, it will tend to break the initial crust that is formed, giving you a slightly 'jagged' split often in the sides of the bread.

Any bread wetter then 70% is rarely worked by hand - instead you have two options, either simply mix in your mechanical mixer and pour the finished dough (*or batter)* into your tin, or if you wish, opt for a double-hydration dough.

double hydration dough

This is a dough where the initial dough mix is made with a lower % of hydration then ultimately desired, eg. around 60%. The dough can be kneaded until springy, allowed to rise, and then returned to the mixer to have the final quantities of liquid added to the dough. In this way it is possible to make a dough which still has a good development of gluten, but also has the slack properties that you desire.

Another reason for a double-hydration dough is where there is a high % of oil, or fat of any kind, to be added (*including eggs*) - or a high level of sweetness used, such as sugar, syrup or honey.

In these instances, such ingredients would impact the doughs properties and the ability of the gluten to form strong strands, so allowing the dough some time to work before adding these ingredients can only improve your dough.

The hydration is very dependent on your flour.

A low-gluten flour will fall apart at high hydration. Therefore you must use bread flour or durum flour for high hydrations, otherwise you'll get a batter instead of a dough.

Sometimes, you actually want a bread dough that is almost a batter, but gluten development is hard to achieve with runny dough. That would be another instance when a double- hydration technique should be used.

formula percentage and total weight

The total or sum of the bakers' percentages is called 'the formula percentage'

The sum of the ingredient weights is called 'the formula weight'

autolyse

Don't be put off by the word, it's a simple technique which will greatly enhance your bread-making.

An autolyse is easily introduced into your bread making routine and delivers a dough that's easier to work with and shape, and has better texture, rise and flavour.

It's a deceptively simple process. **Just do nothing for 20 minutes**.

Combine the flour and water in a bowl and mix until no dry flour remains. **Do not be tempted to knead**. Simply cover the bowl and leave it for anything from 20 minutes up to 3 hours.

During this resting stage, gluten development begins and simple sugars start to form as starch is broken down. Although it may look like nothing is happening, you will notice the difference as soon as you handle the dough because during the autolyse it will have become smoother and more elastic.

Originally the autolyse was used exclusively with just flour and water. However, over time artisan bakers have developed other ways of using it, some adding yeast at the start of the process, and some including all of the ingredients before performing the autolyse.

Generally, breads made with stoneground flour or unconditioned flour benefit from a longer autolyse.

The key thing is to ensure that flour is allowed the time to absorb liquid, before the gluten is strengthened by kneading.

Over-kneading your dough can cause it to oxidise, detracting from the texture, crumb and flavour of your bread. Allowing the grain to absorb liquids before kneading means that the chance of over-kneading your dough becomes very slight. It also makes it easier to achieve a successful loaf.

There are two key things to consider when deciding whether to add all the ingredients to your mix or not, before using an autolyse.

Salt does not kill yeast as used to be thought, but it certainly does slow down its activity (*as you will remember, it also affects gluten development).*

If you are adding yeast to your mixture don't add salt early in the process, you are likely to slow down the whole process because you have compromised the health of your yeast. By all means add yeast early, I prefer to myself, as it helps get the flavours going, but be kind to it and leave the salt for later.

The other consideration is fat. Not just oil but milk, yogurt, eggs, etc. anything that contains fat is not great to add at the start of your process.

The reason for this is that fat has a tendency to coat the flour grains, making it harder for gluten bonds to form. (*It is helpful to remember this when making pastry, as cutting in your fat early before making the flour wet will hep to make a more tender crust, as gluten development will be impeded).*

So a dough with an early high fat content will tend to rise less.

Adding fat later once the bonds have developed is fine.

yukone method (tangzhong)

Yukone (*also known as a 'water roux'*) is a Japanese method for increasing the water content in your bread. It does however has very helpful applications in many other breads.

If you are working with a bakers percentage hydration recipe, you should disregard the ingredients for your Yukone, as they will only take effect once the loaf is baked.

The result of using a Yukone is to increase the life of your bread before it becomes stale, and to make the crumb extra moist and chewy. An ideal application of this method to a western recipe is in the making of bagels, and a recipe is included for you to try.

Making a Yukone is simplicity itself. Using no more than a ¼ of your total flour - add it to 5 x the amount of boiling water *(by weight).*

Stir well, and cook gently for a couple of minutes. You are aiming for the starch to be released from your flour, and for gelatinisation to occur.

Try to avoid lumps by stirring well.

For success with this method, your mixture should reach approx. 65°C. I usually find that just stirring hard when the boiling water is added is sufficient without any additional cooking being necessary. (*This means I can cheat and carry out the process in my stand mixer*). In any case, you are aiming for a similar result to a roux - you should have a thick paste a little like stodgy mashed potato.

Allow the Yukone to cool, then add to your other bread ingredients and continue as normal.

Do try it out, it does make quite a difference to the eating quality of the bread - of course it's not always going to be what you want, but it does offer an interesting and simple additional technique.

knead or fold your dough?

When working with a slack dough, one of the things to consider is why you have made that particular dough as wet.

If it is simply to add richness, have a thinner crust or crunchy bread, any number of reasons, fine - go ahead and knead it.

If it is to encourage the dough to have wild uncontrolled bubbles, then kneading is not your friend.

The purpose of kneading your bread is different, depending upon the process stage that you are working at. Initially, it is necessary to knead your bread lightly before the autolyse.

After a successful autolyse, you should knead your bread to achieve silken elasticity.

If you then want a 'double-hydration' slack dough, once you have mixed in your additional fluid, you should not knead the dough again.

Instead, very gently tip the dough onto your working area and fold the dough, much as you would when making puff pastry.   Leave on the worktop, covered either with an inverted bowl or a damp cloth, until it rises again, then once more gently fold the dough.

Shape into your preferred style *(although a boule is usually the best option for this type of dough)*, invert the bowl over your dough again, and wait for it to rise again.

Another way of dealing with this is to use a willow banneton, lightly dusted with semolina, with the dough inverted. It will allow you to gently tip the dough onto your peel or prepared stone, and maintain the bubbles you have worked so hard to encourage.

why make bread at all?

When I first started making bread in volume, my aim was (*and to a degree, still is*) to replicate the wonderful chewy, flavoursome bread of my childhood. Maltese bread is a treat for me - it has a slightly sweet and sour flavour, a chewy randomly bubble filled crumb, with a slightly shiny interior to the largest bubbles, and a thick crust, often only just on the right side of burnt. Maltese breads also usually have a 'kiss', where the sides of the loaf have risen to touch their neighbouring loaves leaving a resulting scar when they are torn apart.

So, they sound like perfection. But hold on, the very things that made them great have flaws if you are planning on making your own. The flour they are made from is a mixture of local and southern Italian wheat. It is quite strong and has a nutty flavour.

Even within the island of Malta this flour is only available in limited quantities. One massive downside is that the loaves stale incredibly quickly - by the evening, a morning loaf is becoming hard. By the next morning, it is so hard as to be a complete workout for your teeth - by the second evening, you could perhaps use the loaf to break rocks.

This resulted in two associated things - each loaf is generally quite small, a 500g piece of dough as a maximum, rather than any larger. When your loaf is smaller you eat it more quickly, and so it's tendency to stale is not a problem.

When your loaf is only going to be used for a specific meal time, either lunch or dinner, then people are more likely to want a fresh loaf at lunch or dinner time. So unlike bakers in many other countries, in Malta during my childhood, the bakers started early but also finished late. They had a routine of baking fresh batches of loaves every hour, rather than in one session.

There are also a wealth of things to do with stale Maltese bread. The chocolate and sultana sweetness of a 'pudina', crisp pieces of melba toast, tomato salads loaded with cubes of dried and fried leftover bread soaking up the juices. Last but not least of course as breadcrumbs - these are used to thicken soups, make rissoles, and fried with garlic and parsley to add crunch to pasta dishes.

The memory of hunger in Malta lies very close to the surface, not just from the Second World War, but previous wars and sieges back into antiquity. The Maltese love their food, and when I was a child they didn't waste a scrap. Frugality is a virtue which I practice without thinking, and with practice you will too.

The infinite variety of breads which can be made with minimal changes in sequence and ingredients is nothing short of breathtaking.

So, my answer to why make I make and create my own bread is, because I love to do it.

Yes, it costs more. Yes, it takes time & effort. I don't care, it makes me, and those that I love, happy. Hopefully, it will make you happy too.

baking the dough used for fried anchovy balls gives an alternative & interesting bread

Whaligoe hearthbread

This recipe makes 3 x 200g hearthbreads, with a little for tomorrows biga.

This has become my signature recipe. It is a delightful dough to work with, incredibly versatile, and of course, it tastes good.

It is also an excellent bread for diabetics, as using a proportion of apple juice gives a bread that has a lower GI and excellent digestibility due to the extended rise.

ingredients:
500g strong flour
200ml warm water
100ml apple juice
1 tsp easy blend yeast (*or 14g fresh yeast*)
3 tbsp olive oil
2 tsp fine salt
(**optional**) no more than 250g biga

method:

1) Add water, apple juice and yeast to your working bowl. If you are using a 'biga' add it now, pulling it into small pieces to make it easier to mix.

2) Add flour to the liquid ingredients. Mix for a few minutes, until you have a 'rough' or ' shaggy' dough, and leave for 40 minutes. (*This is your autolyse).*

3) Sprinkle the salt and olive oil over the surface of your dough, and knead for at least 5-10 minutes, until you have a smooth, silky and elastic dough.

4) Place in an oiled pot or bowl and cover, leaving it for at least 2 hours before using. (*At this stage the dough may be left for several hours without any problems, or ideally a couple of days, if refridgerated).*

5) Divide the dough into three pieces of approx. 200g each, and gently stretch and ease them into a rough oblong. Try to avoid using a rolling pin as that makes too 'manufactured' a bread, ideally you would like some 'thick & thin' pieces. This means that you get a good combination of crisp and soft parts of your bread.

6) Any leftover dough may be set aside in an airtight bag for your biga for you to use next time you make dough.

7) You may either leave the dough portions in a rough oblong, or you may slash the dough several times in a 'ladder' fashion. If so, pull the dough gently to stretch out. (*Again, this is to give extra crispy edges*).

8) Preheat your oven to 250°C, (*or the highest temperature that your oven will go to*). If you have a baking stone now is the time to use it, otherwise preheat a baking tray to place the breads upon. Should you be lucky enough to have a pizza oven, heat it to 350°C.

9) At the highest temperature, the hearthbreads will be ready in 4 minutes or so, with lower temperatures they can take up to 20 minutes, but they should be quite quick so keep an eye on them. They are ready when golden brown and risen slightly.

10) Usually, bread should be allowed to cool completely before cutting as the crumb is not yet 'set' and you can end up with a sticky mess! However, with a hearthbread, the joy is in eating it warm. Just tear off chunks and use it to mop up sauce, smother it in garlic butter, or dip it in your soup.

If your bread has gone cold, you can bring it back to life quickly by giving it a quick dunk in some cold water, and putting it back into a hot oven for a few minutes.

honey spice twists

This recipe makes one good sized portion.

ingredients:

150g Whaligoe hearthbread dough
3 tsp honey
1 tsp cinnamon
5 tsp caster sugar
sunflower oil for deep frying

method:

1) Heat your oil to 180°C.
2) Mix the caster sugar and cinnamon together.
3) Slice your dough into four pieces, don't worry if they are not even, you want them to be a bit gnarly.
4) Fry the dough until it is golden brown and risen.
5) Drain the dough, sprinkle with your sugar mix and drizzle over some honey. Eat while hot.

barley bannock (barley scone)

makes 1 small bannock, or 4 scones

Bannocks are a generic term for small loaves which are mainly or wholly composed of a grain other than wheat, and which are raised by an agent other than yeast.

They are also usually cooked on a griddle on top of the stove, rather than oven baked. When cut into portions, they are traditionally referred to as scones.

ingredients:
120g barley flour
60g white plain flour (*soft*)
150ml buttermilk (*or ½ yogurt and ½ milk if not available*)
½ tsp salt
½ tsp cream of tartar
½ tsp bicarbonate of soda

method:

1) Mix the flours, cream of tartar and salt together in your working bowl. Mix the buttermilk and bicarbonate of soda together, and add to the bowl containing your dry ingredients.

2) Working quickly, bring the dough together into a soft ball and press it with your hand to form a disc about 2 cm thick. Cut the disc into four if you wish to have separate scones, or cut half way through the dough, if you wish to have a single bannock.

3) Heat a greased griddle (*or heavy frying pan*) on top of your stove, it should not be too hot or the scones will scorch. You should be able to comfortably hold your hand about 2.5 cm above the surface.

4) Cook the bread for approx. 5 minutes on each side until brown. Wrap them in a cloth to keep the outsides soft and eat while warm.

'create your own' multi-grain loaf

this recipe will make one large, or two small loaves.

The ratio given below will give you a successful loaf and you may choose your own variation to suit your personal taste.

Make a few different ones and discover what you prefer.

ingredients:
350g strong flour - white, brown, wholemeal or a mix
10g easy blend yeast (*or 20g fresh yeast*)
15g sugar
3 tbsp olive oil *(or fat of your choice)*
150g other grain flour *(barley, soya, cornmeal, tapioca, rice, rye)*
50g seeds (*sunflower, pumpkin, linseed, caraway*)
1 tsp fine salt
approx 250ml warm water *(this will vary depending upon the choice of grains made, so start with a little and add more as required).*

method:

1) Place all the dry ingredients other than the yeast and salt into a bowl, mix well to ensure they are well combined.
2) Add the water to a separate working bowl and stir in the yeast until well distributed.
3) Add the blended grains to the liquid and combine to just mix.
4) Set aside for at least 30 minutes *(for your autolyse).*
5) Add your chosen oil or fat together with the salt, and knead the dough well until it is smooth and a little 'bouncy'.
6) Shape the dough as required and cover with greased cling film.
7) Leave in a warm place for 1 - 2 hours or until risen, or place in a fridge overnight to develop the flavour. If refrigerated allow to come to room temperature before continuing.
8) Pre-heat the oven to 180°C, and bake for 30 - 40 mins, depending upon the mix of flours used.
9) Depending upon your choice of grains, it may be necessary to bake for longer. The loaf should release easily from the tin or mould when cooked, and sound a little hollow when tapped.
10) Cool on a wire rack before using.

rye sandwich bread

makes 1 large or 2 small loaves

This is a semi-sweet bread, great for toast and makes a great sandwich.

While the addition of the orange oil and seeds is optional, I would heartily recommend it.

ingredients for starter:
55g biga (*if using one*)
215g rye flour
175g water
ingredients for main dough:
rye starter dough
385g warm water
30g molasses or black treacle
15g easy blend yeast (*or 30g fresh yeast*)
55g vegetable oil
30g cocoa powder
680g strong flour
3 tsp salt
optional:
1 tbsp caraway seeds
1 tbsp anise seeds
1 tbsp nigella seeds
¾ tsp orange oil

method:

1) Combine the starter ingredients and mix to a soft mass. Set aside for 6-8 hours in a warm place, or put into an oiled bowl and place in a fridge for up to 4 days.
2) To make the dough, place all your liquid ingredients to a large bowl, add the yeast and mix until well integrated.
3) Cut your starter into 10 - 12 pieces and add to your bowl, mixing again.
4) Add the flour and mix until the dough is soft, supple and very tacky, verging on sticky. Leave to rest for at least 30 mins.
5) Now add the rest of your ingredients, and knead the dough until it is supple - it may well be more sticky then you are used to, this is due to the use of rye flour - don't worry about it, the dough will behave differently to a wheaten loaf.
6) Lightly oil a bowl, add the dough, cover with plastic wrap and allow to rise until doubled in size.
7) Shape your dough and leave to prove.
8) Bake at 200°C for approx. 40 mins, rotating the loaves if necessary.
9) The loaves are done when they have reached an internal temperature of 88°C - you may check this with a probe if you have one, otherwise, just knock on the base for a hollow sound.
10) Cool for at least one hour before storing or slicing.

parker house rolls

makes approximately 36 rolls

ingredients:

2 tbsp easy blend yeast (*or 60g fresh yeast*)
100g granulated sugar
125ml warm water
475ml whole milk
225g butter, divided
4 large eggs
1.5 kg T55 flour *(or strong flour if you can't get it)*
5 tsp salt

method:

1) Melt half the butter into the milk, and stop heating as soon as the butter has melted.

2) Whisk the sugar into the warm milk and butter mixture.

3) Let the mixture cool until barely warm, the temperature should read below 43°C.

4) Whisk the eggs into the milk and butter mixture.

5) Whisk the yeast into the mixture, and pour into a large mixing bowl.

6) Mix the flour into the liquids until you see no more dry flour, and have formed a lumpy shaggy dough.

7) Leave to autolyse for a minimum of 30 mins.

8) Add the salt, then knead the dough for 10 mins. The dough is ready when it is smooth, slightly tacky and holds its shape in a ball when lifted.

9) Place the dough in a lightly oiled bowl, cover and leave to rise until doubled in bulk, 1 to 1 ½ hours.

10) Sprinkle a little flour on your counter, and roll out the dough to a thickness of approx. 2 cm. Cut out rounds using a 70mm cookie cutter, cutting as closely as possible to avoid re-rolling dough. (*Although the waste dough can be used for other purposes, you should not re-roll the trimmings for these rolls*.)

11) Line two baking sheets with baking paper, and melt the remaining butter in a small pan.

12) Dip each round in butter so they are completely coated - using the blunt side of a butter knife, score each round slightly off-centre to make a crease in your dough. Fold the larger half over the smaller half. Pinch quite hard to make sure the rolls stay closed. Transfer the rolls to the baking sheet, and space a little apart.

13) Cover the rolls loosely and let them rise until puffy, 30 to 40 mins. *(at this point, the rolls could be refrigerated overnight, or frozen).*

14) Pre-heat the oven to 180°C, and bake the rolls until they are golden brown, approx. 15 to 20 minutes.

15) Remove from the tray to a wire cooling rack, and brush the tops with more melted butter. Serve warm if possible.

Ukrainian milk dough

makes one medium loaf, or 6-8 buns.

This versatile dough makes a lovely sandwich bread, or may be very successfully used as a stuffed bun.

The buns may be shallow fried or baked, as preferred.

Although savoury fillings are more common, sliced fresh apricots and pitted sour cherries are also a favourite filling.

ingredients:
2 tsp unrefined sunflower oil
250ml milk at room temp. (*preheated to over 80°C and allowed to cool)*
1 tsp easy blend yeast (*or 14g fresh yeast*)
2 tsp granulated sugar
½ tsp salt
400g strong white flour

loaf or rolls method:

1) Whisk the oil, milk, yeast, sugar and salt together in a large bowl, then add the flour gradually to the mix. The dough should be a little damp, but not wet.

2) Leave for 30 minutes to autolyse.

3) Knead well until the dough is elastic and springs back if pressed.

4) Leave until doubled, then knead again on your work surface. The dough should be pleasantly soft, but not stick to your hands.

5) Leave the dough to prove, and use this dough for sandwich bread, or to make fried or baked filled buns.

6) Pre-heat the oven to 180°C, and bake rolls until they are golden brown, approx. 15 to 20 minutes, or a loaf for 30 - 40 minutes.

stuffed buns method:

1) Roll out your dough to approx 1cm thickness, and cut out circles to suit the desired size of your finished buns. You may re-use scraps and continue to cut out circles until you have used all of the dough.

2) Pick up a circle of dough, and holding it with four fingers place a teaspoon full of your chosen filling in the centre, and pinch up to the top centre of the dumpling. Then pinch together the right and left of the remaining spaces, and finally pinch closed all around the seam.

3) You are not trying to fold the dough, it should be 'sticky' enough at the cut edge to become sealed, without increasing the bulk of the dough.

4) Leave to prove until doubled in size.

5) Then either bake as above, or shallow fry until golden brown and well risen.

Italian bread sticks

makes approx 20 sticks

These are quick and easy to make and put commercial bread sticks to shame. This dough may also be used for a very nice sandwich loaf.

ingredients:
450g strong white flour
250ml tepid water
2 tsp easy blend dried yeast (*or 28g fresh yeast*)
2 tsp malt extract
2 tsp fine salt
3 tbsp olive oil
optional:
sesame seeds or poppy seeds for topping

method:

1) Mix the water, salt, malt extract and yeast together in your mixing bowl and stir until well blended.

2) Now add your flour, and mix until you have a 'shaggy' dough.

3) Leave for 20 minutes, then add your olive oil and knead until the dough is smooth. It will be a soft and slightly sticky dough, don't worry about it.

4) Set aside in a warm place until at least doubled in size, then tip the dough out onto an oiled workbench. Cut into 16 pieces, then with a greased or lined baking sheet to hand, gently lift each piece and stretch it.

5) The dough should be sufficiently soft to stretch under it's own weight, and give you a slightly uneven stick. Keep them quite thin, as they will expand when baked.

6) Once you have stretched all your dough, you may either bake it plain or brush with a little tepid water, and sprinkle with either sesame or poppy seeds. (*The water will help the seeds to stick to the surface).*

7) Pre-heat the oven to 200°C, and bake the bread sticks until they are golden brown and crisp, approx. 15 to 20 minutes.

8) Cool on a rack.

wheaten soda bread

makes 1 small loaf

This is an Irish classic, there are many variations and they are usually delicious. Soda breads are quick and easy to make, with no rising time as the baking soda does all the rising in the oven.

Great for breakfast with a fry up, or with soup for supper.

ingredients:
450g soft wholemeal flour
150ml buttermilk *(or ½ yogurt, ½ water)*
150g unsalted butter
2 tbsp honey
½ tsp salt
½ tsp bicarbonate of soda
½ tsp cream of tartar
1 small egg

method:

1) Mix the flour, salt, bicarbonate of soda and cream of tartar together in your working bowl.

2) Cut your butter into small pieces and either by hand, or using a food processor or stand mixer, mix the butter into your dry ingredients until well rubbed in.

(Doing this before any moisture is added will help to coat the flour grains with fat, and ensure that minimal gluten development happens. Unlike a normal loaf, with a soda bread you want to avoid gluten development, as this would make your loaf tough and heavy).

3) Once your mixture is ready mix together the egg, buttermilk and honey, and add this to your bowl. Mix gently, you are only trying to get an amalgamated mix not kneading the dough.

4) Pre-heat the oven to 180ºC.

5) Turn your dough onto a greased baking sheet, and with a sharp knife cut a cross into the top. Cover the loaf with a heatproof bowl or pan that is at least ⅓ larger than the loaf, to allow for expansion.

6) Alternatively, should you have a cast iron dutch oven, line it with baking paper, pre-heat it and place your bread inside - covering with the lid.

7) Bake for 30 minutes covered, then uncover the loaf for the final 10 - 15 minutes to allow it to become golden brown.

Soda bread is best eaten warm and fresh. When cooling it, wrap the loaf in a tea towel if you wish to keep the crust soft. It makes good toast too.

sweet potato buns

makes 8 buns.

These light and tasty buns are perfect for an afternoon snack, they are slightly sweet and very moreish.

Do note that the milk should only be added if necessary to make a soft dough. As potatoes vary so greatly in terms of how much liquid they will take up, the milk should be added slowly, as required.

ingredients:
225g sweet potatoes
225g strong white flour
100ml (*maximum*) tepid milk
120g white sugar
50g butter
1 large egg
2 tsp easy blend yeast (*or 28g fresh yeast*)
ingredients for topping:
250g icing sugar
fine zest & juice of 1 large lemon

method:

1) Start by baking the potatoes in their skins until tender, then peel them, mash the potato pulp with the butter and set aside to cool.

2) Once the potato is below 40°C in temperature, mix the egg, yeast and potato together. Add the flour, and knead until a soft dough is achieved, adding your tepid milk as required.

3) You may need to add more or less liquid or flour, as potatoes will vary in terms of how much liquid they absorb, but you are aiming to achieve a moist but not sticky dough.

4) Set aside to rise for about 1 - 2 hours, until doubled in size. Turn out onto an oiled bench, and divide into two pieces.

5) Shape each piece into a round, and using a greased knife cut each round into four equal pieces. Place on a greased or lined baking sheet to prove for a further 30 minutes, covered with a clean tea towel, while your oven preheats to 170°C.

6) Bake for about 15 minutes, until they are browned and well risen, and cool on a wire rack before topping.

7) While they are cooling, sift your icing sugar, to ensure there are no lumps, and mix the lemon zest into the icing sugar.

8) Now add just sufficient lemon juice to make a firm but spoonable icing - add a spoonful to the top of each bun, but make sure they are cool first as otherwise the icing will just slip off in a sticky puddle. As long as the buns are cool, the icing will gradually drift over the top of your bun, and trickle down gently.

9) Allow them to set before serving, or storing.

Eat them within 2 days, they are wonderful with some butter and honey as a teatime treat.

bulgar wheat toasting loaf

makes 1 large loaf

I adore toast, but it needs to be crunchy outside, soft on the inside and tasty. In my quest for a successful toasting loaf, I've developed this one. It does make excellent toast, but it can be a tad heavy for eating untoasted.

ingredients:
400g strong white flour
200g coarse bulgar wheat
2 tsp easy blend yeast (*or 28g fresh yeast*)
200ml apple juice
200ml warm water
2 tbsp olive oil

risen loaf in willow banneton

1 tbsp fine salt

method:

1) In your working bowl mix the apple juice, water and yeast.

2) Add your flour, and mix to a very wet (*almost batter like*) dough.

3) Leave for 30 minutes, then add your bulgar wheat, salt and olive oil. Knead until well amalgamated - it will still appear quite wet - don't worry.

4) Leave the dough in your working bowl for another 30 minutes, then knead again. The bulgar wheat will have absorbed much of the excess liquid and you should now have a soft dough.

5) Turn out onto your oiled working bench, and shape into a willow banneton if you have one - or if you wish, put the dough into a large oiled loaf tin.

6) Allow to prove until doubled in size, then bake at 180°C for 1 hour.

Bulgarian wholemeal honey bread

makes 1 tall loaf

This is very different bread - almost a cake, perfect sliced and buttered for a teatime treat.

It does have a much higher % of yeast than is normal for a loaf this size, this is to counteract the higher level of sweetness from the honey, and the fat content from the milk and egg.

ingredients:
110g honey
50ml water
100ml milk
1 small egg
1 ½ tbsp easy blend yeast *(or 45g fresh yeast)*
375g wholemeal flour
¼ tsp fine salt
grated zest of 1 large lemon
50ml sunflower oil (*used in 2nd kneading*)
50g chopped walnuts (*used in 3rd kneading*)
to finish:
icing sugar for dusting
equipment:
a plain or fluted Kugelhopf mould or Bundt tin

method:

1) Place the honey together with 50ml of the milk and water into a small pan, and heat very gently until the honey is melted into your mixture. Keep the heat as low as possible.

2) Check the temperature, and if it is 40°C or less, you may beat in your egg. If it is hotter than that, just wait until it cools sufficiently.

3) Place the warm liquid into a large working bowl and add the lemon zest, salt, and yeast. Mix well, then add the flour and knead until moderately stiff and slightly sticky. If necessary you may add the remainder of the milk, but only add sufficient to achieve the dough texture required.

4) Cover with cling film, and leave to rise in a warm place until trebled in size.

5) Knead again without adding any flour, but adding small amounts of the sunflower oil until it is all used.

6) Leave for a second rise in the bowl for about 2 hours, until trebled in size again.

7) Meanwhile, prepare your mould. Oil it well, then dust with flour and tip out any excess.

8) Knead the dough a third time to incorporate the chopped walnuts and shape into a round approximately the diameter of your mould.

9) Wet your hands, then using your wet fingers, press two fingers and a thumb through the centre to make a hole, spreading it slightly. ***(This technique also works well for making the hole in a bagel).***

10) Place it in your mould, which should be slightly less than half filled.

11) Prove in a slightly warmer place than before, it should reach the rim of your mould within an hour or so.

12) Preheat your oven to 180°C, and bake for around 40 minutes. It should be well risen and browned.

13) Cool on a wire rack for a few minutes, then turn out onto the rack and cool completely.

14) Dust with icing sugar before serving.

Finnish pulla bread

makes 2 braided loaves, or 12 small buns

This is a soft and tender cardamom scented bread, lovely with a cup of hot chocolate and some cold butter.

(This is an example of a double-hydration bread)

ingredients:
250ml whole milk
100ml water
1 ½ tsp easy blend yeast (*or 21g fresh yeast*)
½ tsp salt
2 eggs, beaten
110 g white sugar
2 tsp ground cardamom
800g mixed strong and plain white flour
60g melted butter (*cooled*)
to finish:
1 egg, beaten with a little water
2 tbsp sugar nibs & flaked almonds

method:

1) Heat milk until almost boiling, then allow to cool to lukewarm.

2) Add liquid to your mixing bowl, pour in the two beaten eggs, cardamom, and sugar. Mix until well amalgamated, then add the yeast and 400g of your flour. Roughly mix, and leave for 20 minutes to autolyse.

3) Beat until the batter is smooth and elastic, this will help to develop the gluten in your bread. Add the cooled melted butter and salt, beat well, and add the remaining flour. The dough should be quite stiff. Let the dough rest for another 20 minutes.

4) Knead until smooth and satiny. Do not worry if it seems very soft or wet, it will stiffen up as the gluten develops. Place in a lightly greased mixing bowl, and cover. Allow the dough to rise until doubled in bulk, about 1 hour in a warm place. Punch down, and allow to rise again.

5) Divide the dough into two, then each piece into three equal portions, and pull into long strips. Braid the three strips into a loaf.

6) Place each braided loaf onto a prepared baking tray and allow to rise for 20 mins, or as long as necessary to regain its 'plumpness'.

7) Bake at 200°C for 15 mins. The dough should be risen, and the crust 'set' but not completely cooked. Turn the heat down to 160°C, and quickly brush the top of your loaves or buns with the egg wash, and sprinkle with your sugar nibs and flaked almonds.

8) Return to the oven, and bake for a further 30 minutes, but check after 20 mins as the sweet dough can burn easily.

9) Cool on a wire rack before cutting.

bagels

this makes around 14 large bagels

This bagel recipe has been modified to use the Yukone (*water roux*) method, and it definitely helps to keep the crumb chewy and tender for longer. I think it's a great improvement on the standard recipe, and I am indebted to Stella Parkes for the idea.

ingredients for the yukone:
200g strong flour
350ml boiling water
ingredients for the dough:
700g strong flour
30g white sugar
2 tsp easy-blend yeast
15g fine salt
200ml water
to finish:
15g malt syrup
large pot of simmering water

a correctly mixed yukone looks much like mashed potato - don't worry about it

method:

1) Start by preparing your yukone.

2) Using a stand mixer, place the flour into your working bowl, and pour on the boiling water while beating slowly.

3) Continue to beat the mixture until it looks like a pasty mass of mashed potato.

4) Allow to cool to below 30°C, and start on the main dough.

5) Put the water, salt and sugar into your working bowl together with the yeast, and mix well. Incorporate the Yukone into this mix, breaking it up into smaller pieces to help it to mix in.

6) Once you have a homogenous mix, add the flour and knead until the dough is smooth and silky.

7) Now, either cut your dough into 14 equal portions, or weigh the dough for specific sizes of bagel - I like to use 100g portions, for a larger bagel, but anything over 75g will work well.

8) Shape the bagels by kneading into a ball, then using wet fingers (*have a bowl of water to one side on your workbench to dip your hands in*) poke a hole in the middle of each ball, and stretch it out to make a largish (*about 12cm*) hoop. Remember that eventually this will rise and the hole will close up, so don't worry if it seems like a strange shape.

9) Place on a greased baking tray, and cover with cling film.

10) At this point, you may refrigerate your dough for 24 - 36 hours, to develop the flavour, or you may choose to continue. If you do refrigerate the dough, ensure it returns to room temperature before continuing to the next stage.

your initial shaping will be quite rough - don't worry, they will be fine

after their brief bath in malty water, the bagels take on a slightly yellow tone

11) When the bagels have doubled in size, you are ready to poach them. Depending upon the warmth of your room, that may take 1-2 hours from room temperature.

12) Preheat your oven to 180ºC.

13) Prepare a large pot of boiling water, and add the malt syrup - this will help the colour and crust development of your bagel. Turn the water down to a simmer, and add a couple of bagels to the poaching liquid. The bagels will initially sink, as soon as they float remove from the water and place on your greased baking tray.

14) Repeat until all bagels have been poached. Now put them straight into your preheated oven, they should be ready in approx. 20 minutes, but keep an eye on them. You are aiming for a deeply golden blistered crust.

15) If you wish, 5 minutes before the end of your cooking time remove your trays, brush the tops of the bagels with a little lightly beaten egg white, and sprinkle with sesame or poppy seeds. ***(If you do it too soon, the egg white will cause the bagels to over brown).***

16) Cool on a wire rack.

Thanks to the addition of the Yukone to the mix, these bagels keep considerably better than a standard recipe, and are delicious fresh or toasted

aim for a golden brown & slightly blistered crust

a generous basket of bagels is your reward

Maltese bread (Ħobż tal-Malti)

makes 2 small or 1 large loaf.

My search for the perfect recipe will always be to an extent, doomed to failure. Replicating the intense heat of a wood fired traditional oven is not really practical, even in my commercial kitchen, but it's such fun trying.

I am currently working with a recipe that I have tweaked somewhat, with information from the blog of a fellow Maltese chef in New York (*we get around)*. It's pretty good. Not perfect, but pretty good. Try it for yourself.

ingredients for starter:
100g plain flour*
12g gluten*
pinch of easy blend yeast
100 ml tepid apple juice
ingredients to feed your starter:
100 ml tepid water
100g plain flour
12g gluten
ingredients for your loaves:
½ of your biga after at least 6 hours
400g plain flour
48g gluten
7g instant yeast
200 ml tepid water
100 ml apple juice
2 tsp salt

method for starter:

1) Mix plain flour and gluten together, add a pinch of dried yeast, add your tepid apple juice and work into a very sticky dough with a spoon. Cover with cling film and let rise for at least 6 hours.

method to feed your starter:

2) Mix plain flour and gluten together. In the same bowl that has the starter, add the 100ml water and stir the mixture well. Add the flour mixture and mix everything together into a a very sticky dough. Cover and let rise again for 6+ hours.

method to make your bread:

3) Take half of the fed and matured starter and put it in a large mixing bowl. This is your biga.

4) Wrap the other half in cling film or an air tight plastic bag, and store in the fridge for your next baking session *(vacuum packing is ideal).* This will eliminate steps 1) and 2) next time you want to bake this bread again.

5) Mix the water and apple juice. Add it to the bowl with your biga, and mix to a loose consistency.

6) Now add your flour mix *(it's important to sift together the flour and gluten before you do this, to ensure an even distribution of the gluten),* and mix to a shaggy dough.

7) Leave for 30 minutes, before adding the salt and kneading to a smooth elastic dough.

8) Cover the bowl and let rise for about 3 hours. During these 3 hours, you need to fold the dough twice.

9) The reason for folding the dough is to encourage the bubbles that are forming to remain, and become larger. *(Kneading the bread, or 'knocking it back' as is done with traditional British breads would eliminate those large bubbles and give you an even and consistent crumb - not what we want here).*

10) For each folding session, you should fold the dough four or five times, **gently**. So, at 1.5 hours, you fold the dough, and at 3 hours you fold it again.

11) After 3 hours and two folding sessions, the dough should have doubled in size.

12) Place on a floured surface and gently shape into one ball, or split the dough and make two smaller loaves. Press the sides with the palm of your hands. Again, do not knead the dough as you would destroy the air bubbles that have been created with the folding process.

13) In the meantime, preheat your oven to 230°C. If you have a pizza stone, the result will be much better. If not you can bake the bread on a floured baking sheet, but I cannot stress enough the importance of investing in a pizza stone if you intend to bake this bread regularly.

14) Dust your dough well with flour. Cover and let it prove for another 45 minutes. Before popping in the oven, add more flour to the surface or just flip the dough upside down (as the bottom will be uneven therefore more flour sticks to it), dust with more flour on top and pop on the pizza stone. The toasted taste of a good amount of flour on the crust is all part of the appeal.

15) Bake for a good 50 minutes if making one large loaf. If you are splitting the dough to make two loaves, bake them together for 35 minutes. Place them a little closer together then you would normally, to ensure that they 'kiss' in the oven.

16) Cool on a wire rack

Ftira (above)
Maltese Bread (underneath)

ftira

makes 3 or 4 ftira

This is a classic example of how a different shaping process and cooking temperature can cause the same dough to have quite a different finish.

Although it utilises the same dough as the standard Maltese loaf, this Gozitan version is quite different, and equally delicious.

ingredients:

1 batch of Maltese bread dough

method:

1) Divide the dough into 3-4 pieces, depending on how big you want your ftiras to be. Without kneading, gently open up dough into a flat circle and let rest for about 10 minutes.

2) After 10 minutes, continue to expand the dough gently without kneading.

3) Let it rest for another 10-15 minutes, always covered in cling film or a damp tea towel, otherwise the top will dry out.

4) With these resting periods, you will notice that after each rest you can stretch out the dough a little further.

5) Tear a hole in the middle, dust with some flour, place on a floured peel and pop on pizza stone in a 200°C oven for about 20-25 minutes.

6) Cool completely before cutting.

a Maltese sandwich (Ħobż biż-Żejt)

This is the ubiquitous sandwich of Malta. As a child it was always a preferred snack, and could be got from little bars by the side of the beach. Eating one of these at any time brings the tang of the sea to my mind.

It used to be a more humble affair, just dip your bread in a saucer of olive oil, cut a ripe tomato in half, squash it on your bread to render it scarlet, sprinkle with salt, maybe a little chopped parsley and a few capers, and devour.

Now, it has become a different, heartier beast.

Still lovely, in my mind not a true Ħobż biż-Żejt, but probably what you will be served if you are in the Islands today. I have not specified quantities here - it depends how many you are making.

ingredients:
Maltese bread, or Ftira
Maltese tomato paste, or regular sweetened with some honey
tinned tuna
onions - sliced thinly
crumbled ġbejniet *(or goats cheese)*
sliced fresh tomato
sliced olives
capers
fresh mint & parsley
olive oil
balsamic vinegar
sea salt flakes
freshly cracked black pepper
(**optional**) **to finish**: giardiniera salad

ingredients for a typically restrained Maltese sandwich

method:

1) If using Maltese bread, cut a generous slice. If using the Ftira, slice in half horizontally.

2) Dip the cut side of your bread in some olive oil poured in a plate, then thinly spread with your tomato paste (*see sauces*).

3) Layer in the rest of the ingredients, don't add too much mint as it can overpower your sandwich. I prefer to have the giardiniera on the side of my plate, others like it on the sandwich, please yourself.

4) Finally, drizzle with some balsamic vinegar, a good sprinkling of sea salt and lots of freshly ground black pepper.

focaccia

makes one large tray

Focaccia is a half-way house between a bread and a pizza. It often has some toppings but is also usually at least 5 cm thick, so considerably thicker than the thickest crust pizza.

It also has a higher % of oil in the dough, and is usually dimpled by hand before baking, giving you somewhere for the extra oil that is drizzled over to collect.

The recipe given here is for a plain focaccia, but it is common to add sliced olives, peppers or caramelised onions to the top.

Beware though, this is not a fat pizza, it should only have sufficient additional toppings to add some interest and not to overtake the dish.

This dough works well when baked with some steam in the first few minutes, to help develop a crisp crust, so if you have one use an atomiser filled with water to spray inside the oven at the start of your cooking time. *(I find placing a tray on the bottom shelf of your oven works well, as the preheated metal will vaporise the spray easily).*

ingredients:
500g strong white flour
225ml white grape juice
75ml olive oil
2 tsp fine salt
1 tbsp easy blend yeast
olive oil to drizzle over the top
coarse salt crystals to sprinkle over the top

method:

1) Mix the grape juice and yeast, then add the flour and knead until you achieve a 'shaggy' dough.

2) Leave for 20 minutes to autolyse, then add the olive oil and fine salt. Knead again until a smooth dough has developed.

3) It should be a soft but not sticky dough, if necessary add a little more flour / water to adjust the dough slightly.

4) Allow to prove until doubled in size, then using an oiled baking tray with slightly raised sides spread the dough out to fill the tray. Use your fingers to push the dough out to fill the entire tray. If the dough springs back, cover with a cloth for 10 minutes and allow it to relax before pushing again.

5) Leave for a further 30 minutes to regain some volume.

6) Just before placing into a preheated oven (*220°C*), use your fingers to dimple the dough deeply and drizzle with olive oil.

7) Finish by sprinkling with some coarse sea salt and bake for about 20 to 25 minutes. If you wish, spray the oven to achieve some steam at the start of your cooking time as described.

8) Cool completely on a wire rack before cutting.

pizza

A great dish sadly abused by many. I've had more bad pizzas then almost any other single dish. There is a huge variation in styles of what we refer to as pizza, and some come, as expected, from Italy. Many come from the USA where modern pizza was to a large degree re-invented, and others come from less well known origins. Maltese or Gozo pizza is really a deep pie - but unlike a 'Chicago Pizza Pie' it's not sloppy, just crammed full of tasty ingredients. A Sfeeha is a Lebanese pizza, Flammkuchen come from Germany and Croatia has wonderful sour cream pizzas.

One of the most disappointing pizzas I ever ate was in Chicago - a colleague, knowing my 'foodie' tendencies, very proudly took me to what he told me was the original restaurant that the famous 'deep dish Chicago Pizza' originated from. I had high expectations, but was stunned to be served what appeared to be almost a soup within a pizza crust, with a molten lake of cheese bubbling on top. Everyone else enjoyed it - but it was not a pizza to me.

Originally pizza was a product of 'cucina provera', it's a great way of feeding a crowd with a small amount of produce - dough is inexpensive and everything else can be dotted on top. It's now become something that many people (*including me*) are passionate about. It's great hot, it's fabulous cold - I like it thick or thin, chewy or crispy - it just depends what you feel like at the time.

So this section has been designed to show you some pizza styles, not pizza toppings - while there are of course some classics, you don't need me to tell you what to do, just use what you have or buy what you fancy, and have fun.

Adreains' pizza

This has become a signature pizza for me at the restaurant, and it was developed to suit the taste of a good friends husband, Adreain, who is also my most long standing and loyal customer *(not to mention a great guy).*

Adreain likes a large pizza, so I use a 400g dough portion - for a standard 10" pizza use 250g

Other than the dough weight I have not specified quantities of ingredients, this is because with pizza it very much depends upon personal taste. I prefer a pizza with scant toppings allowing the quality of the dough to shine through, others prefer lots of topping.

I also love olives on my pizza, but Adreain does not, so they are strictly optional in this recipe.

ingredients:
250g or 400g Whaligoe hearthbread dough
'chilli & garlic' sauce *(see sauces section)*
rich tomato sauce *(see sauces section)*
chorizo
pepperoni
thinly sliced onion
red pepper flakes
jalepeno chillies
mozzarella cheese
parmesan cheese
(***optional***)
sliced olives

method:

1) Dust your workbench with coarse semolina, and stretch or roll your dough.

2) If you like a thin pizza roll it out larger - I like a medium crust, and Adreain likes a thin one - take your choice.

3) When your dough is at the desired size, create a rope edge crimp around your pizza, this stops the chilli & garlic oil from spilling out of your crust.

4) Make sure your oven complete with pizza stone is heated to 230°C (*unless you are lucky enough to own a pizza oven, in which case you should heat it to 350°C*), brush your dough generously with some of the 'chilli & garlic sauce', and slide it onto your pizza stone (*do buy a peel, even a short handled one will make life so much easier*).

5) Cook until the top is starting to bubble and a slight crust is forming, but the dough is not yet coloured.

6) Remove from the oven, and now spread it with a bit of the rich tomato sauce - not too much, you don't want soggy dough. Now add your pepperoni, chorizo, red pepper flakes, jalepeno, mozzarella and thinly sliced onion, in whatever sequence you prefer.

7) Return to the oven, and bake until bubbling and golden brown.

8) Remove, grate over some fresh parmesan cheese, a good grind of black pepper, and a little drizzle of the 'chilli & garlic sauce' for the finishing touch.

prepare your toppings before starting to bake your pizza

savour

VERB (transitive)

1. to enjoy an experience, activity, or feeling as much as you can and for as long as you can
2. to enjoy the flavour of something as much as you can by eating or drinking it slowly

Reference: Macmillan Dictionary

apple & bacon pizza

makes 3 regular or 2 large pizzas

This is a slightly different take on the pizza crust - it makes a pizza that tends to be crisper than the regular Whaligoe dough crust.

It also has a subtle sweetness from the almond milk, and it makes a terrific semi-sweet pizza.

ingredients for dough:

500g Italian '00' flour
1 tsp easy blend yeast (*or 14g fresh yeast*)
300ml unsweetened almond milk
2 tsp fine salt
50ml olive oil *(or melted lard)*
75g unsalted butter
2 cooking apples or 4 tart eating apples
250g thinly sliced bacon or pancetta chopped into small pieces
100g finely grated fresh parmesan

this sweet & sour pizza is interestingly different
serve it in small quantities to try a different flavour combination

method:

1) Make your dough by mixing the almond milk, yeast and flour in your mixing bowl. Once you have achieved a 'shaggy' dough, allow it to rest for at least 30 minutes before continuing.

2) Add the olive oil *(or melted lard)* and salt, then knead the dough until it is a smooth and springy mass. If it appears a little slack don't be tempted to add much more flour, as it will firm up while proving.

3) Place into an airtight tub with at least twice of volume of your dough, and leave for at least 2 hours, or preferably longer.

4) While the dough is proving, you may prepare your apple-sauce base. Peel and core your apples, and slice them into small pieces.

5) Melt your butter in a heavy based pan, and sauté the apple pieces until they are soft and lightly caramelised, but not burnt. Using the back of a fork, gently mash the apples until you have a slightly lumpy sauce.

6) Season to taste - this should be an agrodolce sauce, both sweet and sour - if you need to enhance the sour note, add a little lemon juice, or a touch of honey to enhance the sweetness.

7) Set aside to cool.

8) Roll out your dough reasonably thinly, and spread with a thin coating of the apple-sauce. Place into your oven *(preheated to it's highest temperature, or if you have a pizza oven, 350°C)* for a couple of minutes, to allow the base to start to firm up.

9) Once the crust is bubbling, remove from the oven, add the chopped bacon, and sprinkle with finely grated parmesan.

10) Return to your oven until crisp and browned at the edges.

Gozitan ftira (a Gozitan pizza)

makes enough to feed 4

This is a typically Gozitan pizza, available across all the islands. However don't expect it to resemble a traditional pizza, it's more of a pie.

Traditionally made in a large family sized pie dish, you slice off however much you please and eat it with a salad.

It's equally good hot or cold, but can be a little crumbly when hot, so if you want a neat slice chill well before slicing.

ingredients:
1 batch of Maltese bread dough
3-4 large potatoes, very thinly sliced
Maltese tomato paste (*see recipe in extras section*)
4 large fresh tomatoes
4 medium, oven roasted, tomatoes
2 dried plain ġbejniet
2 dried peppered ġbejniet
3 tbsp capers
50g pitted olives
2 eggs, lightly beaten
oregano or thyme (*fresh or dried)*
freshly ground pepper
sesame seed
(**optional**)
50g anchovies
OR 3 sliced hard boiled eggs
OR a large can of tuna *(drained)*

method:

1) Place the thinly sliced potatoes into a pot of cold water and bring to the boil. Simmer for 1 minute, then switch off and rinse the potatoes with cool water. Set aside.

2) Set your oven to 220°C, and place your tomatoes for roasting into a tray in the oven while it comes up to temperature. By the time your oven is ready, your tomatoes will be too.

3) Prepare a baking tray - brush it with a little olive oil, and spread out your dough. Use your fingers to push it out to fill the tray, and leave covered for at least 10 minutes to relax. You may need to push it out again, you want to ideally have a margin of dough outside your tray so it should flop over the side at this stage.

4) Spread a little Maltese tomato paste over the dough together with the chopped roasted tomatoes, and sprinkle with herbs. Lay in the cooked potatoes so that the dough is covered up to the edge of the tray.

5) Now add the thinly sliced raw tomatoes, the crumbled ġbejniet and drained tuna flakes, anchovy or hard boiled eggs (*if using them*). Sprinkle over the olives and capers and thinly sliced onions.

6) Carefully pour over your lightly beaten eggs.

7) Fold the edges of the dough which are outside the tray over, and sprinkle the entire thing with some olive oil, ground pepper and if you wish, sesame seed.

8) Bake at 230°C for about 25 minutes, or until the dough is risen and a crisp golden brown. Remove from the oven, and check to see if there is much liquid generated from your tomatoes and fresh cheese - if necessary, tip away any excess liquid and return to the oven for a final 10 minutes baking time.

when assembling your ftira 'tal Gozo, layer in your ingredients

fold over the bread crust, and dust with grated parmesan & sesame seeds

finally, pour over your beaten egg, and bake until golden brown

stromboli or pepperoni pizza rolls

makes about 12 pizza rolls

Another excellent way to use your dough, and particularly good for feeding a crowd as you can pre-prepare trays at a time.

They are easy to pick up and eat with your fingers, and retain their shape more robustly than a slice of pizza might *(depending upon it's thickness of course).*

`The reason for shredding the pepperoni is to make it easier to take a bite from the roll, without dragging out a whole pepperoni slice with your teeth - do take the trouble, it makes it much nicer for people to eat.

ingredients:
1 batch Whaligoe hearthbread dough
rich tomato sauce
pepperoni - shredded finely
sliced onions
thinly sliced olives
mozzarella cheese
parmesan cheese

method:

1) Roll out your dough into a rectangle, and thinly spread the rich tomato sauce over it. Sprinkle over the onions, shredded pepperoni, olives and mozzarella cheese.

2) Roll up the dough from the long side, and press down firmly on the join. Keeping the join underneath, cut the roll into 3cm thick slices, and lay out on a baking tray, cut side upwards.

3) Sprinkle each round with a little parmesan, and bake at 230°C for 15 to 20 minutes, until they are slightly risen and bubbling with golden crusts.

calzone

makes 1 full size calzone

When I was a child in Malta, one of our frequent family outings was to il-Fortizza, a pizza and pasta restaurant on the seafront in Sliema.

That building was originally an artillery battery built by the British between 1872 and 1876. The battery stands on the peninsula that separates Marsamxett Harbour from St. Julian's Bay. It was later used as a searchlight position, and then became a restaurant known as Il-Fortizza (*The Fortress*).

It was there that I first encountered calzone, which became *(and remains)* my one of my favourite pizza styles.

Calzone are in effect a folded pizza, and were probably developed to allow workers to have a portable lunch, much as the Cornish pasty developed in the UK.

In certain parts of Sicily, it is sometimes possible to find calzone sold as 'street-food', deep fried from small carts. I sometimes make a one third size fried version as a party snack, which always goes down well.

(Time moves on for all of us, and il-Fortizza is now sadly a TGI Friday).

ingredients:
200g Whaligoe Hearthbread dough
1 egg
rich tomato sauce
mozzarella
thinly sliced onion
cooked pancetta or ham
thinly sliced artichoke hearts (optional)
(optional) to finish:
rich tomato sauce
hot chilli oil

method:

1) Sprinkle your workbench with coarse semolina, and roll out your dough to a thin oval (*approx. 9″ wide*). Now draw a mental line half way though it at the widest point and sprinkle on some mozzarella cheese in that half oval, making sure that you leave a margin around the edge for pleating the dough.

2) Push aside a circle in the centre of the mozzarella, and crack your egg into this space. If you have done it right, then the egg should be retained by the little wall of mozzarella you have created.

3) Lay over some shredded pancetta or ham, a scoop of rich tomato sauce, some thinly sliced onion, and a final sprinkling of mozzarella. If you are using the artichoke hearts, add them now.

4) To help the filling heat up without bursting your dough, I like to put a couple of slashes into the top half of the oval. It's not essential, but it does work well. Fold the top half over until you have an evenly covered half oval, you may need to gently stretch the dough if the filling is very high. Do try to avoid this though as you don't want to pile in too much, or your calzone will be cold in the centre and your egg uncooked when the dough is ready.

5) Pleat the edges in a neat rope to seal, and place it in your pre-heated oven on a pizza stone. (*A peel is really useful for this*).

6) Bake at 200°C for about 20 minutes, or until the dough is risen and a crisp golden brown. It is cooked at a slightly lower temperature than a pizza to allow the heat to penetrate through to the filling. Don't rush it.

7) You may either serve it as is, or with a side pot of steaming hot tomato sauce, and some spicy chilli oil.

flammkuchen

makes large tray of pizza - enough for 3 to 4

This is a German Pizza.

Popular all over the country, and differently delicious from a Mediterranean pizza.

It should be almost cracker crisp, and smoky from the bacon.

Unlike many other pizza doughs, this is a true flat-bread, with no yeast or raising agent of any kind.

ingredients for dough:
500g plain flour
125ml water
2 tbsp oil
½ tsp fine salt
ingredients for topping:
250ml crème fraîche
2 small onions - thinly sliced
125g smoked bacon lardons a good grate of nutmeg
cornmeal (*or semolina*) to dust your tray.

method:

1) In your mixing bowl pour in the water and oil, and add the flour and salt.

2) Knead until smooth and firm (*about 5 minutes*), and set aside with a cloth over the top to rest.

3) Using a large heavy pan, sauté the bacon to render out the fat and crisp up the lardons. Lift out the lardons carefully and drain on some kitchen paper, saving the fat in your pan.

4) Add your thinly sliced onions to the hot fat, and sauté until lightly caramelised, stirring frequently.

5) Roll out your dough to a thin rectangle the size of your baking tray, and sprinkle the tray quite heavily with cornmeal or semolina.

6) Place your dough onto the tray, and spread the crème fraîche over, leaving a small border around the edge of the rectangle.

7) Dot over the caramelised onions and the crisp bacon pieces, then grate some fresh nutmeg over the whole pizza.

8) Bake at 230°C for about 25 minutes, or until the dough is crisp and the edges are starting to become dark golden brown.

9) Serve immediately.

sfeeha

makes enough for 1

This is an assembly job. It's effectively a small Lebanese style pizza.

Another example of how using the same ingredients in a different way can give quite individual results.

Instructions below are for a single serving, just scale up as needed.

ingredients:
150g Whaligoe hearthbread dough
150g spiced lamb with pine nuts *(see small plates section)*
coarse semolina for dusting.

method:

1) Sprinkle your counter-top with a little semolina.

2) Gently tease and stretch out the portion of dough, laying it flat on your counter and pressing down with your fingertips to dimple it slightly.

3) Using a fork spread the spiced lamb mix over the dough, leaving the edges uncovered to make it easier to move.

4) Preheat the oven to 230°C, (*or the highest temperature that your oven will go to*). If you have a baking stone now is the time to use it, otherwise just put on a tray and bake for 20 mins.

5) When it is golden and bubbling, it's ready.

sfincione (Sicilian pizza)

makes a tray of pizza, enough for 4

This pizza is significantly different from a regular Italian style pizza.

The dough tends to be much thicker (*almost a focaccia style dough*), and cheese is embedded within the dough, rather than sprinkled on top.

The tomato sauce is a middle layer, as it is not desirable to have it soak into your thicker dough, and the top is then sprinkled with a spicy, oily cheesy mixture and baked until crisp.

ingredients:
1 batch of Whaligoe hearthbread dough
3 Sicilian or Maltese sausages (*should contain fennel seeds*)
50g anchovies
50g sliced black olives
rich tomato sauce
100g ricotta
200g provolone cut into small cubes
to finish:
100g dry reasonably fine breadcrumbs
50g very finely grated strong hard cheese
red chilli flakes to taste
olive oil to mix
finely chopped flat leaf parsley

method:

1) Prepare a tray for your pizza *(brush it with olive oil, and dust it with semolina)* and stretch out your dough. You want to have a pretty thick dough, as a Sicilian pizza is more like a bread with topping than a thin pizza.

2) Use your fingertips dipped in olive oil to push and stretch the dough to the edges of the tray. If you are having difficulty with the dough springing back, leave the dough covered for a few minutes to relax then try again.

3) Cover the dough, and remove the sausages you are using from their casings. Crumble them lightly, and fry your sausage in a dry pan until the meat is cooked through and fragrant, with some crispy bits.

4) Push half the cubes of provolone into the dough, then sprinkle over the sausage, anchovies, olives and ricotta.

5) Now spoon over the tomato sauce, and dot with the remaining provolone.

6) Finish by sprinkling over the spiced breadcrumb mix. *(It should have sufficient olive oil in the mix to be damp, but not 'clumpy').*

7) Bake at 230°C for 5 minutes, then turn down the heat to 200°C and bake for a further 20 - 25 minutes, until golden brown.

8) Check the bottom of your pizza is crisp, and if necessary cover with some foil to continue cooking without burning the topping.

Croatian pizza

makes 1 large pizza

I am indebted to Jana Ebury for the introduction to this style of pizza. She asked me to make her a pizza from home. I love it now, and will often have it myself as a treat.

ingredients:
300g Whaligoe hearthbread dough
200ml sour cream
thinly sliced red onion
150g smoked salmon
fresh dill

make a rope edge around your pizza to stop your sour cream topping from spilling outside the crust

method:

1) Roll out your dough into a thin crust, and carefully make a rope edge around the entire circle - the aim is to create a small well on your pizza crust to retain the sour cream at the start of it's cooking time.

2) Place it into your preheated oven (*230°C*) directly on a pizza stone, and bake for 5 minutes, just long enough to 'set' the dough. This makes it easier to handle the pizza when it the sour cream is added.

3) Remove from the oven, and spread the sour cream across the dough up to the rope edge.

4) Sprinkle with the thinly sliced onions, and return to the oven for another 15 minutes.

5) Now lay the smoked salmon over the pizza, and return it for it's final few minutes in the oven - you want the smoked salmon to just lose its translucency but not overcook.

6) Grind over some black pepper and dot with fresh sprigs of dill.

pasta & dumplings

Yum. They exist in most cuisines, they may be large or small but they share a common quality, they are comforting and tasty - you can stuff them with pretty much anything you like, and they make a little filling go a very long way.

I love making them too. There's something so soothing about them (*unless you're on a deadline and having to make 500 at 2am before grabbing a few hours sleep - not so good then*).

They're a great thing to make with friends - get some pals round, crack open a few beers and make a gazillion dumplings while you gossip.

Share them out at the end and you have some very happy people.

Nanna's Maltese ravjul

makes approx. 10 large ravel

These are my much loved nanna's recipe.

She made extra large ravjul, with just 2 or 3 per portion. I remember asking her nanna why don't you make smaller ones, like the ones in the shops? She fixed me with what I can only describe as a steely glare and said 'should I dry my own salt too?'

I love these large ravioli, and I also appreciate the time saved.

Please note though, that they are not like Italian ravioli, the dough is not laminated so it is thicker, and the high egg content makes for a slightly raised dough - they are more like a dumpling than pasta.

They should have a slight chew to them, and are a hearty meal.

ingredients for dough:
200g '00' pasta flour
150g fine semolina
½ tsp fine salt
3 beaten eggs.
ingredients for filling:
300g ricotta
50g freshly grated parmesan cheese
1 tsp cracked black pepper
1 tbsp finely chopped parsley
1 tsp grated nutmeg
1 beaten egg
10 small whole eggs *(if you can get them, pullet eggs are perfect)*

method:

1) Make your dough with the dough ingredients, and knead until smooth. If the mixture appears too stiff add a few drops of water, but don't be impatient, if you add water and it's unnecessary it will spoil your pasta.

2) Rest the covered dough at room temperature for 1 hour.

3) To make the filling mix the ricotta, parsley, nutmeg and a bit of salt to taste - check for flavour and adjust seasoning at this stage. Add half of your beaten egg and mix well. Set aside the rest of the egg while you prepare your pasta.

4) Sprinkle your work surface generously with fine semolina, and roll out your pasta dough to a thin sheet - but not too thin, this isn't like an Italian pasta dough which is laminated for strength, Maltese pasta dough is softer.

5) Use two pasty cutters to cut our your tops and bottoms - you want a size larger for the top to allow for the extra size of the filling. Use 100mm cutters for the top, and 90mm cutters for the base. I tend to cut them in pairs, to make sure I have enough sets of each size. Set the trimmings aside under some clingfilm, and then knead them together and roll out for your final few pairs.

6) Lay out your bottoms in a grid, and before adding any filling just brush the entire bottom pasta circle with the beaten egg - it's much easier to do this then to have to go around your filling at the end. Now, put a heaped spoonful of the ricotta mixture on the base, and make a well in the middle with a teaspoon.

7) Once you have put the ricotta on each base you can start to prepare your eggs. (*Save the egg whites for another recipe*). Work with one egg at a time to avoid breaking the yolk.

8) Carefully slide an egg yolk into the prepared well in each of your bases, then gently lay the larger circle over the top and press down on the outer edge - if you wish you can use a fork to indent the pasta all around. Set aside on a baking tray lined with baking parchment, and cover with a clean cloth.

9) If not using immediately you can keep them in the fridge for a few hours. Cook them the same day though, or you will find that the dough will toughen and they might crack when cooked.

10) To finish, bring a very large pot to the boil with lots of salted water, carefully lower in the ravioli, they will sink and then rise to the surface as they cook.

11) Cook for no longer then 3 minutes, and serve immediately either with some Maltese tomato sauce, or some simple melted butter, and a scrape of parmesan.

12) If you have some spare, which have dried out a little, try deep frying them - they make great little fried pastries.

Italian pasta dough

makes sufficient dough for 5 or 6 people.

Italian pasta dough has different proportions, and may either be rolled out by hand *(which many feel gives a better result after practice)*, or rolled through a pasta machine *(which is considerably easier, but according to purists can affect the texture of your pasta adversely).*

In either case, you should still end up with pasta that is superior to the majority of commercial fresh pasta available.

However, personally I would only usually bother making my own pasta if I intend to stuff it - as then you can control the quality of the filling.

It's also worthwhile if you are flavouring the pasta.

For regular spaghetti, tagliatelle etc., like most Italians, I prefer to use a good brand of dried pasta which can then be cooked 'al dente'. It's not really possible to cook fresh pasta like that, as it cooks within about 10 seconds of the pasta hitting the boiling water.

ingredients:
(note this is a straightforward ratio, simple to scale up or down)
3 eggs
300g '00' flour *(or plain if you don't have '00')*
pinch of fine salt

method 1 - making pasta by hand:

1) Put your flour directly on your workbench, and make a well in the centre.

2) Break your eggs into this well, and using your fingers break the eggs up and mix lightly. Then, using one hand to mix and keeping the other ready in case the wall of your flour well needs reinforcing, draw flour from the inside of the well into your egg.

3) Once the eggs are no longer runny, cover the entire mass with the flour and start to mix your dough.

4) If the eggs were particularly large you may end up needing some additional flour, but in any case you should never exceed 130g flour per egg used - so if you are adding flour, make sure you weigh what you add.

5) Once you are happy with the dough you have achieved, clean your hands and the workbench, and knead your dough until it is smooth and elastic.

6) Allow the dough to rest for at least 30 minutes.

7) It's hard to rollout more than a 3 egg quantity of dough at one time, so if you have made more, divide the dough, cover it well with clingfilm to ensure it does not dry out, and work with one piece at a time.

8) Do try and use a pasta rolling pin if you have one - they are extra long and make it easier to manipulate the pasta.

9) When rolling you initially want to create a simple circle, of approx. 3mm thickness with your dough.

10) Next you roll the top of the circle around the pin, and holding it with your hand roll the pasta towards you, stretching as you go. Repeat this and turn the circle as you go, until you have a dough that is paper thin and almost translucent. It's something that comes with practice - don't worry, it will come.

11) If you want to use this dough as flat pasta, go ahead and cut your preferred shapes - but personally I like to stuff my pasta, and there are any number of excellent things you can stuff them with.

12) Remember, fresh pasta cooks significantly quicker than dried, so pop it in boiling water, and lift out as soon as the pasta floats to the surface - for this reason, it is usually best to only use fillings that are either pre-cooked, or require minimal cooking time, to ensure that you do not end up with an unpleasant raw centre in your pasta.

13) Serve immediately on hot plates, as cold pasta can be nasty.

method 2 - making pasta with a machine:

1) Place your flour, fine salt and egg into the bowl of your food processor, and blitz until you have a smooth dough. Stop as soon as the dough is formed *(should take approx 30 seconds)*.

2) Cover the dough with cling film and allow to rest in the fridge for 30 minutes.

3) Return the dough to your workbench, and knead gently. Divide your pasta into two parts, wrap one while you work with the other.

4) Clamp your pasta machine onto your workbench, and with it set on the first setting pass the pasta dough through the rollers. Fold into three, and pass it again. Fold into three in the opposite orientation, and pass it again. Repeat this three times, to give you a laminated dough.

5) Move the pasta rollers onto the next setting and pass through your dough, continue to move up the roller settings giving you thinner and thinner pasta, until your reach the thickness you desire for your product.

6) Either use the fancy cutters with the machine to give you specific pasta types, or cut and stuff as desired.

Asian dumpling dough

This is a simple and very useful dough. It may be boiled, panfried, deep-fried and steamed.

There are lots of options with fillings, and the dough is easy to handle allowing you to practice different shapes.

A good place to start to work with Asian filled goodies.

ingredients:
300g plain flour
180 ml (*or grams)* of freshly boiled water

method - for making the dough by food processor:

1) Put the flour in the bowl of your food processor, and with it running add the water in a steady stream.

2) As soon as all the water is added stop the machine, and check the dough. It should look a little rough, and feel soft but firm enough to hold it's shape. If necessary, add additional water or flour by the spoonful until you have achieved your desired dough.

3) Run the machine for a further 10 seconds to work the dough, but don't overwork it, you just need to run the machine long enough for the dough to form a ball around the blade.

method - for making the dough by hand:

1) Just add the flour to a mixing bowl, add the water in small amounts kneading as you go, to achieve the same result as above *(with a little more effort).*

2nd dough stage - kneading & proving:

1) Once the dough is together, give it a final minute or so of hand kneading to produce a nearly smooth and slightly elastic dough - if you press the dough, it should spring back slowly with a slight impression of your finger remaining.

2) Place the dough in a zip lock bag, expelling as much air as possible, or use a vacuum bag if you have one. Rest at room temperature for a minimum of 15 minutes, and up to 2 hours. The dough will become soft and pliable *(earlobe soft)* which makes the wrappers easy to work with.

3) You may now either use the dough, or refrigerate overnight, but if doing so, you must allow it to return to room temperature before trying to form wrappers from dumpling dough

3rd dough stage - shaping

1) It's a three stage process forming your wrappers; first portion, then flatten, then finish.

2) To portion your dough, you may weigh each piece if you want to be precise, but I just roll the dough into a long roll, and divide it into the number of dumplings I am making. It also has the advantage of giving you basic circles to start with.

3) To flatten, you may use a rolling pin, but I use a tortilla press - this wonderfully useful gadget must however be lined with plastic top and bottom *(or silicon baking paper works well too)*, then just position your small circle of dough and press down, job done.

4) Set these circles aside, keep them covered to avoid them drying out.

5) To finish, use a thin dowel rolling pin if possible. What you want to achieve is a circle with a thicker 'belly' in the centre. This is so that when you have gathered up the edges to seal your dumpling, the dough is of an even thickness throughout and will cook consistently.

6) Use your rolling pin to apply pressure on the outer edges of the wrapper with one hand, and use the other hand to rotate the wrapper so that you roll around the entire wrapper.

7) If the dough sticks you may use a little flour, but avoid adding too much as it will spoil your dough. If you have having trouble, let the dough rest for a few minutes and try again.

8) The wrapper should resemble a flattened fried egg shape when correctly rolled. The actual size of the wrapper required will depend upon the filling and use of the dumpling, individual recipes will usually suggest an optimum size.

portion your dough, and use a tortilla press to make the initial shape

flavouring your dough:

Below are some suggestions for dough flavourings and colours.

Don't be held back, be adventurous, all of these can be used with any of the styles of dough, Asian, Italian, Maltese.

Have fun using them, and making your own combinations.

carrot dumpling dough

1) Use 100% carrot juice to replace the water in your recipe.

spinach dumpling dough

1) Blitz 500g of spinach with 100 ml of water in a blender, adding more water if required, until there is a vibrant green and smooth mixture.

2) Heat the mixture until it comes to a near boil - look for foam around the rim of your pan, and turn off the heat.

3) Stir to blend the mixture well, then use as much as necessary for your dough.

4) Any excess may be frozen for use another time.

golden dumpling dough

1) Mix ¾ tsp ground turmeric into your flour before adding the water. The dough will develop colour as it rests.

extra-chewy dumpling dough

1) For extra elasticity and sweetness, combine 25% of glutinous (*sweet*) rice flour with your all purpose flour. This dough is firmer then the basic dough, you may find that the rice flour makes it a bit easier to manipulate.

black pasta dough

1) Add a couple of sachets of squid ink to your liquid before mixing with the flour. This gives a dramatic dark colour to the dough, and marries well with seafood fillings.

parsley dough

1) Add a large bunch of parsley to 200ml water, and blitz until smooth. As with the spinach dough, ensure that you heat to scalding point and stir well before use. Again, any excess can be frozen for use another time.

rosemary dough

1) Rosemary works well as a flavour for doughs containing chicken or pork. Strip the needles from the stalks and discard the stalks. Be aware that rosemary has a very strong flavour so only use a few sprigs initially, and taste as you go until you achieve the desired level of flavour.

lemon zest dough

1) Grate some lemon zest into your flour before combining with water in the usual way, this pairs well with seafood fillings, chicken fillings and cheese fillings.

2) It also works really well with sweet pasta. Particularly a ravioli filled with sweet ricotta and candied fruits, then deep fried and tossed in icing sugar.

Mongolian meat & caraway dumpling

This is a simple and flavoursome filling which may be used with any of the wrappers. It is traditionally encased in a wheat wrapper and deep fried to chewy crispness.

ingredients:
350g minced beef or lamb
100g finely chopped onion
2 cloves crushed garlic
1 tsp salt
1 ½ tsp caraway seeds (freshly toasted and ground)
½ tsp black pepper
2 tbsp olive oil
75ml water

method:

1) Mix together the salt, caraway seeds, pepper, oil and water in a small bowl.
2) Pour over the meat and stir with a fork or spatula to mix well. There should not be any visible chunks of meat.
3) Wrap with cling film and leave for at least 30 minutes to develop flavour.
4) Using a heavy based pan, sauté the onion and garlic until golden, then add your meat mixture and cook until lightly browned. Set aside to cool before use.
5) Again, you can leave this in a refrigerator for up to 24 hours, but bring it to room temperature before using.
6) Use your chosen dumpling dough and either deep fry, steam or boil. Serve with some blisteringly hot chilli sauce.

wonton skins

This recipe makes approx 48 wonton skins.

These skins are more similar to a pasta dough then a standard Asian dough, and can be successfully made using a pasta machine if you wish or simply rolled by hand.

In any case, they are fun to make, easy and tasty. They don't freeze particularly well though, and can turn slightly grey if you keep them in the fridge - so make them fresh and use them fresh.

ingredients:
200g plain flour
¾ tsp fine salt
1 large egg
75g water
cornflour for dusting

method:

1) If using a food processor, blend the flour and salt for a few seconds to mix well.

2) Combine the water and egg, and beat lightly, then through the feeder tube add the liquid to your flour mixer with the machine running.

3) Run the machine only until a large slightly sticky ball of dough gathers, if it's too dry add a very small amount of water, if too wet adjust with some flour.

4) On your worktop, knead the dough for at least 2 minutes, or if you have mixed by hand for at least 5 minutes.

5) Rest the dough in an airtight bag at room temperature for up to 3 hours, or refrigerate overnight and bring back to room temperature before continuing.

6) If you are using a pasta machine, treat the dough in a similar way to an Italian dough, in that you should laminate the dough 5 or 6 times when using the widest setting. Once that is done, a single pass through the narrower settings will suffice.

7) Dust your work surface and the surface of your dough with a light sprinkling of cornflour to help the dough become silky thin.

8) To laminate, shape one third of your dough into a rough rectangle *(keeping the rest under cover to stay moist),* then feed it through the machine on the widest setting. Then take that rectangle, and fold it like a letter, with one end towards the middle and the other end on top to cover. Pass the unfolded ends through the machine, and repeat.

9) As you work through the rollers, remember to add some cornflour to both sides of your dough before passing it through the machine.

10) When you have achieved your desired thickness, you are ready to cut your dough.

11) For wonton skins the usual size is a square of approx 8 cm, so measure the width of your dough, and if possible ensure that you can either hand roll it to a 16 cm width, or keep it at 8 cm, in any case don't waste your dough - any leftovers can be gathered up and re-rolled.

12) Once you have cut your wrappers, keep them covered with a dry cloth to avoid them drying out.

pork & shrimp dumpling

makes lots

This filling is traditionally used in pot-stickers or Japanese gyoza, but can be used in any of the dumpling shapes. However, remember that if using a raw filling, the dumpling should be cooked for longer then when a cooked or vegetable filling is used.

ingredients:

200g finely shredded cabbage
2 cloves crushed garlic
1 tsp grated fresh ginger
2 tbsp chopped scallions or chives
180g minced pork
100g chopped prawns
¼ tsp sugar
¾ tsp salt
½ tsp black pepper
1 ½ tbsp soy sauce
1 tbsp sake
1 tsp sesame oil

excess dumplings may be successfully frozen to give you a quick & easy treat

method:

1) Toss the cabbage in a large bowl with ½ tsp salt, and set aside to draw as much moisture as possible from the cabbage.

2) Drain in a colander and rinse to remove excess salt, then drain again and spin to dry.

3) Add the garlic, ginger, chives, pork and prawns to the cabbage, and stir and combine the ingredients.

4) In a separate bowl, combine the remaining ¼ tsp salt, sugar, pepper, soy sauce, sake and sesame oil. Mix well, and pour over your pork mixture.

5) Stir well to combine the ingredients into a well amalgamated mixture.

6) To develop the flavours, wrap the bowl and set aside at room temperature for at least 30 minutes. If you wish, you can refrigerate the filling for up to 24 hours, but bring it to room temperature before using.

7) Now assemble and cook the dumplings as per the individual recipe being used.

Remember, if you want to use this filling in a quickly cooked dumpling, you should fry the filling well first and allow it to cool before using.

Uncooked fillings should only be used in dumplings which are cooked for a longer time, such as gyoza or pot stickers.

wheat starch dough

makes approx 500g

This dough is malleable, snowy white and gluten free.

When cooked, the dough has a translucency that allows the filling colour to be visible.

Wheat starch on it's own would make too firm a dough, so tapioca starch is also used to add elasticity.

ingredients:
125g wheat starch
60g tapioca starch
4 tbsp oil *(I prefer olive oil)*
approx 250ml just boiled water
large pinch of salt

method:

1) Combine the wheat starch, tapioca starch and salt. Mix in about 200ml of the water.

2) Work at a slow speed, to prevent the fine starches from flying out of your bowl.

3) The dough will look translucent first, then become mottled, whitish and lumpy. A smell of wheat will be evident. Now add the oil, and work in.

4) If the dough looks a little dry, work in more of the water until you achieve a medium firm texture. If you add too much water, add additional wheat starch by the tbsp until the dough forms a rough ball that feels a bit bouncy.

5) Transfer the warm dough to an un-floured board, and knead for a couple of minutes until smooth and resembling 'play-doh' in texture. It should not crack if you squeeze it. If it does crack, lightly oil one hand and knead the additional oil into the dough to increase it's suppleness.

6) Cut the dough into three or four pieces to work with and form into your desired skins.

7) Roll the piece of dough you are working with into a log, then cut into the number of skins you wish to make from it. Now use either the oiled flat side of a cleaver to press into a circle, or a plastic covered and lightly oiled tortilla press *(or an oiled rolling pin).*

8) Once pressed, assemble a batch of your dumplings before forming more wrappers from your next portion of dough.

Thai tapioca pearl dumpling dough

makes 24 dumplings.

A natural segue from stuffed dough skins, these tempting morsels are halfway to a more European style of dumpling, but still wonderfully strange.

ingredients:
175g small tapioca pearls
125ml just boiled water
¼ tsp salt

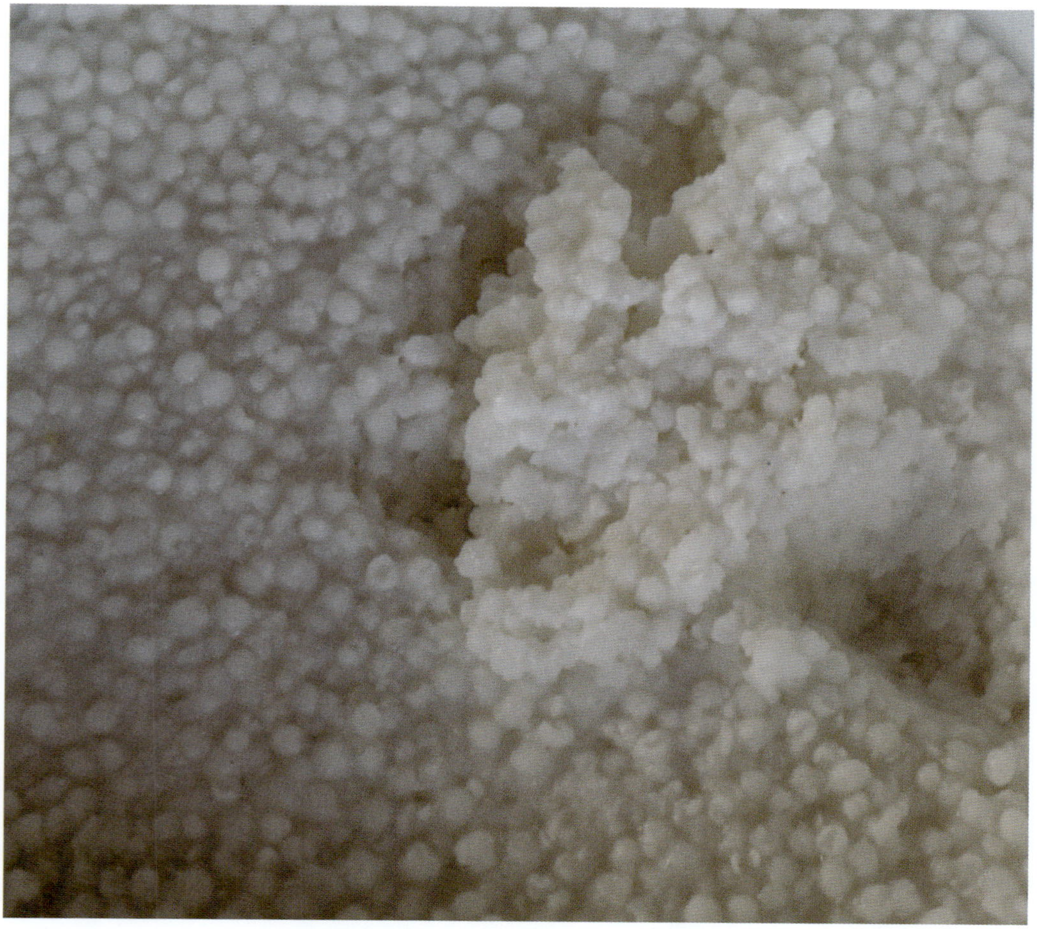

weird looking, but honest it works...

method:

1. Put the tapioca into a bowl, add hot tap water to cover, swirl twice, then immediately pour into a fine mesh strainer. Shake the strainer to get rid of excess water. The tapioca should have bloomed.

2. Transfer the tapioca to a dry bowl, stir in your just-boiled water and salt, and combine well. Cover the bowl, and leave for 1 hour.

3. Transfer the tapioca mixture to an un-floured work surface. *(You will initially work with slightly wet hands to avoid stickiness, and later use tapioca starch to form the dumplings).*

4. Knead the dough with wet hands for about a minute, into a bumpy ball of tapioca pearls. It will be a bit squishy, that's fine. Cut the dough in half and return half to the bowl, covering it with cling film.

5. Dampen your hands, and roll the working dough into a 30cm log, cut it into 12 pieces, and with damp hands roll each piece into a ball.

6. Now wash and dry your hands thoroughly.

7. Lightly dust your hands with tapioca starch, and pick up a dough ball. Form an indentation in the centre with your thumb, and rotate the dough to form a small cup.

8. Fill it with about ½ tsp of your chosen filling, and close the opening by pressing the dough inwards. If there is a hole in the dough, pinch it together and dab on some tapioca starch to seal.

9. Steam the dumplings for 20 minutes over boiling water, turn off the heat and remove the steamer lid. After about 3 minutes, the tapioca pearl dough should go from translucent to mostly clear. If it does not, steam for a further 5 minutes.

10. Serve with a lettuce and herb garnish, or in soup.

Tibetan beef & pepper dumplings

These are hearty and fragrant with ginger, garlic and Szechuan peppercorns, and are often served with a spicy roasted tomato sauce.

ingredients:

350g minced beef (*lamb or dark chicken meat may also be used)*
100g finely chopped onion
50g finely chopped chives or scallions
2 ½ tbsp minced fresh ginger
3 cloves crushed garlic
1 tsp salt
¾ tsp Szechuan peppercorns *(toasted and crushed)*
2 tbsp olive oil
90ml water

method:

1) Combine the beef (*or lamb or chicken*), with the onion, chives, ginger and garlic in a bowl. Mash together well to mix thoroughly.

2) Stir together the salt, Szechuan peppercorns, oil and water then pour over the meat mixture and mix well.

3) Develop the flavours by setting aside for 30 minutes, or refrigerate for up to 24 hours. Always bring back to room temperature before using.

4) Use a standard wheat wrapper, and either steam or deep fry these dumplings.

5) Bear in mind that this is an uncooked filling so the dumplings should not be too large, to allow the centre to cook through without overcooking your chosen wrapper.

6) Serve with a spicy tomato sauce.

Thai dumplings

This is a distinctive combination of flavours. The filling may be used very successfully within a standard dumpling wrapper that is then either fried, steamed or boiled.

It can also be absolutely terrific served in a translucent wrapper submerged in a spicy chicken broth, and a works as a successful filling in tapioca pearl dumplings.

Whatever you do with these, I'm sure you will enjoy them.

ingredients:
100g hand chopped fatty pork or dark chicken meat
2 tbsp finely chopped shallot
2 tbsp finely chopped unsalted roasted peanuts
1 ½ tsp finely chopped coriander stems *(or roots if available)*
1 tsp crushed garlic
2 tsp fish sauce
1 tbsp palm sugar *(or brown sugar)*
¼ tsp white pepper
1 tbsp olive oil

method:

1) Heat the oil in a medium pan, add the coriander stems and ginger, and cook until fragrant and light golden.

2) Add the shallot and pork or chicken, stirring well to ensure that the meat is crumbly.

3) Cook for about 1 minute, until the meat has lost it's pinkness, then add the fish sauce, palm sugar and white pepper.

4) Continue cooking for another 3 minutes or so, until some of the meat has browned and the mixture is bubbling.

5) Add the peanuts, stir well to combine, and remove from the heat.

6) Adjust seasoning with salt and sugar as needed, aiming for an intense salty-sweet flavour.

7) Allow to cool completely before using.

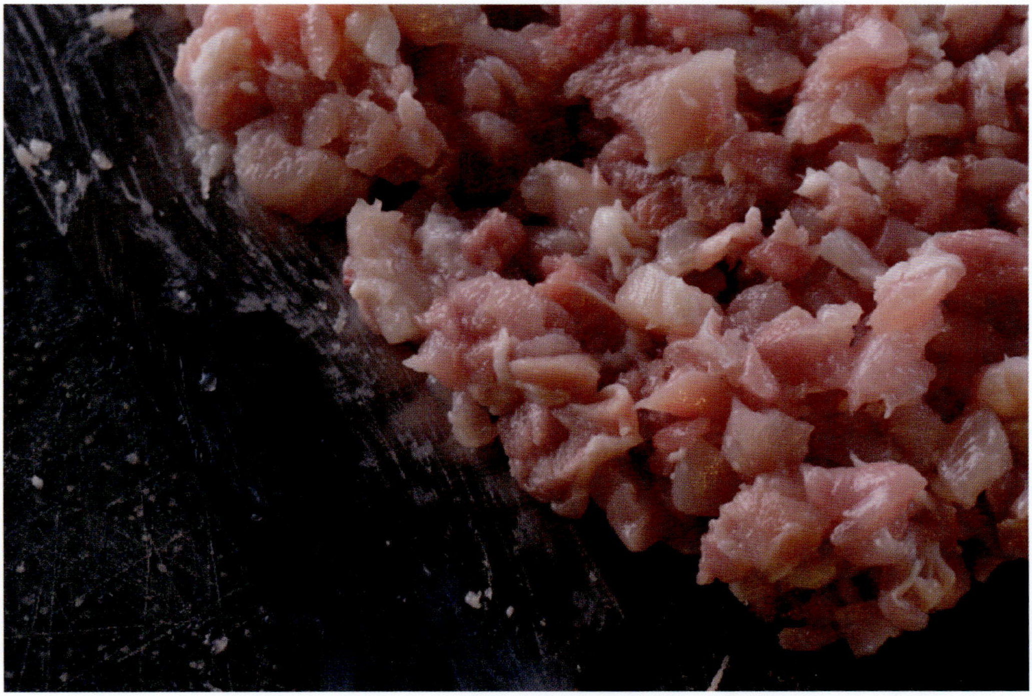

chicken & spring onion pot stickers

Pot stickers are one of my favourite things. The contrast with a succulent filling, tender but chewy skin and crusty bottom is wonderful.

ingredients:
1 batch basic dumpling dough
300g coarsely chopped cooked chicken
150g chopped spring onion
2 tbsp finely chopped fresh ginger
½ tsp salt
100ml chicken stock
2 tbsp light soy sauce
1 tbsp rice wine
1 ½ tbsp olive oil
1 ½ tbsp sesame oil pepper to taste
to serve:
Chinese black vinegar
tangy soy dipping sauce (*see extras*)

only use a small amount of filling, to avoid bursting your dumpling

method:

1) To make the filling combine the chicken, spring onion and ginger in a bowl. Mix well to start to combine the flavours.

2) In a separate bowl stir together the salt, pepper, chicken stock, soy sauce, rice wine, olive oil and sesame oil. Mix well, and add to the meat mixture, stirring and folding the ingredients together.

3) Develop the flavour by setting aside for at least 30 mins, or refrigerate overnight. If you do, bring up to room temperature before filling the dumplings.

4) Divide your dough in half, and make 16 wrappers from each half of the dough.

5) Scoop up about a tablespoonful of filling, and position it in the centre of the wrapper.

6) Pleat the edges, and press down on the dumpling to give it a flat stable bottom.

7) Keep the finished dumplings on a lined baking sheet, covered with a dry cloth, until ready to use.

8) To pan fry, use a large non-stick pan and heat 2 tbsp of oil, place the dumplings sealed side up in a winding circle pattern. Fry for a couple of minutes until they are golden brown on the bottom.

9) Pour over some boiling water *(or stock if preferred)*, and immediately place a lid over the pan.

10) Cook for a few minutes until most of the liquid is absorbed, then remove the lid, pour over a little black vinegar and serve with a tangy soy dipping sauce.

traditional British suet dumplings

This is a simple ratio recipe, simply make as much as you need for whatever you are using them for!

These are usually cooked and served within a stew or soup, but can also be boiled in plain water (*or stock*) and added to your dish.

For additional texture, you can also add them to the top of a stew and bake them until the top is crunchy. Definite comfort food.

ingredients:
150g self raising flour
75g suet (*beef or vegetarian*)
1 tsp salt
2 tsp finely chopped parsley

method:

1) Mix the flour, salt, parsley and suet until well combined. Add just sufficient water to bring to a soft dough.

2) Portion into dumplings, allowing for approx. 50% expansion - don't make them too large.

3) Place into your soup or stew, but be aware they will suck up quite a lot of moisture, so if your stew looks quite thick or you have scant soup, cook in a separate pan and place into your stew or soup once they are cooked.

4) In any case, once you have put the dumplings into the simmering liquid, cover and cook for approx. 30 minutes.

butter dumplings

This is a variation on the traditional recipe. I think using butter gives you a tastier dumpling. Another flavour enhancer is to use cold stock (*either chicken or vegetable*) instead of water when mixing the dough.

These are particularly good made quite small, and simmered in a clear soup.

ingredients:
150g self raising flour
75g cold unsalted butter
1 tsp salt
2 tsp finely chopped parsley

method:

1) Mix the flour, salt and parsley until well combined.

2) Grate your cold butter into the mix, and ensure that the butter is well distributed.

3) Continue as per the standard dumpling recipe.

Polish dumplings (kopytka)

I spent over a year living and working in Wroclaw, Poland and learned to love beetroot, sauerkraut and most of all, dumplings. (*Oh, probably vodka too*)

These are potato based, and may be filled with either cooked minced meat, cabbage or mushrooms.

ingredients:
50g finely chopped onion
25g butter
250g minced meat
500g potatoes - cooked and mashed
1 egg - beaten
100g plain flour
to finish:
sour cream

method:

1) Fry the onion until golden, add the minced meat and continue to fry until well cooked. Season to taste, and set aside to cool.

2) Make the dough by adding the flour to your mashed potato together with the beaten egg, and mix well to combine. If necessary, you may add a little more flour but avoid adding too much.

3) Make the dough into a roll, and cut into slices. Place a tsp of meat and onion filling in the centre of the slice, and bring up the edges to seal.

4) Roll the dumpling into a ball in your hand and set aside.

5) Cook in simmering salted water for 5 minutes, and serve with sour cream.

lazy dumplings (leniwe pierogi)

makes enough for 4

These dumplings are quick and easy to prepare. They are referred to as 'lazy' because there is no need to fill them, the cheese is incorporated into the dough, and they are simply sliced into portions from your dough roll.

ingredients:
225g curd cheese
1 tbsp milk
½ tsp sugar & ½ tsp salt
1 egg - separated
175g plain flour
2 tbsp breadcrumbs
25g butter

method:

1) Mix the cheese, milk, sugar, salt and egg yolk, then beat well.

2) Whisk the egg white until just stiff, and fold into the mixture, folding in half the flour at the same time.

3) Put the rest of the flour on your workbench, and turn out your mixture onto this. Knead the mixture, working in the rest of the flour and continue until the dough is no longer sticky.

4) Make into a long roll, approx 2.5cm wide, and flatten slightly. Cut diagonally into pieces approx. 4cm long and cook in plenty of boiling salted water.

5) As the dumplings rise to the surface, let them simmer for another 2 - 3 minutes, then drain.

6) Melt the butter, and fry the breadcrumbs - add the dumplings and fry for a few minutes more to colour them slightly, and serve.

pierogi filled with sauerkraut & mushrooms

makes enough for 4

ingredients for dough:

300g plain flour

1 egg

½ tsp salt

ingredients for filling:

450g sauerkraut

150g butter

1 onion (*finely chopped*)

110g mushrooms *(diced)*

to finish:

2 tbsp dried breadcrumbs

25g unsalted butter

sour cream

method:

1) Make a soft dough by mixing the flour, egg and salt with just sufficient warm water *(a couple of tbsp should suffice)*.

2) Rest the dough.

3) To make the filling, chop the sauerkraut finely, and sauté in the butter together with the diced onion and mushrooms.

4) Set aside to cool in a strainer, to allow any excess liquid to drain away from the filling.

5) Divide the dough into quarters, and keep the rest covered while you work with one portion.

6) Roll out the dough thinly, and cut out circles of approx 8cm diameter.

7) Place a heaped tsp of filling in lower half of each circle of dough, fold over and press the edges together firmly.

8) Cook in boiling salted water.

9) When they rise to the surface, turn the heat down and simmer for 3 minutes.

10) Drain well and keep warm.

11) Melt the butter in a small frying pan, and toss in the dried breadcrumbs. Cook for a few minutes, until the crumbs are crisp and buttery.

12) Remove the cooked pierogi from your oven, and sprinkle the fried breadcrumbs over.

13) Serve with sour cream.

curd cheese dumplings with strawberries (jahodové knedlíky)

makes 16 small dumplings.

These divine little treats from Prague are delicious. They can also be filled with plums, chocolate, apricots or whatever you fancy but strawberry is my favourite filling.

ingredients for dumplings:

250g curd cheese
25g soft butter
2 egg yolks
1 tbsp of vanilla sugar
180g fine semolina flour *(you might need more depending on the curd used)*
1 tsp lemon zest a pinch of salt
a pinch of baking powder
16 small strawberries

ingredients for sauce:

200g strawberries
150g sour cream icing sugar to taste

method:

1) Put the curd in a fine sieve for at least 15 minutes to drain any excess fluid away.

2) Heat up a large pot of water so it's almost at a very light boil, and keep it at that temperature. Wash the small strawberries and pat them dry, then remove their hulls and coat them in sugar.

3) Beat together the strained curd cheese, melted butter and egg yolks in a big bowl. Zest your lemon directly into the mixture.

4) Add vanilla sugar, salt, baking powder and mix well.

5) Finally, add the fine semolina and combine until you can form the dough into balls *(if the dough is still sticky, you can add more semolina, but your dumplings will turn out firmer in the end).*

6) Form the mixture into two logs and cut each into 8 equally sized pieces. Lightly flour your hands and shape little circles, then place a strawberry in the middle of each, and wrap it firmly with the dough to make a little dumpling, and flour it lightly if necessary.

7) Carefully slide the dumplings into the lightly boiling water, stir gently every now and then to make sure no dumpling is stuck to the bottom of the pot, and let them simmer at low heat for 10 minutes.

8) Meanwhile mash the remaining strawberries, icing sugar and sour cream with the back of a fork.

9) Melt some butter in a pan over medium heat. As you take the dumplings out of the water with a skimmer, let them dry a moment and toss them in the pan with the melted butter.

10) Put a little bit of strawberry sauce into a bowl and add a few hot dumplings.

11) Dust with icing sugar, and top with more strawberry sauce.

gnocchi

makes enough for 6

A staple in Italy, and surprisingly popular in the north of Scotland.

ingredients:
1 kg floury potatoes
250g fine semolina
2 beaten eggs

method:

1) Cook the potatoes in their skins until just tender, and peel them while still hot.

2) Put through a mouli or potato ricer, and drop straight onto a worktop dusted with semolina.

3) Make a well in the centre of your potato mixture, and pour in the beaten egg and some of the semolina.

4) Work the egg and semolina into the fluffy potato, and add more as required to achieve a soft but not sticky dough. Do not overwork the dough, and put in the minimum amount of semolina necessary, to maintain a good potato flavour.

5) Section the potato dough into four portions, and roll each one out into a long rope, around the thickness of your thumb.

6) Cut off 3 cm lengths from the potato mix, and toss in more semolina to ensure the cut pieces do not stick together.

7) If necessary, refrigerate until needed. (*They will keep well in an airtight container, for several days, as long as each layer in the container is separated by some baking paper).*

8) Cook in plenty of simmering salted water, dropping them in carefully with a slotted spoon.

9) They should float to the surface and be cooked within 2 - 3 minutes.

10) Alternatively, you may sauté them in butter, or deep fry them, for a different but equally delicious texture.

11) Serve with your chosen sauce, or sprinkle with some fresh thyme, or buttery fried sage leaves.

I like my gnocchi sautéd in butter, with a sprinkle of fresh thyme leaves

gnocchi poutine

serves 4 hungry people.

These are absolutely totally comfort food.

ingredients:
1 batch of potato gnocchi
45g unsalted butter
45g plain flour
500ml good beef stock
½ tsp brown sugar
few sprigs fresh thyme,
2 finely chopped shallots
75ml red wine
to finish:
25g unsalted butter
300g Camembert *(or other soft melting cheese)* in thick slices

method:

1) In a small pan, melt the butter and add the flour.

2) Whisk it until it is well combined, and cook gently until you have an amber colour and nutty fragrance. *(this is your roux)*

3) Remove from the heat and set aside.

4) In a heavy based pan, sauté the shallots in a little olive oil until they are golden, then deglaze the pan with the red wine and reduce for 1 minute.

5) Add the beef stock, brown sugar and thyme together with the roux and whisk well.

6) Season to taste, and simmer and reduce the sauce until you have a good consistency.

7) To finish the sauce, whisk in a final 25g unsalted butter for extra gloss and mouthfeel.

8) Simmer the gnocchi in plenty of salted water for 2 minutes, then remove with a slotted spoon, and sauté gently in butter until slightly crisp and golden.

9) To serve, put individual portions of gnocchi in a bowl, pour over a ladle full of gravy and top with some camembert.

10) Place under a pre-heated grill until the cheese is melted and bubbling.

11) Serve immediately.

Simplex

sauces

Essential for pasta but also used for so many other dishes.

While this is not meant to be an exhaustive list, it is hopefully a clear explanation of some basic sauce techniques from where you can progress to develop your own special style.

Sauces, more than any other type of cooking, can be magical.

Part science, part art, part sheer inspiration - when they work, they're fabulous. When they don't, they can be hard to fix - generally chalk it up to experience and start again.

The days of simply thickening a pallid uninteresting liquid with some cornflour and declaring it a sauce are thankfully behind us.

Sauces may be simple or can be complex - in either case, they should sing. Some will take hours *(or days)* while others can be ready in minutes.

You just need to have a clear idea of what you want, and then take the necessary steps to achieve it.

Easy.

Pitzcalzean House duck with chocolate

makes enough for 2

My lovely customers from Pitzcalzean House in Ross-shire have sponsored this recipe, and their three ingredients from which I could make a choice were chocolate, salt and coffee.

For this recipe I have combined all three, to make an unusual and complex light meal. The sauce will take approx. 1½ hours to make, but don't be tempted to hurry it, as it is likely to scorch if the heat is too high. Be patient, and enjoy the results.

Serve it with a crunchy salad for some contrast.

ingredients for sauce
100g thinly sliced shallots
50g unsalted butter
250ml well flavoured beef stock
50ml strong espresso
1 black cardamom pod
½ star anise pod
½ tsp grated ginger
1 tbsp honey
1 tbsp pomegranate molasses
100g very dark chocolate (min. 75% cacao)
to finish:
15g unsalted butter

ingredients for duck:
2 x duck breasts
2 tbsp Mycryo
(*optional*) to finish:
2 tbsp caster sugar
blow torch

method for sauce:

1) Using a heavy based sauté pan, sauté the shallots in the unsalted butter over a moderate heat until they are caramelised and golden brown, but not scorched.

2) This will take approx. 30 mins, do stir them frequently to ensure they do not catch on the bottom of your pan.

3) Once you have achieved sufficient caramelisation, pour over the espresso and beef stock, and bring to a gentle simmer.

4) Add the cardamom and star anise, and season lightly with salt and pepper.

5) Simmer gently for at least 1 hour, until the liquid is reduced. Taste frequently, and when you feel there is sufficient flavour from them remove the cardamom and star anise - set aside on a saucer as you may add them back in later.

6) Add the finely grated ginger and pomegranate molasses, and stir.

7) Slowly start adding your chocolate pieces to the sauce, whisking well after each addition. The heat of the mixture should be sufficient to melt the chocolate. Taste as you go, you should achieve a spicy, earthy and rich sauce.

8) Adjust seasoning as required, and if you wish, whisk in a final knob of unsalted butter to add gloss and consistency to the sauce.

9) Place in the top basin of a bain-marie to keep warm. If you chill this sauce and need to bring it up to serving temperature, use a bain-marie as heating the sauce directly could cause the chocolate to scorch.

method for duck:

1) Preheat your oven to 180°C
2) Bring a ridged cast iron grill pan up to a moderate to high heat (*you should only be able to hold your hand above the surface for a moment*).
3) Sprinkle the skin side of your duck breasts with Mycryo, and salt lightly.
4) Place the duck breasts in your pan skin side down, and if possible, weigh them down with a press (*or heavy lid*).
5) Sear for no more than 2 minutes, then turn the breasts and sear again for only 1 minute.
6) Turn the breasts again so that they are skin side up, and place in your preheated oven for 8 minutes.
7) Remove from the oven, and leave to rest for 10 minutes.
8) Once you are ready to serve the duck, sprinkle the skin side with the caster sugar and dust off any excess.
9) Using a blowtorch and moving quickly to avoid scorching any particular area of the skin, caramelise the duck skin.

10) Rest for a moment, then cut into thick slices, and place on your serving dish, with the coffee sauce & a side salad.

serve with a crunchy salad as a foil to the rich duck and chocolate sauce

rich tomato sauce

makes approx. 5 litres of sauce.

This sauce takes several hours to make, but keeps (*and freezes)* extremely well, so make a large potful.

It is also useful as a base for many other dishes.

ingredients:

2 litres chopped tomatoes
2 litres tomato passata
50g tomato purée
200g brunoise cut onion
100g brunoise cut carrot
100g brunoise cut celery
3 thinly sliced garlic cloves
4 tbsp pomegranate molasses
2 tbsp verjuice
small bunch of parsley - finely chopped
2 tsp ground cinnamon
¼ tsp ground cloves
1 tbsp red pepper flakes
3 bay leaves
½ tsp fennel seeds
finely grated zest of an orange

method:

1) Using a large heavy based pan, add a generous glug of olive oil and sauté your onion until translucent.

2) Add the garlic, celery and carrot and continue to sauté the mixture (*your soffrito*) for another few minutes. Try not to brown the onions.

3) Now add the chopped tomatoes, tomato passata, tomato purée and 500ml of water to the pot. Stir well, and simmer for approx. 10 minutes.

4) Once you have heated your tomato mixture well, add the pomegranate molasses, cinnamon, cloves, red pepper flakes and fennel seeds - together with a good grind of salt and pepper.

5) Mix well and simmer on a very gentle setting for at least 1 hour, and preferably 2 hours, stirring periodically to ensure that the sauce does not catch.

6) Now add a handful of chopped parsley, half the zest of an orange and the verjuice, mix in then taste. Adjust the sauce as necessary. (*You are aiming for a rich, complex and slightly spicy sauce. There should be a zing of freshness from the orange zest and parsley plus a sour/sweet back note from the pomegranate molasses).*

7) Serve as it is, or use as a base for other dishes.

This sauce is very good used with pizzas.

fresh tomato sauce

makes approx. 2 ½ litres of sauce.

This is a fresh and tasty sauce, very different from the rich cooked sauce but equally useful. It is served 'raw' and should have a good mix of texture and crunch from the finely chopped vegetables.

Very refreshing on a summer's day.

ingredients:
2 litres chopped tomatoes
2 garlic cloves
150g shallots
100g celery
50g finely diced green pepper
segmented flesh of 2 blood oranges *(or normal oranges if out of season)*
grated zest of 1 lemon
handful of chopped parsley
to finish:
wine vinegar & olive oil to taste

method:

1) If you are lucky enough to have some lovey ripe tomatoes, prepare those by scalding them to remove the skin, then chop them into small dice retaining as much of the juice as you can. Otherwise, use the best quality tinned tomatoes you can get.

2) Place the tomatoes in a large bowl, and finely chop the onion, celery, green pepper and garlic *(you may use a food processor to mince them if you wish)*. Add the chopped vegetables to your bowl.

3) Peel your blood oranges, and remove the flesh from the sour pith. Chop the segments roughly, making sure that you remove any pips from within the flesh.

4) Add to the tomato mixture, and add a generous grind of black pepper and some sea salt.

5) Leave to combine flavours for 30 minutes at room temperature, then add the finely chopped parsley and lemon zest.

6) Combine well again, and taste - if you wish to add a little sharpness, you can add some wine vinegar or verjuice, but it will depend upon your choice of tomato.

7) Finally, stir in a little olive oil and the chopped parsley, and taste again. Adding the olive oil will open out the flavours and add some extra 'mouth feel' to your sauce, but don't overdo it as you want to retain that fresh taste.

8) If you put this sauce in the fridge it will deaden the flavour. If you are storing the sauce before use, you must always allow it to return to room temperature before using.

Maltese style kunserva

this makes a large potful - but it keeps & freezes really well.

This is midway between a rich sauce and a tomato concentrate.

In the past, families would simmer down their ripe tomatoes from scratch to make this delicious staple. With an abundance of fresh ripe tomatoes this is the sensible way to go, however we are not all so lucky.

I have developed what I consider a good compromise, and use good quality tinned produce together with flavour enhancers to achieve a similar result to that remembered from my childhood.

ingredients:
800g tomato purée
2.5 litres tomato passata
50g finely chopped onions
10 garlic cloves *(finely sliced)*
200g thyme honey
50ml olive oil
6 padron chillies or ½ a small green bell pepper *(finely chopped)*
1 tbsp chopped mint
1 tbsp fresh thyme leaves
3 tbsp finely chopped parsley
3 bay leaves
finely grated zest & juice of 1 orange

method:

1) Mix all the ingredients together, and bring to a gentle simmer.

2) Simmer gently in a closed pot *(this will spit all over your cooker if left open)*, for at least 1 hour and preferably 2 hours.

3) Stir frequently, to ensure that the pot does not 'catch'.

4) Remove the bay leaves, taste the sauce, and season with salt and pepper. If desired, add some extra orange zest to bring out the tomato flavour.

5) Allow to cool completely, before packing in zip lock bags to freeze, or bottling if preferred.

This is a great standby to have in the fridge, it is used in many of my recipes, and is also great with a burger, or spread on some fresh bread.

pistachio & basil pesto

This makes approx 600g of sauce.

This sauce is quick and simple to make, although some care must be taken to ensure the nuts are toasted correctly, and the garlic is tempered. Once made, it's terrific just smeared on some freshly baked bread, but it also makes a superb pasta sauce.

Simply add a generous scoop of it to some cream *(or olive oil, for an oil based sauce)*, heat, and toss your pasta in it. Pretty much instant sauce.

It may be kept refrigerated for several weeks, or frozen successfully.

ingredients:
400g shelled pistachio nuts
5 cloves of garlic
200 ml extra virgin olive oil
150g fresh basil
grated zest of 2 lemons.

method:

1) Toast the pistachio nuts in a moderate oven until fragrant.

2) Chop the garlic, and gently simmer in the olive oil to remove the 'raw' flavour.

3) Add all ingredients to a food processor, and blitz until you have achieved your desired consistency - I prefer to keep some crunch in the paste, but you may continue until it is smooth if you prefer.

4) Store in an airtight container in the fridge, but allow to come to room temperature when using it 'raw'.

wild garlic sauce

I've been making this for several years, and it's great. Always fun to make something tasty from foraged produce and I'm lucky enough to have friends who have a huge amount of wild garlic available to pick in early spring.

I usually try to get a batch made before I get busy in the restaurant after Easter, and generally I make enough to last me through to the end of the year.

ingredients:
At least one large bucket full of wild garlic leaves
(cut them with a sharp knife at the base of the leaf blade)
1 small bottle of dijon mustard
4 bottles of olive oil
6 (*or more*) green chillies
zest & juice of 12 lemons
A bottle of food safe, taint free disinfectant.

method:

1) Fill your sink with lots of cold water, and add the appropriate amount of disinfectant to act as a sterilising agent.

2) Carefully put in the cut leaves, and leave them to steep for around 30 minutes, then wash them gently as you want to avoid bruising the leaves at this stage if at all possible.

3) As you wash each bundle remove them from the sink and place in a draining area. Once all the leaves are washed, you need to remove as much excess moisture from them as possible, so in small batches run them through a salad spinner.

4) Start by blending 100g of the dijon mustard with the peeled zest and juice of your lemons. Add the chillies and blend again. Add sufficient olive oil to bring the level in your blender up to half, and stuff in your first handful of leaves. Blend again.

5) Keep adding more leaves until your blender is reaching capacity.

6) Tip the blended mixture into the basin, pour more oil into the blender to approx half fill it, add more leaves, and blend again.

7) Repeat until you run out of oil. If you run out of leaves first, you skimped on your bucket! Whisk the mixture in your basin gently to ensure that it is all well mixed, then put some in your blender, and add more leaves.

8) Continue to do this until you run out of leaves. Whisk the basin of sauce well, and taste - adjust the seasoning and the heat level of the sauce using more mustard, chilli or lemon as you prefer.

9) When you are happy, put around 500ml into an air tight container to be kept at ambient temperature, and freeze the rest in zip lock bags. They will be perfect, and the sauce will just need to defrost overnight and be stirred to taste as fresh as the day it was made.

garlic & chilli sauce

This is a very useful standby to have in your kitchen…

It will keep well for a couple of weeks on the shelf, or a bit longer in the fridge. However, if you're keeping it in the fridge the olive oil will solidify, so it must be brought back to room temperature before use.

It is simplicity itself to make, but do try it.

ingredients:

500ml extra virgin olive oil *(use a good one)*
very finely chopped garlic *(at least 10 cloves)*
3 fresh red chillies *(or more)*
3 fresh green chillies *(or more)*
1 large bunch of flat leaf parsley
finely grated zest of 1 lemon

method:

1) This is an instance when using a food processor to chop your vegetables is not recommended. Please hand chop your garlic, chilli and parsley as finely as possible. If you blitz them you will end up with an emulsion, which is not what you want.

2) Stir your finely chopped vegetables and lemon zest, add the olive oil, and season to taste with salt and freshly ground black pepper.

3) Leave for at least 30 minutes before tasting again, and adjust the seasoning, or heat, of your mixture as you wish. Remember, the power of the chilli will continue to develop, you should be aiming for a sauce that will 'prickle' in the mouth, rather then blowing your head off.

keep the sauce quite chunky for great bursts of flavour
use a few spoonfuls with cooked pasta for a quick and tasty supper

this sauce is also fantastically useful as a garnish,
on anything from some hummus to a fresh green salad.

salmon roe & fruity tomato sauce

makes enough for 4.

Based on an old Maltese recipe, from the days that sea urchins (rizzi) were cheap and readily available. In the fish market, the individual stalls would specialise in various fish, but there was also an 'ugly' stall, where all the oddities that were caught were displayed.

Deep sea fish in particular tend to be rather challenging looking, but nonetheless, delicious. Sea urchins were often on this table, and made a delicious pasta sauce.

I am lucky enough to have some keen divers as customers, and will sometimes wake to a knock on the door and a bucket of sea urchins in seawater on my doorstep. A real treat.

These days sea urchins (*or uni as the Japanese call them)*, are rather expensive. If you are lucky enough to get hold of some, keep it simple, and try this sauce.

Otherwise this sauce can be made very well with salmon roe, which is becoming quite readily available, and has a similar flavour profile.

ingredients:
8 Sea Urchins or 100g of salmon roe (*or caviar*)
1 large shallot
2 very ripe tomatoes
25 ml anisette or ouzo
1 tbsp finely chopped parsley
1 tsp orange zest
1 small orange - segments removed from their membrane
to serve:
600g fresh pasta or 400g dried pasta

method:

4) If using sea urchins, prepare them by cutting off the tops (*carefully*) with a pair of scissors, and gently scooping out the orange flesh. Set aside until the end of your cooking time. (*It can help to wear gloves to do this*).

5) Prepare your sauce by gently sautéing the shallots and ripe tomatoes (*which will ideally have had their skins removed, and be chopped into small dice*). Once they are softening, add the anisette or ouzo, and cook off the alcohol for a few minutes.

6) Add the orange zest, orange segments and parsley, and stir through to combine. Taste and season lightly.

7) Cook the pasta in plenty of boiling water, until it floats to the surface. Remember, fresh pasta cooks in seconds not minutes, so be prepared.

8) Drain the pasta, and stir through your prepared sauce, and top with either the sea urchin mixture or your salmon roe.

9) Serve immediately.

béchamel sauce (white sauce)

makes approx. 500ml

This is the first sauce I learnt to make, I remember my grandmother helping me to stir it. *(I needed a stool to reach the pan, so I must have been quite young)*. It's a classic, and is the base of an infinite variety of other sauces.

It's a straightforward ratio sauce - use 1/10 the quantity of butter and flour to the quantity of liquid. To make 500 ml of sauce, use 500 ml of milk and 50g each of butter and flour.

You can make a very simple variation by adding a handful of finely chopped parsley at the end to make a parsley sauce, which may be a little old fashioned but is still perfect served with fish.

ingredients:
500 ml whole milk
50g unsalted butter
50g plain flour
1 small onion
1 bay leaf
couple of whole cloves
nutmeg

method:

1) First, infuse your milk to add flavour to your sauce. Peel the onion, halve it, and stud each half with a clove. Add the onion and bayleaf to your milk, and bring up to scalding point *(just below the boil).*

2) Remove from heat, and allow to cool for at least 30 minutes. This can also be left overnight for a fuller flavour.

3) When ready to use, strain the milk discarding the flavouring ingredients, and bring up to scalding point again. Set aside.

4) Using a heavy based pan melt the butter, taking care not to burn it. Add the flour, and stir constantly for 1 minute to absorb the butter and create a thick paste. *(This is called a 'roux', and is a simple paste of equal quantities of butter and flour.)*

5) Taste a small amount of the roux to ensure that the 'raw' flavour of the flour has been cooked out - if necessary, cook for a little longer *(30 seconds or so)* but do not overcook. If you cook your roux for too long, the flour will lose it's thickening properties and your sauce will be thin.

6) Once your roux has cooked out, start to add the scalding hot infused milk. Use a whisk at this stage to quickly combine the milk, and as it is incorporated, add more.

7) Cook until it reaches boiling point, and simmer gently for a few minutes.

8) Season with salt, white pepper and nutmeg to taste.

3 cheese sauce

makes approx. 1.25 litres of sauce.

This is another simple variation on the classic béchamel sauce recipe.

ingredients:

1 litre whole milk
100g unsalted butter
100g plain flour
2 medium onions
1 bay leaf
2 tbsp wholegrain mustard
100g grated parmesan
150g grated cheddar
100g marscapone
50g finely chopped spring onions

method:

1) First, infuse your milk to add flavour to your sauce. Peel the onions and slice into thick chunks, add to your milk together with the wholegrain mustard. Bring the mixture to scalding point.

2) Remove from heat, and allow to cool for at least 30 minutes. This can also be left overnight for a fuller flavour. However, rather than discarding the onion, blend the mixture to achieve a smooth liquid.

3) Now make as per the standard béchamel sauce recipe, but at the point that the sauce is thickened, but not completely cooked, add the marscapone and whisk in.

4) After a couple of minutes, when the sauce is cooked, remove from the heat, and whisk in the grated cheddar and parmesan cheeses, together with the finely chopped spring onion.

5) Mix well, and taste to adjust seasoning.

savour

verb [T] uk us savor UK /ˈseɪ.vər/ US /ˈseɪ.vɚ/

to enjoy food or an experience slowly, in order to enjoy it as much as possible:

Reference: Cambridge Dictionary

Loch More - a beautiful view with excellent company

pastry - sweet & savoury

What an amazing thing.

One of the fascinating things about learning more about other nations cooking styles, is how elements of them are the same, but different. Great minds are thinking alike, across centuries and continents.

A middle eastern baklava type pasty is akin to an Austrian strudel. Dutch butter pastries are much like the rich biscuits of Scandinavian countries.

One of my biggest surprises was to find that the Maltese spiral pastry used for pastizzi, which gives a different spin on a puff or flaky pastry, also has a close relative in a classic Chinese flaky pastry. Not quite the same, but certainly a strong similarity exists.

It's one of the joys of cooking. Somehow, seeing how other people cook helps you to feel connected. We may deal with things in different ways, we may tackle problems in different ways, but at the base there is a deep connection in the way we think.

rich short pastry

This is the basis of many savoury and sweet dishes, it is easy to use, quite robust and forgiving. It can be kept in the fridge for a week, or a freezer for up to 3 months. If you wish to make a less rich dough, then replace the egg with some additional water.

ingredients:
250g plain flour
125g unsalted butter - slightly softened
1 egg
1 tsp caster sugar
½ tsp fine salt
approx 40ml cold water

method:

1) If using a food processor, add the butter and flour to the bowl, and pulse until it appears similar to fine breadcrumbs.

2) Add the sugar, salt, and egg, and pulse again. If necessary add a little of the cold water until the dough collects in a ball around the blades.

3) Alternatively, make on the workbench in the same way you would make pasta - tip the flour on your bench, make a well in the centre, and rub in the softened butter.

4) Then add the egg, sugar and salt into the mixture, and if necessary, add sufficient water to mix to a soft and pliant dough.

5) In either case, knead gently 4 or 5 times until the pastry is smooth, then wrap in cling film and refrigerate until ready to use.

rough puff pastry

This is an excellent pastry - it rises well, *(although not as well as a classic puff pastry I must admit)*, but it takes a fraction of the time. It's the only recipe I use for puff pastry any more.

Again, it's a ratio recipe - equal quantities of flour and butter, and ½ quantity liquid.

ingredients:
500g plain flour
500g ice cold butter
1 tsp fine salt
250ml ice cold water

method:

1) Using a food processor, blitz the flour and butter together until the butter pieces resemble little grains of rice - don't make them any smaller, you want to keep some visible butter pieces.

2) Add the salt and gradually add the ice water until it is incorporated. The dough should be slightly soft.

3) Wrap in cling film, and refrigerate for at least 20 minutes.

4) Now flour your work surface, and roll out the pastry into a rectangle approx 40cm x 20cm. Fold it into three, and give it a quarter turn. Roll the pastry out again, and once more fold it into three. Wrap the block in cling film, and refrigerate it for 30 minutes.

5) Return to the workbench, and repeat the process above to give the chilled pastry another two turns.

6) Rest again for 30 minutes in the refrigerator, the pastry is now ready to use.

sour cream pastry

makes enough for a 23cm tart tin

This is a classic pastry that is equally delicious when paired with sweet or savoury fillings. I particularly like this when paired with feta cheese in my cheese and honey pastries.

ingredients:
250g plain flour
200g unsalted butter
125 ml sour cream

method:

1) Dice the butter, and blitz with the flour until you achieve a fine breadcrumb consistency.
2) Add the sour cream, and pulse until a dough ball forms around your blades.
3) Remove the pastry from your processor, and wrap in cling film.
4) Rest in the fridge or a cool counter for at least 20 minutes.
5) I like to roll this out fairly thickly, about ½cm, and use as required.

flan pastry

Another classic pastry, which is a useful workhorse. It's not too delicate, tastes good, and has a crisp texture.

Again, when well wrapped it can be kept in a fridge for up to a week, or be frozen.

A very useful pastry to have in your repertoire.

ingredients:
250g plain flour
125g unsalted butter
1 egg
1 tsp caster sugar
½ tsp fine salt cold water to bind

method:

1) Blitz the plain flour, butter, caster sugar and salt until it resembles fine breadcrumbs.

2) Add the egg, and blitz again.

3) Using just sufficient to bind the dough, slowly add some very cold water to your mixture while the processor is running.

4) As soon as the dough is formed, switch off and put your dough on your workbench.

5) Knead gently until smooth, wrap well and rest for at least 30 minutes before use.

pâte sablée

This is a classic french pastry, used for sweet tarts, it's quite fragile and delicate to work with. However, it's fantastic and worth the effort.

It also *(if well wrapped)* keeps in the fridge for up to a week, and freezes well.

While it may not be the first pastry one should attempt, it's really just a case of being gentle with it.

You can of course work this in the traditional way on your workbench by hand, but using a food processor means it's made in a couple of minutes.

It is such a delicious pastry that it is often used as it is, to make thin and crispy biscuits, referred to simply as sablée.

ingredients:
250g plain flour
200g unsalted butter, diced
100g icing sugar (*sifted*)
2 egg yolks
pinch of fine salt

method:

1) Blitz the flour, salt, icing sugar and cubed butter in your food processor until it resembles fine breadcrumbs.

2) Add the egg yolks, and blitz again. If the dough has not formed yet, add a little very cold water a teaspoonful at a time, until it forms around the blades.

3) Turn out onto your workbench, and knead a few times until the dough is beautifully smooth.

4) Wrap in cling film and rest for at least 30 minutes, before using as desired.

samosa pastry

This is a pastry that I have developed because I love samosas, but often find them a little too tough and oily.

Oddly, having a moderately high % of butter in this mixture seems to make a more tender and flaky pastry, which seems to absorb less oil.

It is not particularly authentic, as usually samosa pastry contains little or no fat. In any case it works well, and is simple to make.

ingredients:
800g plain flour
250g unsalted butter
1 tsp fine salt
2 tbsp cumin seeds

method:

1) Rub the butter into your flour, and mix in the salt and cumin seeds.
2) Use just sufficient cold water to bind the mixture, knead lightly, and rest for at least 1 hour.
3) Roll out thinly, cut out large circles (*I use a side plate for this*). Cut the circle in half, and pick up half a circle in your hand.
4) Overlap the edges to make a pocket, and seal with a little water if necessary.
5) Stuff the pocket with your chosen filling, and seal the top edge.
6) Deep or shallow fry your samosa until golden brown and bubbling.

potato & red onion samosa filling

(makes enough for a dozen)

I love the freshness of this filling, it's spicy and cool.

ingredients:
4 medium sized potatoes (*cooked in their skins*)
100g cooked peas
30g chiffonade of fresh mint leaves
50g finely sliced green chillies
100g thinly sliced red onion
1 tbsp crushed coriander seed
2 tbsp finely chopped coriander leaf

method:

1) Peel the cooked potatoes, use your fingers to crush them lightly, and place into a working bowl.

2) Add the rest of the ingredients, and mix well to combine.

3) Season to taste, and use to fill your samosa pockets.

ricotta qassatat

makes 3 large, or 5 smaller qassatat

These are a very popular Maltese snack, they can have a variety of fillings but are most often filled with ricotta cheese.

They are much easier to make than pastizzi, so give them a try first.

ingredients:
1 quantity rested rich short pastry
500g well drained ricotta cheese
200g finely grated pecorino or parmesan cheese
100g fine semolina
2 small eggs
salt, black pepper & ground nutmeg to taste

method:

1) In a large bowl mix the ricotta, grated cheese, semolina and seasonings to taste.

2) Gradually mix in the beaten eggs. You should have a reasonably firm mixture, only add sufficient egg to make the mix bind.

3) Save any leftover beaten egg, to egg wash the pastry before baking.

4) Now set the filling aside to mature, and roll out your pastry to a thickness of approx ½ cm.

5) Cut out circles of approx 12 cm diameter and put a couple of spoonfuls of mixture in the centre. Bring the circle up to almost encase the filling, but leave the centre uncovered. Pleat the edges to rotate around the circle, making a sort of 'purse' of the pastry.

6) Brush the outside with the remaining egg wash to glaze the pastry, and bake at 200°C for approx. 30 minutes, until golden brown.

feta pastries with honey

makes enough for 6

While these are not traditional Maltese pastries, there is no doubt that they are influenced by the Maltese love of sweet and salty flavours.

I make these as fairly small pastries, as they are quite rich. They make a good side dish, and are a lovely snack with a salad.

ingredients:
400g feta cheese
1 rested batch of sour cream pastry
2 tbsp chopped flat leaf parsley
3 tbsp brunoise cut shallot
6 tbsp thyme honey *(or regular if none is available)*
1 egg, beaten with a little water
white sesame seed

method:

1) Crumble up the feta cheese into a basin.

2) Mix in the chopped parsley and shallot, and season to taste with plenty of cracked black pepper and a little salt.

3) Roll out your pastry to a thickness of approx 0.5cm, and cut out circles with a fluted pastry cutter.

4) Put a generous portion of the feta mix into the lower half of your circle, and fold over to make a semicircle.

5) Press down on the edge to seal, and place on a baking tray lined with silicone paper. Brush with the egg wash, and sprinkle with some sesame seed.

6) Bake in a preheated oven at 175°C until the pastry is golden. Serve warm, drizzled with the thyme honey.

Maltese pastizzi

makes lots and lots

These are absolutely my favourite snack in the whole world. *(Well, OK, I say that a lot, but they really are).* They taste great, they're not low fat, but nor are many other delicious things.

Don't eat them every day, but do eat them.

Traditional fillings tend to be ricotta cheese *(as in the Qassatat recipe)* or a dried pea, onion and black pepper mixture *(much more appealing than it sounds)*, given after the pastry recipe.

This particular pastizzi recipe was given to my sister Fiona by Carmello who used to run the pastizzi shop a few doors away from my grandmothers house in St Paul's Street, Valetta.

He seemed old when I was a child, but Fiona persuaded him to not only give us the recipe, but spent a day working with him being shown exactly what we should do.

Her photo's and instructions are invaluable, and I thank them both for their kindness in sharing. As the pictures are quite old now, the quality is not great, but the information they contain is priceless.

There's no denying it - this is a time consuming pastry to make, and it's quite messy too. Make an afternoon of it, these pastries freeze extremely well, so prepare a big batch.

ingredients for pastry stage 1:

500g plain flour

60ml olive oil

1 tsp fine salt

250ml water

ingredients for pastry stage 2:

250g soft vegetable fat (*such as Trex or margarine*) or lard

100g butter (*softened*)

method:

1) Mix the flour, olive oil, salt and water to make a smooth dough.

2) Knead for at least 5 minutes if using a machine, or 10 minutes if making by hand.

3) Set aside to rest at room temperature for at least 1 hour.

4) Meanwhile mix the butter and vegetable fat or lard, and beat them until they have a soft creamy consistency.

5) Divide your fat into two portions, and do the same with your dough.

6) Taking one portion of dough, roll it out into as large a rectangle as you can. Don't flour your workbench, if the pastry is sticking you may lightly oil your bench and rolling pin.

7) Once you have a large rectangle, spread the softened fat mixture over it as evenly as possible, then starting at one end roll into a long sausage shape. As you go, pull and stretch the pastry to make it even thinner.

8) Having achieved a long rope like pastry, you should now start to roll it up from one end to make a spiral. Using your quite greasy hands, smooth over the top of the spiral to cover it with some fat.

(The reason for the spiral is to make it easier to store the pastry in your fridge while it rests - if you have lots of space, then just make a loop, it's a bit easier to work with).

9) Cover your pastry with cling film, and repeat for the other portion of dough and fat.

10) Keep in the fridge until ready to use the dough.

pea filling for pastizzi

ingredients:
500g dried marrowfat peas
2 large onions finely diced
1 tbsp garam masala
1 carrot finely diced
plenty of freshly ground black pepper

method:

1) Follow the packet instructions for soaking your peas.

2) When ready to cook, start by sautéing the finely diced onion in a little olive oil. Add the garam masala and freshly ground black pepper to the mix, (*do not add salt at this stage)* then stir in the soaked peas, and cover with either water, or if available, vegetable stock (*or chicken stock if you prefer*).

3) Simmer until the peas are tender, but not completely collapsed, you want to have some texture left in them. By this stage, the majority of the liquid should have been absorbed.

4) Taste, and adjust seasoning, adding salt as required at this stage.

5) Check the texture of your peas, you should have a fairly thick paste - if there is still some liquid in the mix, cook it out until it evaporates.

6) Allow to cool completely before using to fill your pastizzi.

shaping the pastizzi:

1) Take the chilled dough from the fridge, and working from the outside edge cut a piece of dough from the end of the spiral (*or rope*) of approx 5cm.

2) Holding the cut portion upright, use your fingers to smooth the dough outwards - you should see rings in the dough *(a bit like tree trunk rings)*, and this is what will make your pastry flaky.

3) Holding between thumb and forefinger, hollow out to a disk approx. 10cm in diameter, then put a generous portion of the chosen filling in the centre, and pinch the sides together leaving a small gap in the top of your pastry.

4) This allows for the expansion of the filling when it is baked, and stops the pastry breaking..

5) At this stage, they may be refridgerated, or frozen for future use.

6) Bake at 190°C for approx. 20 - 30 minutes until golden brown. If you wish, towards the end of baking time you may brush them with a little egg wash, and sprinkle with a little coarse sea salt for extra crunch.

Now take a look at how the professionals do it.

Carmelo's pastizzeria in St. Pauls Street, Valletta

Carmelo mixing the first stage of the pastizzi dough

kneading the first stage dough

preparing the mixture of fats for the second dough stage

preparing the dried pea filling for his pastizzi

portioning the rested dough into manageable sizes

spreading the softened fat mixture on the stretched dough

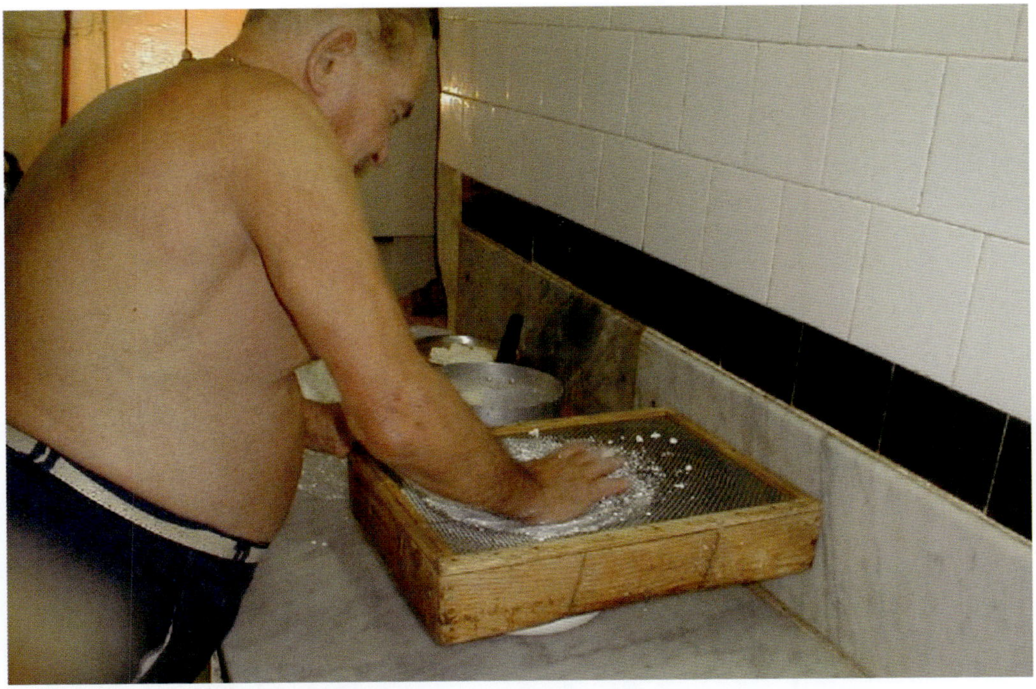
pressing ricotta through a drum sieve to make a smoother filling

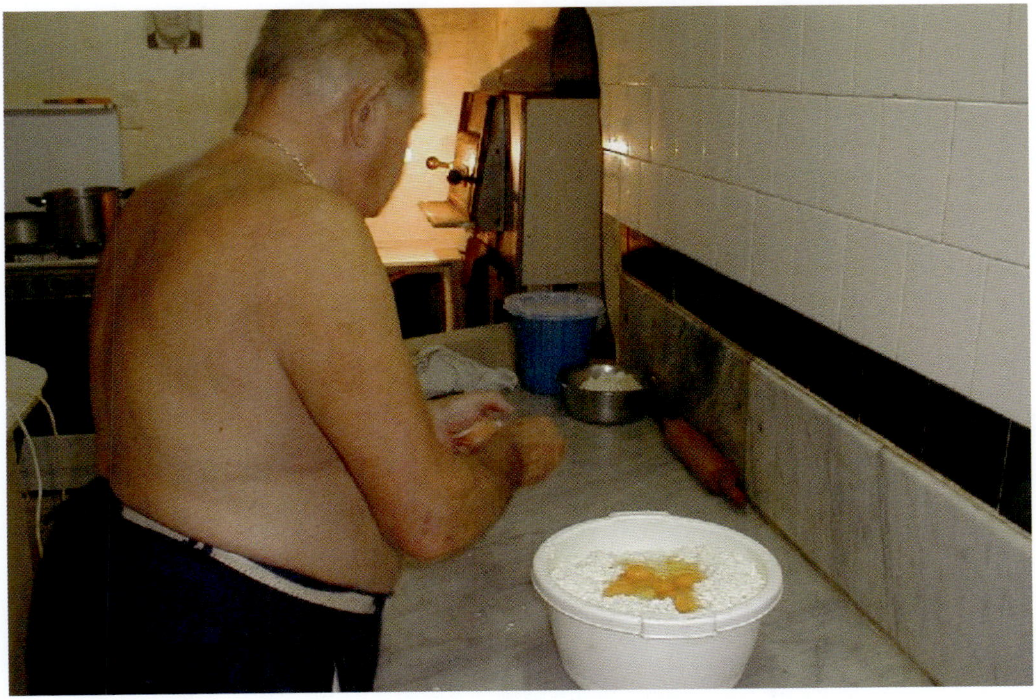
mixing the sieved ricotta with eggs and semolina to complete the filling

rolling up the greased dough

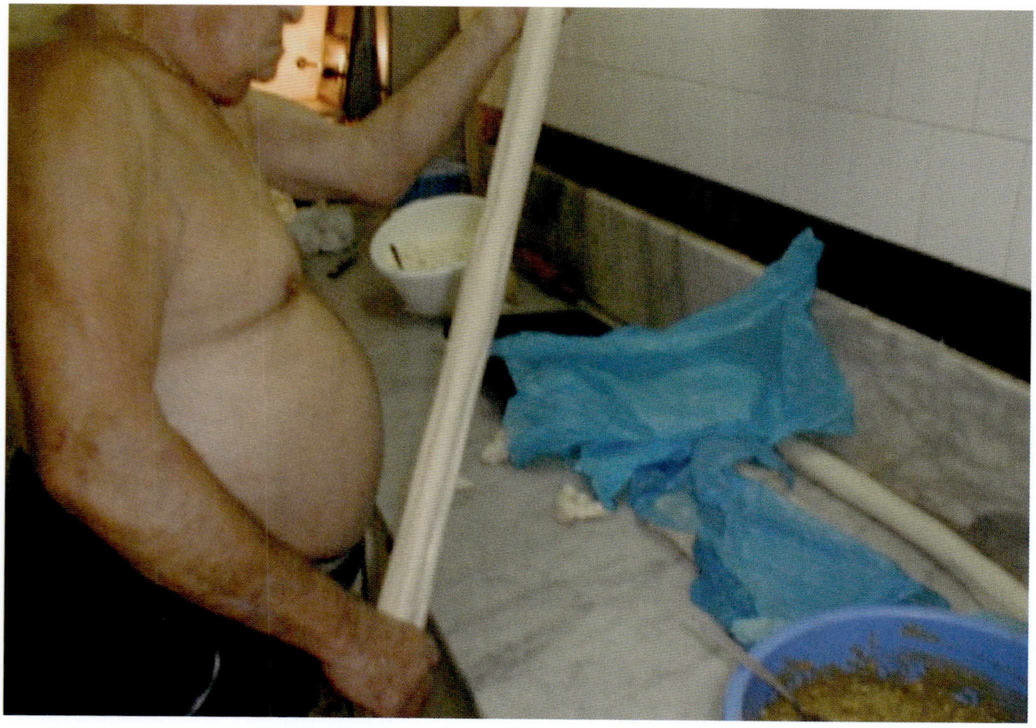

stretching the rolled dough into thinner rolls

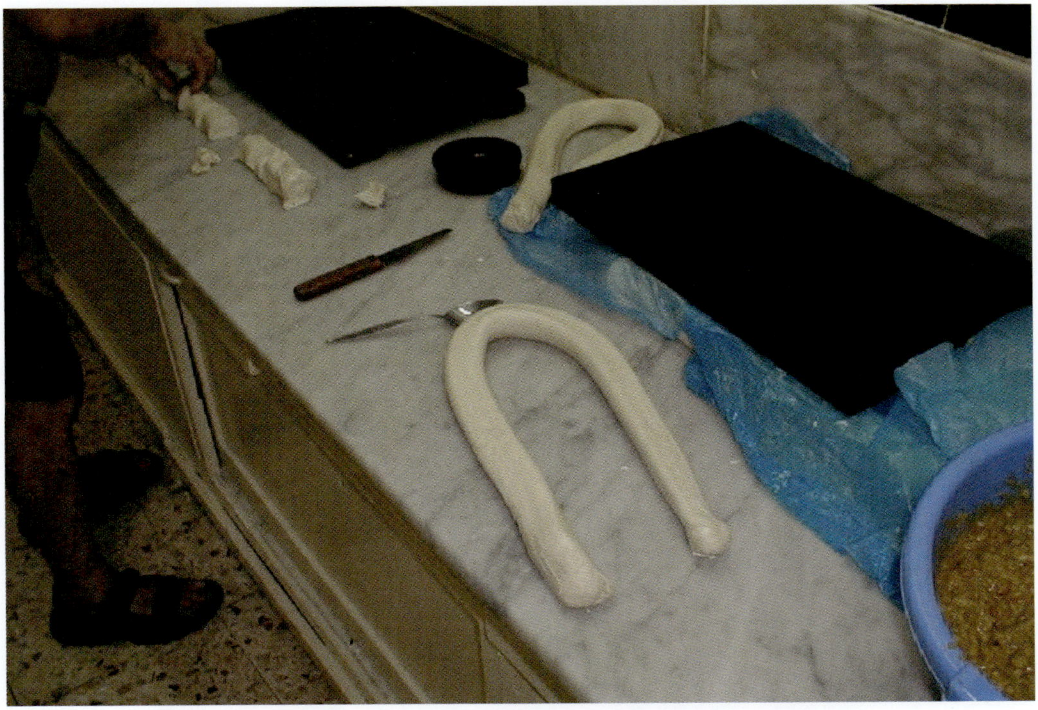

pastry loops are ready, Carmelo is portioning the dough

a relatively small amount of pastry is sufficient for each pastizzi

opening out the pastry to make the circular pouch for the filling

pinching the ends to make the distinctive pastizzi shape

bake at a high heat to achieve a crispy crust

a lifetimes practice offers perfection - something for us to aspire to

Maltese lampuki pie

makes 6 individual pastry topped pies

This is a pie stuffed full of fish, it is savoury and filling, and the vegetables added are by way of a 'soffrito' to add flavour, not to dilute the flavour of the pie.

ingredients:
2 kg lampuki
150g finely diced onions
100g finely diced celery
100g finely diced carrot
2 bay leaves
500g tomatoes
100g tomato paste
150g sliced black olives
50g capers
2 tbsp finely chopped mint
flour to dust the fish
600g rough puff pastry
to finish:
1 beaten egg with a little water for egg wash

method:

1) First make your rough puff pastry, as per the instructions in the pastry section. While it is resting in the fridge, you may start on the pie filling.

2) Make your soffrito by gently sautéing the onions, celery and carrot together with the bayleaves, until tender but not coloured.

3) Set aside to cool, and prepare your fish. As you will be removing the bones after cooking, just clean them well, dust in flour and shallow fry. You only want to lightly cook the fish, to allow the flesh to come away from the bones more easily, as it will be cooked further within the pie.

4) Now, while it is still warm, flake the flesh from the bones of your lampuki. Try to keep the pieces as large as possible, and set the bones and head aside to freeze for stock later.

5) Return to your soffrito, and add the chopped tomatoes and tomato purée, together with the olives, capers and chopped mint. Mix well, and cook for a few minutes to allow the tomato purée to thicken your sauce. Once you have a good consistency, remove from the heat and add the flaked fish.

6) Stir carefully to avoid breaking the fish up more than necessary, and adjust seasoning to taste.

7) Divide the mixture into six heatproof dishes and top with your puff pastry, sealing the edges well to avoid leakage, and adding a small vent hole to the centre of your pastry.

8) Brush with a little egg wash for a golden finish to your pastry.

9) Bake at 190°C until the pastry is risen and gilded.

Serve with a green salad.

sweet things; cake, pastries & puddings

Even the most die-hard savoury fan has a weakness for something sweet. However, many traditional recipes relied upon a high sugar content to improve their keeping qualities and this is often unnecessary now.

As a diabetic pastry chef, the consideration of whether sugar is integral to a dish or whether it may be scaled back, or even replaced, is something that I consider every day. The result is that where appropriate, I use less sugar, but ultimately the answer is to eat and enjoy all things in moderation.

The Maltese have a notoriously sweet tooth, and will travel across town to buy a particular favourite from a specific bakery. In Valetta when I was a child, there were two competing attractions, Café Cordina had the best cakes, but Café Premier (*now unfortunately gone*) had the best pastizzi, so much indecision would ensue. It was not unusual to start a meal sitting at the tables belonging to one café, and end it at the tables of the other.

However if we were in Mdina, there was no contest, the best place to go was the Fontenella perched on top of the city walls, and offering views across the Island, terrific cakes and ice cold Kinnie.

Bliss.

meringues

Firstly, a confession - I used to **hate** meringues.

Making them, eating them, the sugary dry texture of them, sometimes they worked, sometimes they didn't, and they made me ill - BLEH.

However, a good friend of mine became gluten intolerant, and decided that for her wedding she wanted meringues, lots and lots of them. What can you do, friends are friends. I had to figure out a way of making meringues that were reliable, pretty and delicious.

It took a while, but ended up being really simple. The quantity of sugar to egg white must be exactly double, and all crystals should be dissolved before beating starts. That's it. Really.

ingredients:
this is a simple ratio recipe 2:1 - sugar to egg white

(Use whatever amount of egg white you prefer, but as a rough guide, I would normally expect 200g of egg white to provide you with approx. 6 decent sized meringues, using exactly double the weight of egg white in caster sugar).

eg. if you use 200g of egg white, you must use 400g sugar.

method:

1) Weigh your egg whites into a metal bowl (*one that will fit over a pan of simmering water)*, and add exactly double the amount of caster sugar.

2) Using a wooden spoon or spatula, mix them together until combined, but don't try to whisk them - you're just gathering the sugar into the whites. You will see that the colour of the mixture is quite white.

3) Place over a pan of simmering water and heat for approx. 5 mins, stirring every now and then, you want to ensure that the mixture is heated evenly.

4) It is important that you do not overheat this mixture, as you don't want sweet scrambled egg - you will see that the mixture will become less 'white' as the sugar melts - when it reaches around 42°C the sugar should be melted. Ideally use a thermometer to check the temperature to start with, but you can do it by eye if necessary.

5) Remove from the heat, and scrape into the bowl of a stand mixer.

6) Whisk at high speed for about 5 - 10 minutes, until the meringues have fluffed up and cooled.

7) You now have a batch of plain meringue, and can flavour and colour it to suit your requirements.

8) Once you have flavoured your basic mix, you are ready to prepare your baking tray.

9) Always line your tray with silicone baking parchment, and to keep it in its place, dab a small amount of meringue mix in each corner of your tray before pressing down your lining paper.

10) Then if you like a rough swirl of meringue, scoop out large spoonfuls of the mixture and space them out well on your tray. They will expand slightly as they cook, so don't allow them to touch if possible.

11) Place your tray into the oven, which should be set to a temperature of 110°C. (*No need to pre-heat, just set the oven when you are ready)*

12) If you have made large individual meringues, then bake them for 2 hours, if you have made smaller ones you may cut the baking time.

13) If you are unsure as to whether or not the meringues are cooked, gently try to peel one away from the baking paper - if it comes away cleanly, it's ready. If not, don't pull it but return the tray to the oven and practice patience.

14) When the meringues are ready, cool them on a wire rack, before storing them in an air tight tub or jar for up to 2 weeks. Do note, although they will have a good crisp shell they should still have a gooey centre.

rose meringue

Colour delicately pink with gel food colours *(liquid colours make your meringue too sloppy)*, and use rose water for a subtle flavour, or rose oil for a more intense experience.

chocolate meringue

Use brute cocoa powder sifted into your meringue, and don't over mix. I think it looks prettier when it is streaky rather then a uniform brown.

cardamom meringue

Use cardamom extract for flavour, and colour a pale green.

raspberry meringue

Fold dehydrated raspberry pieces through the mix, and once they are shaped, sprinkle with a little raspberry powder for tang.

chocolate chip, walnut & orange meringue

Use bake stable chocolate chips, and fold them through the mixture, together with chopped toasted walnuts and some oranges zest

salted honeycomb meringue

Use chunks of home made salted honeycomb crunch. The honeycomb will lose some of its crunch, but becomes deliciously chewy.

nutty noodle meringue

Sounds bizarre I know.

Make a basic soft pasta dough, but instead of rolling it press it through a potato ricer to make squiggly noodles.

Bake them at around 180ºC until toasted pale golden, and allow to cool. Then crumble them into small pieces.

Mix with flaked toasted almonds, and stir through your meringue mix.

They will be strange, but an amazing texture and flavour. Try them at least once, they're worth the effort.

vanilla meringue

Plain basic vanilla, but always a treat if you use a high quality extract, or better still scrape the seeds from a fresh pod.

small meringues make a delightful addition to a selection of sweet treats

chocolate fondant

makes 8 ramekins

A chocolate fondant will only be as good as the chocolate you use, so don't skimp. I prefer to use Callebaut single origin chocolate, but whatever you pick, make sure it has a minimum of 70% cacao.

The great thing about this recipe, is not only is it simple and reliable but it will keep in the fridge for several days before cooking, wrapped in cling film. It can then be simply baked to produce a crowd-pleasing treat.

This recipe scales up or down very well, and is a simple ratio, so feel free to change it as needed.

It also freezes well, although if baking from frozen you should bake at a slightly lower temperature for a little longer, to ensure that you do not have a frozen centre.

ingredients:
200g good quality dark chocolate (*minimum 70%*)
200g unsalted butter
4 eggs & 4 egg yolks
100g caster sugar
100g plain flour
to prepare your ramekins:
approx 50g melted unsalted butter
approx 50g brute cocoa.

method:

1) Prepare a pan with simmering water, and ensure you have a metal basin that will fit over it. Preheat your basin, then add the 50g butter for your ramekin preparation and melt.

2) Using a pastry brush, coat the inside of each of the ramekins with melted butter, and place them into the freezer for a few minutes.

3) Add another layer of melted butter, and chill again.

4) After a few minutes, remove them from the freezer, and dust each buttered ramekin with the cocoa.

5) Tap the ramekins to ensure that the sides are well coated, and shake out the excess into your basin containing the leftover butter.

6) Melt the rest of the butter in your basin, and add the chocolate callets *(or pieces)* to the butter.

7) Remove the basin from the heat and stir the mixture until the chocolate has been melted by the heat of the butter. Set aside to cool a little.

8) Place the eggs, yolks and sugar into a stand mixer, and whisk until light and fluffy.

9) Fold the flour into the egg mix, then fold the slightly cooled chocolate into the whisked mixture. Be gentle, as you want to retain your volume from the beaten egg and sugar mix.

10) Put the mixture into a jug, and pour into each ramekin - try to make sure that you do not smear the edges of your ramekin, as the rise will be impaired if there is mixture dragging on the side.

11) Chill the ramekins for a minimum of 1 hour, but up to 5 days before baking, or freeze them for future use.

12) Bake at 180°C for 10 minutes, *(or if cooking from frozen, allow 15 minutes)* and serve immediately if leaving them in the ramekins.

13) To turn out, wait a minute for the fondant to cool a little, run a knife around the edge of the ramekin to ensure a good release, and tip it on it's side. You should be able to gently tip it into your hand, and then place on your plate.

using excellent quality chocolate is the first step to a successful chocolate fondant

glazed egg custard or crème brûlée

makes 4 or 5 portions, depending upon dish size.

This is a recipe which was very kindly given to me by the talented chef at Ratho Wine Bar and Restaurant, in Falmouth, Cornwall. I ate there once while travelling for business with a couple of colleagues, and we were served a truly superb meal, but for me the pinnacle was his delicious egg custard. Something that I have a weakness for, but can so often be disappointed by. Not that time, it was wonderful and he generously wrote out the recipe.

I still work from that paper, as a memento of a lovely evening.

The recipe is still perfect.

ingredients:
400 ml double cream
150 ml milk
6 egg yolks
75g sugar
½ vanilla pod

method:

1) Split your vanilla pod lengthwise, and scrape the seeds from one half. Add seeds and scraped pod casing to a small pan with your milk and cream, bring up to scalding point. *(Just below the boil).*

2) Meanwhile, whisk the egg yolks and sugar together slightly thickened and pale.

3) Add ½ the hot cream and milk mixture to the egg yolk mixture, whisking constantly. Then add that back into the remaining cream and milk. (*This process is referred to as 'tempering' the mix, and helps to avoid your mixture becoming lumpy when adding cold ingredients to hot).*

4) Sieve the mixture into a jug, trying to minimise any froth - this would spoil the top of your custard.

5) Pour the mixture into your chosen mould - I prefer to use shallow ceramic dishes, as you get a good surface area for your sugar crust. Whatever you choose, ensure that you are able to place it within a baking tray, to create a water bath with a water level which is up to the height of the mixture in your serving dish.

6) Bake in the oven at 170°C - the time needed will depend upon the depth of your mixture, but expect 20 - 25 mins for a shallow individual dish, or 40 mins to 50 mins for a large dish.

7) Remove from the oven when there is still a little 'jiggle' in the centre of your custard, and cool. Refrigerate for at least 1 hour, or keep for 2 - 3 days before using.

8) To glaze, remove from the fridge and holding the dish over a tub of caster sugar, sift a fine covering over the custard. Invert the custard to shake out any excess, then wipe the rim of your dish to give you a clean edge.

9) Using a blowtorch, caramelise the sugar and serve.

buttermilk panna cotta

this makes approx. 6 portions

The recipe below is simplicity itself, but gelatine can be a tricky beast. You must follow the proportions of fluid to gelatine exactly, or you won't get that sexy wobble. (*Remember, melted sugar is a liquid too...*)

ingredients:
400g buttermilk
300g double cream
100g caster sugar
4 leaves professional gold leaf gelatine
1 vanilla pod

method:

1) Break your sheets of gelatine into smaller pieces, and put them into a small bowl of **cold** water. Leaf gelatine must 'bloom' before use - it will absorb some of the liquid and become soft and jelly like. This will take about 5 - 10 mins, don't be tempted to leave it much longer than that, as after about 15 mins the ability of the gelatine to set your liquid will start to degrade.

2) Split your vanilla pod lengthwise, and scrape the seeds out with the tip of a teaspoon - add the pods and seeds to a small pan which contains the cream and caster sugar. Heat gently, you don't want to boil this, but bring it up to scalding point and then allow the vanilla bean to infuse.

3) Once the gelatine is ready (*feels soft all over when touched)*, drain it from its soaking liquid and squeeze out as much moisture as you can.

4) Remove the vanilla pod from the hot cream, and whisking gently, add the bloomed gelatine and allow it to melt into your mixture. Unless your cream has cooled significantly (*which means you're left the gelatine too long also)*, you should not need to re-heat the mixture.

5) Place the pan on a set of scales, and weigh in the buttermilk.

6) Whisk gently to combine, taste to check the flavour balance, and adjust if necessary.

7) Pour into small dariole moulds and place in the fridge to set for at least 1 hour, or if preparing ahead - up to 3 days ahead.

8) To serve, prepare a bowl which is deeper then the height of your mould, and a jug of boiling water. Place the mould in the empty bowl, pour around the boiling water to just under the rim of the mould, then immediately remove from the bowl.

9) I like to scatter the sides of my panna cotta with chocolate splitters.

banana cake (from the Maldives)

makes 1 large sheet cake, or a layer cake if preferred

When I was heavily pregnant with my son Nicholas, I thought that a low stress holiday in the Maldives would be the perfect destination. Lovely beach, and gentle snorkelling to keep me cool.

If you've ever tried to press a rubber ball under water, you can imagine what trying to snorkel with a belly the size of a whale is like - great buoyancy, but a tendency to spin around, leaving you facing up and breathing lots of sea.

So, I actually spent quite a bit of time in the cool restaurant area, looking out at the view, and eating this banana cake with great big chunks of fresh mango and papaya. On my last day, the pastry chef Mohammed (*who I had of course been chatting to*) brought me over a nicely wrapped piece of cake for my journey home, and the recipe. A very kind man.

I use it regularly, and it's always a winner.

ingredients:
500g caster sugar
7 large eggs
500g banana purée
250 ml sunflower oil
100 ml milk
500g plain flour
4 teaspoons sodium bicarbonate
scatter of sugar nibs

method:

1) Mix the banana purée and sodium bicarbonate together, and keep cool for 30 mins.

2) Beat the sugar and eggs together until you have a pale thick mass, then slowly add the oil and milk to your mixture.

3) Alternately, fold in the flour and banana mixture into the main mix - ensure there are no lumps of flour, as they would be unsightly (and unpleasant) in your cake.

4) You may either bake this as a single sheet cake, a layer cake, or as individual cup cakes.

5) Scatter the surface with some sugar nibs, this greatly enhances the look of the finished cake, as it adds a little visual interest and a pleasing crunch to the surface.

6) Depending upon which depth of cake you choose to make, expect to bake the mixture from 25 mins to 55 mins at approx. 170°C.

7) Check the cake is cooked by pressing the top for 'spring', or using a wooden skewer which should be withdrawn cleanly from the cake, or finally, you could simply use a temperature probe - if the cake is about 95°C internally, it's cooked.

8) It will be quite a brown cake, this is a result of the reaction between the banana and the bicarb, and gives a lovely caramel flavour, it will be moist and will keep well for several days.

9) Allow to cool in the tins if they were used, and either leave plain, ice with your choice of a whipped marscapone, or a vanilla sugar glaze.

churros with chocolate

makes enough for 4 to 6

My son loves these, and can sit and eat a plateful then turn pleading eyes towards me for more.

The mixture is a combination of a batter and a choux style dough, it's very simple to make, and keeps well in the fridge for up to a day.

This means that it's simple to prepare ahead for a crowd, then just fry to order - don't try to pre-cook these, they take hardly any time to fry, and are just not the same re-heated.

ingredients for churros:
400g plain flour
400 ml water pinch of salt
1 tsp bicarbonate of soda
to finish:
1 - 2 litres of sunflower oil, for deep frying your churros
caster sugar to toss over the top
ingredients for chocolate ganache:
400 ml double cream
200g good quality dark chocolate
finely grated zest of an orange
freshly grated nutmeg
(***optional***) small pinch of chilli flakes

method:

1) First make your batter.

2) Using a heavy based saucepan, bring your water to the boil and add the salt and bicarbonate of soda, whisking them quickly to dissolve them throughout your liquid.

3) Turn your heat down to a minimum, and using a wooden spoon or spatula, beat the flour into your water ensuring that no lumps form. When all the flour is incorporated, raise the heat slightly and cook for about 2 minutes, while stirring to ensure that your batter does not catch on your pan.

4) Remove from the stove, and scrape the batter into a bowl which you should cover with cling film, and leave to rest for at least one hour.

5) Meanwhile you can prepare the chocolate. This is effectively a loose ganache. Bring the cream up to scalding point in a small pan, and whisk through the orange zest, nutmeg and if using, chilli flakes.

6) Remove from the heat, and add the chocolate which should either be in callets, drops or pieces, to ensure that it melts quickly and evenly.

7) Whisk gently to amalgamate the chocolate and cream, and set aside for later use. Bear in mind that if you choose to chill this, it will set, and need to be re-warmed before use. So save some washing up, and leave it in the small pan you've made it in.

8) When you are ready to serve, heat your oil for deep frying to approx 170°C. No hotter or they will burn, and not too much cooler or they might fall apart. If you have a fryer with a temperature setting, that's perfect.

9) Put the batter into a (*disposable*) piping bag with a 1 cm star nozzle, and use a small cable tie to secure the top of your piping bag if you have one (*it makes life much easier*).

10) Pipe loops, sticks or coils directly into the hot oil, but don't overcrowd your pan as you want to keep the temperature constant and the churros separate.

11) They will take approx 4 - 5 minutes per batch to prepare.

12) If you're making lots, have a warm oven ready so that you can stack them in there until you have finished frying - although if your house is anything like mine, you will have a queue of hungry ones holding out their plates to catch the freshly fried morsels.

13) Sprinkle your plate with lots of caster sugar, and serve with a small pot of the warm chocolate sauce. Happy dunking!

Should you end up with more dough then you need to cook - get a baking tray which is lined with parchment, and pipe your churros directly onto the parchment.

Place in your freezer, and once frozen solid, remove from the tray and place into a bag for easy storage. You can then cook them directly from frozen, they just take an extra minute or two in the fryer.

A fantastic standby treat.

hazelnut & banana cake

makes a circular 23 cm cake (enough for 8 to 12 portions)

This cake came about because I have been making the traditional Middle Eastern orange and almond cake for many years, but I love banana's and hazelnuts.

ingredients:
6 large eggs
200g caster sugar
500g fresh bananas
500g ground hazelnuts
200g chopped hazelnuts
1 tsp vanilla extract

method:

1) Prepare a 23 cm round cake tin by lining the bottom with baking paper, and lightly oiling the sides.

2) Sprinkle a little ground hazelnut around the sides, so that the oil is covered.

3) To prepare the cake, beat the eggs with the caster sugar and vanilla until pale and fluffy, then fold in the mashed bananas and ground hazelnuts.

4) Pour into your prepared tin, and sprinkle the top with the chopped hazelnuts.

5) Bake at 180°C for between 35 to 45 minutes, until the cake is firm when touched. It will still be slightly soft, but will firm up further as it cools.

6) Serve with whipped cream and caramel sauce for complete decadence.

chocolate & chestnut cake

makes a circular 23cm cake (enough for 8 to 12 portions)

This is an excellent reliable cake, quite dense, almost mousse like, but it truly melts in the mouth.

ingredients:
200g dark chocolate
6 eggs (*separated*)
135g caster sugar
335g chestnut purée
1 ½ tbsp dark rum
to prepare your baking tin:
a little melted butter
cacao powder
to finish:
brute cacao powder

method:

1) Preheat oven to 180°C, and prepare your cake tin.

2) Use a 23cm spring-form round cake tin, and line the base with baking paper. Butter the sides of your pan, and dust lightly with cocoa powder.

3) Melt the chocolate in a double boiler, remove from heat and allow to cool slightly.

4) Meanwhile, whisk together the egg yolks and sugar until pale, and thick enough to hold a ribbon trail.

5) Add the chestnut purée to the yolk mix, and combine, then stir in the melted chocolate and rum.

6) Whisk egg whites until soft peaks form (*do not over whip, or it will be much more difficult to combine into the cake*).

7) Mix one third of the whites into the chestnut mixture, beating well to loosen the mixture and combine the whites thoroughly. Now very gently fold in the remaining egg whites, making sure that you have no specks of white remaining, as these would be unsightly in the finished cake.

8) Spoon into your prepared tin, and bake for 35 mins to 40 mins until risen slightly and firm to the touch.

9) Cool well before dusting with some cocoa powder to finish.

10) Serve with fresh berries.

Middle Eastern orange & almond cake

makes a circular 23cm dense cake.

This is one of the oldest cake recipes I am aware of. It is at least 500 years old, and has been only slightly modified over the years. It's delicious, easy *(now - with the advent of food processors - not so much in the past)*, and can be used as a base model for many other wheat free cakes.

ingredients:
6 eggs
250g ground almonds
250g caster sugar
2 medium oranges or 4 tangerines
50g flaked almonds
prepare your baking tin:
some melted butter
2 tbsp ground almonds
to finish:
150g honey
your reserved orange cooking water

method:

1) Start by preparing your orange pulp. Place the oranges (*or tangerines*) into a small pan, and cover with water. Simmer for 30 minutes to 1 hour (*depending upon the size of the fruit*), until the fruit is soft when pierced with a sharp knife.

2) Remove from the water (*which you should reserve*), and split in half, making sure that you remove any seeds within the fruit, as they would make your cake bitter.

3) Place the oranges into a blender, together with the eggs and blend until smooth.

4) Pour your egg and orange mix into a basin, and add the caster sugar and ground almonds. Stir well, until you have a cohesive mixture.

5) Use a 23 cm springform cake tin, place a sheet of baking paper on the bottom, reattaching the spring.

6) Use some melted butter to brush the sides of the tin, and chill for a few minutes to allow the butter to set.

7) Brush again, to make sure that no parts are missed, and chill once more.

8) Finally, use a couple of tablespoonfuls of ground almonds to dust around the sides of the tin.

9) Fill the tin with your mixture, and sprinkle the top with some flaked almonds.

10) Cover the tin with a baking sheet or some foil, and bake at the centre of a preheated oven set to 175°C for 20 minutes.

11) Remove the cover, and continue to cook for a further 30 minutes, until golden brown and softly set.

12) While the cake is cooking, place the reserved orange cooking water in a small pan with the honey, and gently simmer until only about 200ml of liquid remains.

13) When the cake cooked, before removing it from the tin, pour over the orange and honey syrup, and allow it to soak into the cake.

14) Once cool, remove from the tin carefully *(as the moist cake can be quite fragile)*, and serve with a little whipped cream.

chocolate, cherry & almond cake

makes a circular 23 cm dense cake.

This cake is inspired by the classic Middle Eastern almond and orange cake previously noted, and is a variation which I feel is as delicious (*if not more so for chocolate fans*).

It was devised as a birthday cake for my friend Islay, who loves all things chocolate, and it went down pretty well.

Be warned, it's very rich. Cut your slices smaller than usual.

ingredients:
6 eggs & 4 egg yolks
200g caster sugar
500g ground almonds
100g brute cacao
200g chocolate chips
500g drained weight bottled sour cherries - split into two parts
to prepare your baking tin:
a little melted butter
cacao powder
to finish
50g sugar nibs or flaked almonds
to serve:
200 ml double cream
150g dark chocolate callets
50 ml kirsch

method:

1) Use a 23 cm spring-form round cake tin, and line the base with baking paper. Butter the sides of your pan, and dust lightly with cocoa powder.

2) Blend the 6 eggs, 4 egg yolks, caster sugar and 250g of the drained cherries until smooth.

3) Place the blended mixture into a working bowl, and stir in the ground almonds, cacao, chocolate chips and the remainder of your cherries (*I prefer to halve the remaining cherries, but it is not essential).*

4) When the mixture is well amalgamated, and there are no lumps of almond visible, pour into your prepared 23 cm circular cake tin and scatter either the sugar nibs, or flaked almonds, on the top of the cake.

5) Now bake at 165°C for 1 hour.

6) At this point check the top, your cake should still be quite soft, but not wobble. If necessary, leave for another 10 minutes, then remove from the oven and allow to cool completely before cutting.

7) While the cake is cooling, prepare your pouring sauce.

8) In a small pan, heat your cream to scalding point, then remove from the heat and whisk in the chocolate callets.

9) Whisk until the chocolate has melted into the cream to produce your ganache, then add the kirsch and whisk again.

10) Keep warm until needed. If the sauce does completely cool, it will stiffen up due to the high chocolate content - if you wish, rewarm the sauce gently (*ideally in a bain marie*) before use.

ricotta kannoli

makes lots of shells - they keep well in an airtight tub

These are great, crunchy, totally wonderful. They must however only be filled shortly before serving, as they will otherwise become disappointingly soggy.

This recipe makes a larger quantity of tubes than filling, the filling may be prepared and kept in the fridge for several days in an airtight container, however the pastry tubes may be kept well for several weeks. Making extra tubes means that you will be able to produce a pastry with only a few minutes assembly time.

However, you should note that if you want to make these, it really helps if you have some kannoli tubes, or lengths of thick wooden dowel, to use as formers for the pastry.

ingredients for kannoli pastry:
700g strong flour
500 ml warm white wine (*no more than 43°C*)
30g caster sugar
40g easy blend yeast (*yes 40g - really - not a typo*)
60 ml olive oil
1 tsp ground aniseed
1 beaten egg with water for egg wash
sunflower oil for deep frying
ingredients for filling:
500g well drained ricotta
100g caster sugar
100g chocolate chips
100g chopped glacé cherries
finely grated zest of 2 oranges
to finish:
chocolate splitters
icing sugar

method:

1) Add the wine and ground aniseed to your mixing bowl. Stir in your easy blend yeast and mix in the bread flour until you have a shaggy dough. Leave to rest for 20 minutes, then add the oil, salt and sugar and knead until it forms a smooth dough.

2) Coat the entire dough ball in a light film of oil, and cover with cling film. Leave to rise until it has doubled in volume.

3) Punch the dough down, and split into four equal pieces, working with one at a time.

4) Roll out your dough, it should be around ¼cm in thickness, and cut out circles to suit the size of your former. Take care to oil your former before it's first use - you should aim to over-wrap the former.

5) Use egg wash to seal the join, and deep fry at 170°C in small batches to a golden brown. The pastry should bubble up. Drain well and set aside to cool completely before storing.

6) Pastry scraps may be set aside in an airtight container to relax, then re-rolled once the main dough is finished.

7) To make the filling, mix the drained ricotta with the caster sugar, orange zest, cherries and chocolate chips.

8) Fill your pastries shortly before serving. The easiest way to do this is to use a disposable piping bag with a large plain *(or fluted)* tip. Once filled, sprinkle some chocolate splitters (*or toasted chopped nuts) over the exposed cream filling at the end of your pastry*).

9) Finally, you may dust with icing sugar.

imqaret

makes lots, deep fry some for immediate pleasure, bake the rest for later

Just outside the main city gates of Valetta was the bus terminus, and surrounding the buses were a plethora of stalls selling everything from pastizzi to fresh milk.

However, there was one stall that cannot be ignored - if imqaret are being fried, you can smell them before you leave your bus, and a determined hustle will get you there before the queue becomes too long.

This is my version, it's a little richer than the one you find by the buses, and if you want to make some to keep as a biscuit, it can be baked - but it does taste better fried.

A trade off with the baked version though is that it keeps really well - up to a couple of weeks in an airtight tub, whereas there's no denying, the fried ones are only at their best while warm.

Try them both ways, fry a few for a treat, and bake the bulk of your batch for a healthy snack.

ingredients for pastry:
500g plain flour
100g butter
1 tsp baking powder
1 tsp crushed aniseed
ingredients for filling:
300g chopped pitted dates
300g chopped figs
zest of 3 lemons, 2 oranges and 4 clementines
1 tbsp aniseed
juice of 2 oranges and 4 clementines
2 tsp ground cinnamon
1 tsp ground cloves

method:

1) Combine the flour, baking powder, and aniseed in your food processor bowl. Blitz in the butter until it resembles fine crumbs.

2) Add just sufficient cold water to make a fairly stiff but pliant dough.

3) Knead on your workbench for a minute or so until smooth, then cover with cling film and set aside at room temperature to relax.

4) In a large heavy based pan, combine the citrus juices and zests, chopped figs, dates, and spices.

5) Heat gently, to create a sticky mass, you want to ensure that this is quite a stiff mass as you don't want the filling to leak out of the pastry, so if it seems a little wet just reduce the filling down a bit.

6) Place in the fridge to cool once the mixture is well combined.

7) Divide your dough into two portions, and roll out into a large rectangle. Try to keep the dough even.

8) Cut into long strips, and smear some filling down the centre of each strip.

9) Fold over the dough, and if necessary, use a brush with water to moisten the edges to seal.

10) Press down to create a flat long shape, then cut diamond shapes for the individual pastries.

11) These freeze really well, but don't keep terribly well in the fridge (*they have a tendency to seep sugar syrup*), so either use them reasonably quickly, or freeze them. They can be very successfully cooked from frozen.

12) If frying, cook in hot oil until golden, drain on kitchen paper, and if you wish, dust with some caster sugar to finish. (*Try not to burn your mouth on them - the filling stays really hot*).

13) If you're baking these, preheat the oven to 170°C, and bake for approx. 15 minutes, until golden brown.

14) Cool before storing.

Marti Negri's thyme honey mousse with hazelnut daquoise

makes enough for 8

This recipe is dedicated to Marti Negri (*another very talented glass person).*

Her three ingredient choices were thyme, mint or lamb. I decided to surprise her with a dessert, this is fun to make, and none of my recipe testers have left a scrap on a plate. Always a good sign.

This recipe is designed to also show how individual elements may be combined to give a special result, without being too difficult to make.

I have used Silpat sheets and moulds to make this dessert. They can be expensive and hard to find, but will give you years and years of reliable service, unlike some other silicon moulds that I have had. They are the professional's choice, and if you are serious about desserts, try to get yourself a couple of interlocking sizes if you can.

special equipment:
2 sizes of hemisphere mould (*Silpat if at all possible*)
Silpat sheet (*seek one out if you don't have one*) or silicon baking sheet
to serve (*optional*):
chocolate mint marshmallows *(see recipe in sweet things)*
crumbled daquoise
fresh thyme leaves

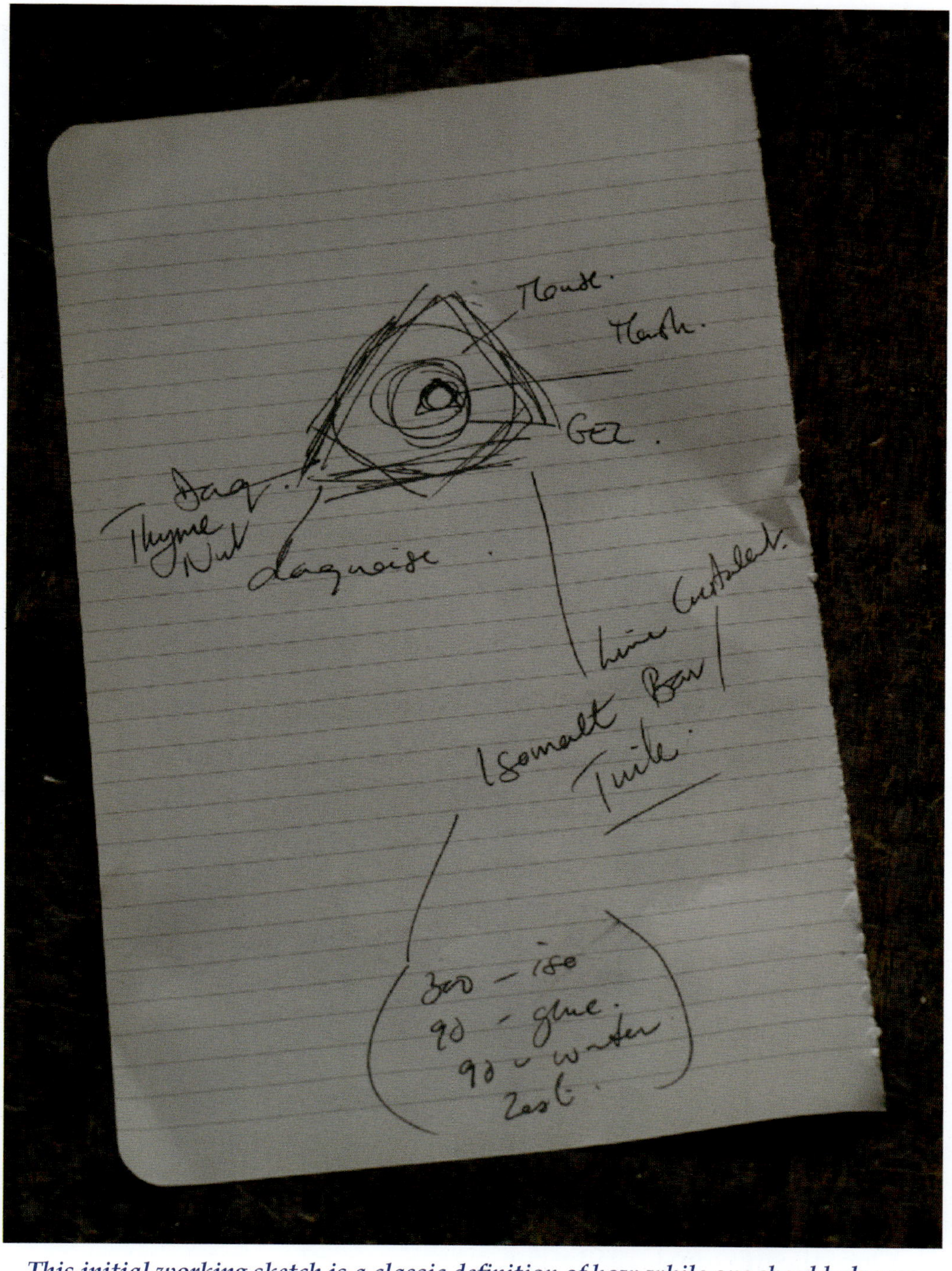

This initial working sketch is a classic definition of how while one should always have a plan, its also good to have a backup plan (or two). Initially, I intended using a triangular mould (but didn't like the way it looked). I was also going to use chopped nuts for texture, but preferred the crumbled daquoise. Finally, I thought of using a tuile, or caramel shard - but wanted something soft instead, hence the marshmallow addition to the recipe.

I am very happy with the final result, but working through the options meant that a future dessert may contain some of those elements instead.

ingredients for the orange gel:
finely grated zest & juice of 4 oranges
equal weight of caster sugar as zest & juice
50ml Curaçao (*or similar, such as Triple Sec*)
100% pectin powder (*slow set)*

method for orange gel:

1) Zest your oranges, and add to a small pan together with their juice.
2) Add an equal amount of caster sugar to the pan, and warm it gently until the sugar is dissolved.
3) Set a jug on your scales, and set them to zero. Pour the warmed mixture into the jug, and add the Curaçao.
4) When working with pectin powder, it is important to use accurate weights. So, check the weight of the ingredients in your jug, and in a separate small dish weigh out your 100% pectin powder, to the ratio of 30g of pectin for every 1 kg of mix.
5) Place the top on your blender, and start it up - open the feeder hole, and while the blender is running at a medium speed, spoon in the pectin powder.
6) Allow the mix to run for approx. 5 minutes, to ensure that the mixture is well sheared in. Pectin powder can be difficult to disperse into a liquid, so allow the mix to run for the full time.
7) Once the mixture is ready, you may pour it into a tray to set, or directly into some moulds if you prefer. (*This makes a very soft set gel, almost a jam rather than a gel, so I freeze it to make it easier to handle).*
8) Set your moulds on a tray, and freeze them until you are ready to assemble your dessert.

the bright orange gel will become opaque once frozen, but will regain it's transparency once it returns to room temperature

ingredients for the hazelnut daquoise:

500g egg whites
500g caster sugar
500g icing sugar
400g ground hazelnuts
100g plain flour

method for daquoise sponge:

1) Whisk the egg whites with the caster sugar until soft peaks are formed

2) Fold in most of the sifted icing sugar *(reserving a little to sprinkle over the top of your sponge)*, together with the flour and ground hazelnuts.

3) Spread out on baking parchment (*or Silpat sheets if you are lucky enough to have some).*

4) Sift your remaining icing sugar over the top of the sponge, and bake at 160°C for 20 to 25 minutes. Do keep a close watch on them from around 18 minutes on, as you don't want to burn the daquoise.

5) Remove from the oven when golden and set with a slight crust, and allow to cool on a wire rack before removing from the baking parchment or Silpat.

6) Once completely cool, use a 100mm cutter to cut out a circle from the daquoise, and then use a 20mm cutter to remove the inner circle from your daquoise, leaving you with a torus (*or doughnut*) shape.

7) Make sure you have 8 shapes ready, then store them in an airtight container until they are needed.

8) Break up the remainder of your sponge, and blitz in a food processor until it becomes chunky crumbs. This will be used to finish your dish, and any remaining crumbs are fantastic on ice cream.

Whisk your egg whites & caster sugar to soft peaks, and make sure that your sifted icing sugar, flour and ground hazelnuts are well mixed

gently fold the dry mixture into your softly whipped egg white, and spread out in a shallow baking tray or silicon mould, to a depth of approx. 1 cm

allow to cool completely before cutting
cut out your outer circles first, then remove the centre carefully

ingredients for the thyme honey mousse:
500ml chilled whipping cream
200ml double cream
350g dark chocolate callets
75g thyme honey *(see extras section)*

method for honey mousse:

1) In a small pan, warm the double cream and honey until the honey is melted in.

2) Add the chocolate callets, and whisk gently to blend the chocolate into your honey and cream mixture.

3) Set aside to cool slightly.

4) Whisk your whipping cream into soft peaks, then add your slightly cooled chocolate and honey mixture.

5) Fold gently into your cream, to create a slightly swirled mixture.

6) Using the larger of your hemisphere moulds, fill to ⅔ depth with the honey mousse mixture.

7) Once your moulds are all partially filled, remove the orange gel hemispheres from your freezer, and place one into the centre of each of the honey mousses.

8) Place the filled hemisphere moulds into your freezer, and leave them there until ready to assemble your dessert. *(approx. 15 minutes before serving is ideal).*

ensure that your cream is only whipped into the softest of peaks, then gently fold in your thyme honey and chocolate mixture to create a swirled soft mousse

partially fill your larger hemisphere moulds with the honey mousse, before removing the frozen gels from their moulds to insert into the centre of your mousses. you will see that the gel defrosts very quickly, so work fast, and get the moulds back into the freezer until 15 minutes before they are due to be served.

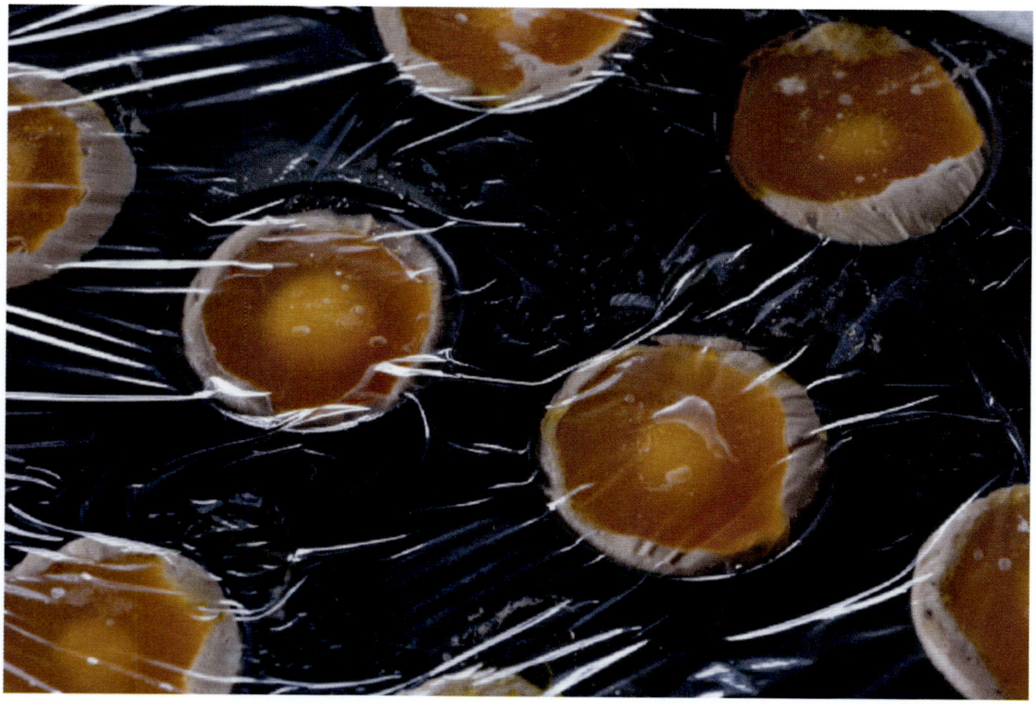

method for assembly:

1) Place a daquoise 'doughnut' onto your serving plate.

2) Working quickly, remove a frozen hemisphere from the freezer and place it on the 'doughnut'. (*The shape means it is unlikely to slip around on your plate once it is assembled*).

3) Remove a second hemisphere, and place it offset on top of the other (*while you could make it a complete sphere - I like the visual of the slipped hemisphere - take your pick, either works well*).

4) Sprinkle over some of the crumbled daquoise, together with some fresh thyme leaves.

5) Add a few chocolate mint marshmallows for additional textural interest.

6) Serve within 10 minutes, as the honey mousse will collapse if left for too long.

position your daquoise base in your individual serving dish
place the 1st hemisphere on the base, at a slight slant, so that it appears to be on the verge of tipping over (but is not)

I rather love the slight 'car crash' element of this plating - by all means, have a smooth sphere with a surprise filling if you wish,
but there's something rather appealing about my approach I think.
If you have some chocolate mint marshmallows, do add them to the plate.

thor cake

makes a 23cm square cake - approx. 12 pieces

This cake is based on an old Yorkshire recipe, but I have modified it quite extensively to give me an extremely useful standby.

It's gluten free, vegan, tastes great and keeps well (*wrapped up*) for a couple of weeks.

A fantastic energy boost to pop in your pocket before a windy walk on the beach (*and trust me, up here, there's no other kind*).

ingredients:
200 ml sunflower oil
100g black treacle
100g honey
250g medium oatmeal
100g rolled oats
250g rice flour
150g demerara sugar
150g chopped candied peel
2 tsp Chinese 5 spice powder (*or powdered ginger if not available)*
1 tsp baking powder
1 tbsp xanthan gum
1 tbsp vanilla extract

method:

1) In a heavy based pot combine the sunflower oil, honey and black treacle, together with the demerara sugar.

2) Stir gently until they are well combined, and the honey and black treacle are fluid.

3) Add the vanilla, baking powder, 5 spice powder and xanthan gum and stir well.

4) Add the rolled oats, oatmeal and rice flour. Stir well (this will take a bit of effort), finally add the chopped peel and give one last mix.

5) Line your square tin with baking paper, and bake in an oven preheated to 165°C for 30 minutes.

6) Leave in the tin on a cooling rack until completely cold, before removing from the tin by grasping the edges of the baking paper and lifting upwards carefully.

7) Even when cold this cake has a tendency to crumble somewhat, so cut carefully with a serrated knife, and I wrap each individual slice in cling film before storing in an airtight tub.

prinjolata - a Maltese celebration cake

makes a very large cake - approx 20 portions

This recipe is dedicated to John McMaster. I didn't originally intend adding this recipe to the book, as it is rather an elaborate confection. However, he pointed out that I'd been making it for over 30 years, so it would be a shame to leave it out.

Also, I think he wanted to have a piece to eat himself. For someone who doesn't have a particularly sweet tooth, that was sufficient reason to change my mind. The fact that I love him madly didn't hurt either.

This is my version of the classic Maltese cake - it differs in some significant ways - I use a Crème Chiboust as part of the filling, rather than the more traditional buttercream and meringue mix - it gives a lighter finish. I also don't particularly like angelica, so I don't use it.

My cakes tend to vary depending upon how quickly they will be eaten, and how they will be displayed. I've taken these on camping trips, and executed the final assembly on a trestle table with blowtorch and candlelight (*yes, I admit it, probably a bit of an exhibitionist*), but they are always crowdpleasers.

Whatever you do, remember to serve it in small portions, it is very rich.

As it is a recipe with several stages, I have broken down the ingredient lists to each element to make it easier to follow. Do make sure that you read through the whole recipe before starting, to ensure that you don't find half-way through that you are missing a vital ingredient. Also, expect it to take a couple of days to complete. On the up side, it does keep extremely well for up to a week in the fridge.

You will note that when it comes to the nuts and chocolate, I don't specify quantities - these are expensive ingredients, use what you can afford, but be generous if you can, as that is the spirit of this cake.

ingredients for sponge:
500g self raising flour
500g eggs
500g caster sugar

method:

1) Pre-heat your oven to 180°C.

2) Whisk your eggs in a stand mixer together with the caster sugar until the mixture is pale and fluffy, and leaves a ribbon trail when the whisk is lifted.

3) Gently fold the self-raising flour into the mixture.

4) Line a large baking tray (*or sheet pan*) with baking paper, and gently smooth out the sponge mix to a depth of approx 2 cm.

5) Sprinkle the top of your mixture with granulated sugar to add a little crunch to the finished sponge.

6) Bake for 15 minutes, then keep a close eye on it, and remove from the oven as soon as it is risen slightly and golden brown. The top should spring back if pressed lightly.

7) Cool on a wire rack, and remove from the baking paper once cold.

8) Cube the sponge cake and allow to air-dry a little, as a slightly dry sponge will soak up more liquid in the next stage.

don't worry if your sponge doesn't look pretty
it's going to be broken into cubes and compressed to within an inch of it's life

just make sure it's properly cooked through, and a pale golden brown

ingredients for Crème Chiboust (*crème pâtissière element*):

500 ml whole milk

1 vanilla pod

8 egg yolks

100g caster sugar

50g plain flour

4 sheets gold leaf gelatine

2 tbsp orange liqueur

ingredients for Crème Chiboust (*Italian meringue element*):

8 egg whites

250g caster sugar

pinch of salt

method

1) Break up the gelatine sheets to fit into a bowl, and cover with cold water. Set aside to bloom while you continue with the crème pâtissière.

2) Slice your vanilla pod into two halves lengthwise, exposing the seeds, and place them into a medium sized pan with your milk.

3) Bring up to scalding point.

4) Meanwhile, beat your egg yolks and caster sugar together until thick and creamy, and fold in your flour until mixed in well.

5) Remove the vanilla pod from your scalded milk, and scrape out any seeds you can with the tip of a knife, and return the seeds to your pan. *(Set the pod aside to rinse and dry, then add it to a pot of sugar for flavouring)*.

6) Add some of the scalded milk to your egg mixture, whisk well, and return the whole mixture to your pan.

7) Gently whisk while continuing to heat, and bring up to boiling point.

8) Cook for a few minutes, until the mixture is thickened, but be sure not to allow any of the mixture to catch at the bottom of the pan, as it would ruin your crème.

9) Once the mixture is thickened, remove it from the heat.

10) Squeeze the maximum amount of moisture from your bloomed gelatine, and add it to your hot crème. The residual heat within your mixture should be sufficient to melt the gelatine.

11) Cover the surface of your mixture with cling film to avoid a skin forming, and set it aside on your counter while you continue with the Italian meringue.

12) In a stand mixer, whisk your egg whites with a pinch of salt until they achieve soft peaks.

13) Meanwhile, in a small heavy based pan melt the sugar with a little water (*just sufficient to wet the sugar*), and once it has melted, bring it up to 121°C.

14) Pour the hot sugar syrup into your egg whites, beating at medium speed, and trying to avoid hitting the whisk with the sugar as this could cause it to solidify on the metal.

15) Once all the sugar is beaten into the egg whites, continue to beat until the meringue is glossy and only slightly warm.

16) At this stage, beat in a few large spoonfuls of the slightly cooled crème pâtissière.

17) Remove your mixing bowl from the stand mixer, and continue to fold in the rest of your crème pâtissière gently. Mix well until fully amalgamated, and either use straight away, or refrigerate until used.

ingredients for interior layers:

Marsala wine
flaked almonds
pistachio nuts
pine nuts
chocolate chips

line your mould with a double layer of cling film before you start

add a dollop of your Crème Chiboust, sprinkle with your filling ingredients and place a layer of sponge over the top

sprinkle the sponge layer with some Marsala wine, add another dollop of Crème Chiboust and repeat, repeat, repeat

finish with a smooth layer of Crème Chiboust
and cover with a couple of layers of cling film

refrigerate overnight at the very least, but ideally for 2 days,
to allow the flavour to mature and the sponge to become completely soaked

you can make this cake in any conical mould, but I have to admit that this
Stark colander is a rather fine beast for the job.
(thank you Simon, for the present long ago)

to finish: (*Italian meringue element*):
8 egg whites
250g caster sugar
pinch of salt
to finish: (*decorative elements*):
pine nuts
pistachio nuts
flaked almonds
chocolate drops
chopped citrus peel
coloured sugar nibs

method:

1) Make your Italian meringue in the same way you did earlier.

2) Whisk the egg whites with a pinch of salt until you achieve soft peaks, meanwhile heat the sugar with a little water to 121°C.

3) Pour the hot syrup into your egg whites while beating at a moderate speed, and keep beating until the meringue is glossy and only a little warm.

4) Take care not to over beat the meringue, as this would cause it to split and appear unsightly when spread on your cake.

5) Demould your cake, and place it on a cakeboard to make it easier to move about.

6) Cover the outside with the Italian meringue, and scatter your decorative elements all over.

7) Using a blowtorch, toast off the meringue to give you golden brown edges to your cake. Try not to set light to the cake, it does happen.

8) When serving, it is usually sliced in horizontal sections from the top down, then sliced into individual portions. Keep them small.

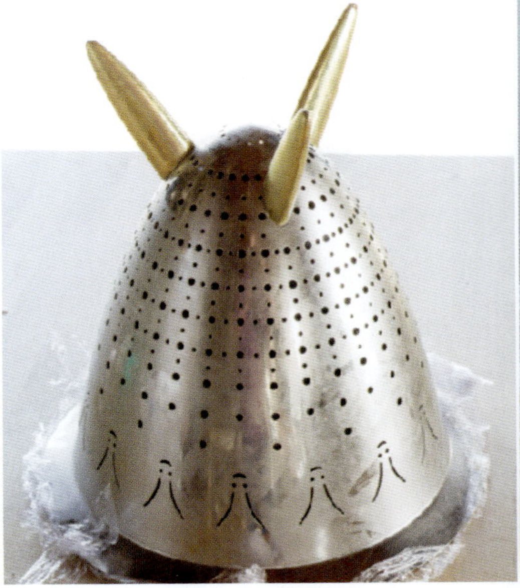

remove the top layer of cling film from your cake, and place a cake board on top
invert your mould, and remove the inner layer of cling film from your cake
start to apply the Italian meringue - try to make sure that the entire cake is covered

biscuits, crackers & oatcakes

Given the choice I'd generally rather have a savoury biscuit than a sweet one, and yet, although most people are happy to make sweet biscuits, they rarely seem to make their own savoury biscuits.

Living in Scotland, oatcakes are pretty much everywhere, but I like something with a little more crunch, and maybe a bit more interest.

I started to make my own oatcakes here in the restaurant, and it turns out that lots of people felt the same. I now make different savoury biscuits every week, there are some consistent favourites, but I pretty much ring the changes with them.

Try out a few recipes, see what you like, and develop your own 'house special'.

Of course, there are also many delicious sweet biscuit recipes - however, I tend to make lower sugar versions of most of them.

Where this is not possible, I just make them a bit smaller. It means that I can indulge myself in a small treat, and anyone who wants more can always have two *(or three)*.

I hope you enjoy this chapter, it's also an ideal way to kick-start children's interest in baking, as the smell of fresh biscuits of any kind is usually divine.

Whaligoe oatcakes

makes approx 175g of crackers

I have developed this as an ideal cracker to serve to my gluten free customers, however, I have to admit it's probably one of my favourites to eat as a snack at pretty much any time.

Although it works really well with cheese, salmon, and pretty much any savoury spread, I like it with just a little bit of butter and some crunchy Maldon salt.

This recipe makes one large oatcake, I usually make several batches but this is a recipe that does not scale particularly well.

The dough needs to be rolled out while still warm as it cracks when cool, so making a large batch is counter productive. You may certainly mix up a larger batch of the dry ingredients, but stick to mixing a smaller amount at a time, to ensure that it does not get cold and crack.

ingredients:
100g oats (*I like to use a mixture of rolled & pinhead*)
50g rice flour
25g crushed sunflower seeds
1 tsp honey
1 tbsp olive oil
¼ tsp fine salt
¼ tsp red pepper flakes
¼ tsp spice mix
1 tsp chopped herbs
hot water to bind.

method:

1) Mix all ingredients other than the water in your working bowl, then add just enough hot water to bind.

2) Lay a sheet of baking parchment on your bench and put the dough mix on the paper.

3) Place another sheet of baking paper on top of the mix, and roll gently until fairly thin. Carefully remove the top parchment - this can be re-used for your next batch.

4) Place the paper and oatcake directly on your oven shelf without a tray. Bake at 160°C until the top is dry, then remove from the oven, peel the backing parchment, flip it over, and return the oatcake to the oven to complete cooking.

5) You should aim for a dry biscuit, which is only very lightly coloured.

6) Allow to cool completely, the oatcake will crisp up as it cools.

7) Break up into random shards & store in an airtight container.

Scottish oatcakes

makes a small batch

Unlike my own version, traditional oatcakes are not usually gluten free, but rely upon the binding properties of wheat flour to hold the oat mixture together.

They also tend to be thicker, and not as crisp.

ingredients:
100g oats
75g wheat flour
1 tbsp sugar
1 tbsp fat (*melted butter, olive oil or lard*)
¼ tsp fine salt
hot water to bind.

method:

1) Place all the ingredients other than the water in your working bowl, and mix together well.

2) Add the water gradually, and only add enough to bind your dough without making it too sticky, but do work quickly as the dough rolls better when warm.

3) Roll out to desired thickness (*usually about ½cm*) and cut rounds or triangles from your dough. If the scraps cool too quickly and you are having difficulty re-rolling them, just pop them in a microwave for a few seconds to re-heat.

4) Bake at 165°C until lightly coloured and starting to firm up.

5) Allow to cool completely, they will crisp up a little as they cool.

6) When cold, store in an airtight container.

parmesan melba toast

This is such a delicious way of using up stale Maltese bread, that I frequently make an extra loaf to ensure that I have some left over.

My son devours this by the tubful, and it's a lot healthier than a bag of crisps.

ingredients:
A leftover portion or loaf of Maltese bread, or Ftira
freshly grated Parmesan cheese
(***optional***) dried red pepper flakes

method:

1) Using a serrated knife, cut very thin (*no more than 2mm*) slices of your bread. It will be impossible to do this with a very fresh loaf, which is why it is ideally made with slightly stale bread.

2) Preheat your oven to 160°C, and lay out your slices on a baking tray. Sprinkle lightly with the parmesan, but keep it a light dusting as you want to end up with slightly toasted speckle, rather than a cheesy lump.

3) If using it, sprinkle over some red pepper flakes, and bake for 10 -15 minutes, checking them frequently towards the end of the cooking time.

4) The pieces should dry out and become a very pale golden at the edges, but should not be over browned. They will curl up and become twisted - that's part of the pleasure of a home made toast.

5) Cool, and store in an airtight tub.

Maltese galletti

This is a very popular biscuit in Malta. It's often served with cheese and pickles, but is equally popular served plain with a cup of tea.

Sold in large plastic bags across the island, pretty much every bakery will make it's own slightly different version.

Here is mine.

ingredients:
100g plain flour
75g semolina flour
1 tsp easy blend yeast
¼ tsp salt
1 tsp crushed toasted fennel seeds
35g melted butter
approx. 50ml warm water.

method:

1) Mix all ingredients to make a pliable but rather dry dough.

2) Work a little at a time, rolling out thinly, cutting into rounds and docking to make a pleasing pattern in the centre if wished.

3) Bake at 200°C until just coloured, they should blister up slightly.

4) Cool completely and store in an airtight tin.

rye & sesame seed crackers

makes approx. 300g of crackers

I love the taste of rye, but when using it in breads it has some challenges. When you're using it in crackers, you can pretty much disregard them, and enjoy the flavour to the full.

ingredients:
200g dark rye flour
50g white sesame seeds
50g black sesame seeds
1 tsp fine salt
½ tsp cracked black pepper
1 tbsp olive oil
1 egg yolk
to finish:
1 egg white, beaten with 2 tbsp of cold water
mixed black & white sesame seeds

method:

1) Mix the dry ingredients until well distributed. Add the olive oil, egg yolk, and sufficient water to make a fairly stiff dough.

2) Roll out thinly on baking parchment, and if necessary add a little oil on your pin to stop the dough from sticking. (*But be aware, due to the pentosans in rye grains, any dough containing rye will always be quite sticky)*

3) Either cut into bars, or bake as one large cracker which you will break later. In either case, brush the surface with your egg white wash, and sprinkle with the remaining sesame seeds.

4) Bake at 160°C, until dry to the touch and lightly browned at the edges.

flaky parmesan biscuits

makes approx. 500g of biscuits

These light flaky biscuits are great served with cheese, but are equally good just as a snack on their own.

They are tender, and melt in the mouth, but are not very crisp - more pastry than cracker, but people seem to love them anyway.

ingredients:
300g plain flour
1 tsp baking powder
150g unsalted butter
75g grated parmesan
1 egg
1 tsp fine salt
1 tsp honey
enough cold milk to bind the dough
to finish:
egg wash
freshly ground salt

method:

1) In the bowl of your food processor, blend the flour, baking powder, parmesan, salt and butter. Stop when you have achieved a fine crumb.

2) In a small bowl, beat the egg, honey and a splash of cold milk.

3) Add to the food processor, and blitz. Add just sufficient additional cold milk to make a fairly stiff dough.

4) Knead on your workbench, and roll out to approx ½cm thickness. I like to use a small fluted cutter to press out my crackers.

5) Place on a lined baking tray, brush with egg wash and grind over some fine salt.

6) Bake at 165°C, until dry to the touch and golden. (*This should take about 15 minutes - if you have multiple trays in your oven, rotate them ½ way through the cooking time).*

7) They will puff up slightly - you can dock them to prevent this if you wish, but I think it's part of their charm.

8) Allow to cool before storing - if they do not crisp up sufficiently once cool, bake for a further few minutes to ensure they are completely cooked through, but bear in mind that they are a tender biscuit rather than a crisp one.

Scottish shortbread

yield - 32 small biscuits (using a 60mm cutter)

These are delicious crumbly tender biscuits.

However, my method is not the traditional way to make these. If you follow a traditional method, you cream the butter first, then mix and chill before shaping. It works, but is a fragile dough which has a high failure rate in terms of broken biscuits.

My method, of blending the butter with your dry ingredients first ensures that you still have a crumbly biscuit, as the gluten in the strong flour does not have a chance to develop, but it is a stronger dough.

I then shape it before chilling and baking. It means you have almost zero wastage in this recipe, (*always good for your profit margin*) and makes delicious biscuits.

I use a small cutter for these shortbreads, as I prefer a smaller biscuit, and also because I sometimes use them in sandwich form for my take on a millionaire shortbread, this variation is listed next.

Do try that too, for absolute decadence in a biscuit.

ingredients:
250g unsalted butter - cut in small cubes
250g strong white flour
125g semolina or rice flour
125g caster sugar
1 tsp vanilla extract
¼ tsp fine salt
to finish:
caster sugar for dusting

method:

These biscuits are ideally made in a food processor, but a stand mixer may also be used successfully.

1) Mix the strong flour, rice flour, icing sugar and salt together, and add them to the bowl of your processor.
2) Blitz until they are well mixed. Add your butter to the mix, together with the tsp of vanilla extract. Now blitz again, until you have a mixture resembling fine breadcrumbs.
3) Working very carefully, add water to your processor while it is running - literally only a few drops at a time - I usually expect to need only 1 or 2 teaspoonfuls of water.
4) As soon as the mixture comes together to form a dough, stop adding water, and mixing.
5) Turn the mixture out onto your work surface, which should be well dusted with rice flour. Knead gently, just enough to bring it together.
6) Roll out to a thickness of ½cm, and ideally using a 60mm fluted cutter, cut out your biscuits.
7) Transfer them to a lined tray, and in between each cut, dip your cutter into more rice flour.
8) Once only scraps remain, bring them together again, and once again roll out to ½cm thickness. Continue to cut until no dough remains.
9) These biscuits will spread a little even when cooked from cold, so do make sure when laying out the tray that you allow some space around each round. You should fill two trays with this mixture.
10) Chill your tray of biscuit dough for at least 1 hour, as they must be baked from cold to avoid them spreading too much as the soft butter melts.

11) Preheat your oven to 160°C, and bake for 12 minutes. The shortbread should remain pale in colour, with a slight golden tinge around the fluted edges.

12) Remove from the oven and leave on the tray for 5 minutes, before transferring each biscuit gently to a cooling rack.

13) When completely cold, toss in caster sugar and store in an airtight tub.

rolling your biscuit dough before it is chilled helps to avoid unsightly cracks
do use plenty of rice flour sprinkled on your workbench to avoid the biscuits sticking

cherish

verb [with object]

1. Protect and care for (someone) lovingly.
   'she needed a man she could cherish'

Reference: Oxford Living Dictionary

Steve Klein's millionaire shortbread sandwich

makes 16 sandwiched pairs

Millionaire shortbread is very popular throughout Scotland, however I usually find it rather disappointing, overly sweet and made with chocolate flavoured toppings rather than real chocolate.

Steve Klein (*another awesome glass person and great man*) had a diverse choice of apple, cinnamon or spinach as his ingredient choices.

I really didn't want to make an apple pie, but thought it would be the ideal opportunity to make a different take on the millionaire sandwich.

Small but perfectly formed, the chocolate you use may be either dark or milk (*although in this instance, unusually, I prefer milk)*, but it must be excellent quality, and tempered well to ensure that the biscuit remains crisp.

I use an authentic South American 'Dulce con Leche', which is a little more complex in flavour than a standard caramel, and only use just enough to stick the pairs together - I want it to be there for the taste and texture, but it shouldn't be the dominant flavour.

Finally, I've used cinnamon to flavour my Maldon salt, giving a surprising twist to the salted caramel, and served it with some freshly caramelised apples sprinkled with a little more cinnamon salt.

This biscuit is all about balance, the crisp and crumbly biscuit, fine layer of chocolate and a sweet (*and salty*) hit of caramel and cinnamon, with the bursting freshness of apple.

They're really very good indeed.

ingredients:
1 batch of Scots shortbread, baked as per my recipe.
150g milk or dark chocolate (*single origin high quality only please*)
1 tbsp Callebaut Mycryo (*cocoa butter*)
100g Duche con Leche
1 tsp ground cinnamon
3 tbsp Maldon salt
to finish:
1 small apple per person - cored and sliced into 8 wedges
caster sugar for caramel

method:

1) Prepare your shortbread biscuits as described in the Scots shortbread recipe, up to the point that you are cooling the shortbread, but don't toss in caster sugar.

2) Once the biscuits are cool, turn over so their underside is facing upwards.

3) Melt your chocolate over a pan of boiling water, and whisking well, ensure that you have good movement in the melted chocolate.

4) Check the temperature, and if you are around 30°C add your tablespoon full of Mycryo, whisk it in, and set the bowl of chocolate on a stable surface. (*You have tempered your chocolate - so easy with Mycryo, it's worth seeking it out*).

5) Mix the salt and ground cinnamon together to make your cinnamon salt component. It should be quite strongly flavoured with the cinnamon to balance the large crystals of Maldon salt.

6) Use a brush to coat each uppermost surface of the biscuits, and allow the chocolate layer to dry. (*Note that as it dries, the colour darkens*). This is normal, don't worry about it.

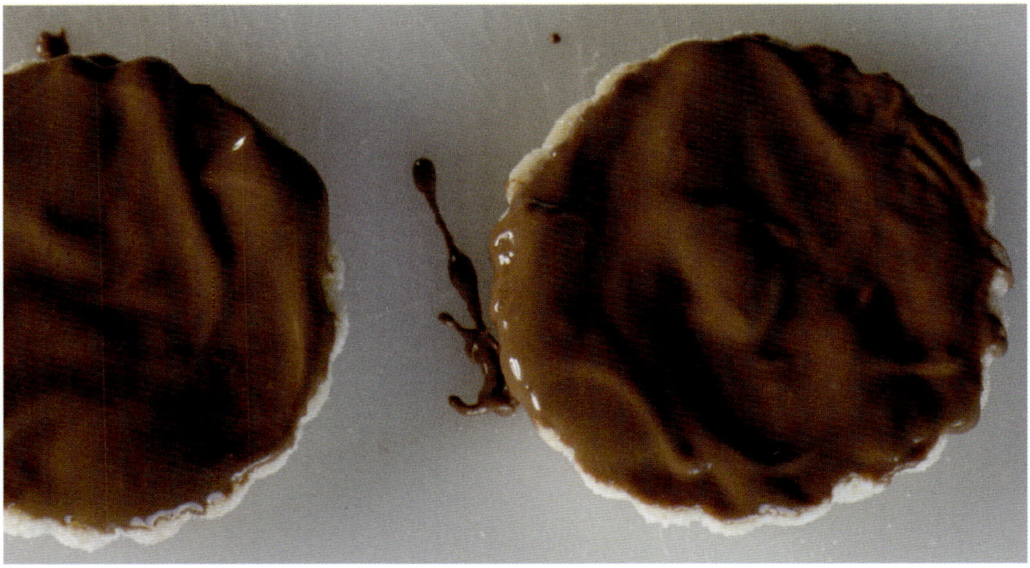

7) Place a small teaspoon full of the dulche con leche onto each biscuit, *(or if you wish to, you may choose to only place it on one of each of the pair)* and then spread out a little to make a fairly thin layer.

8) Sprinkle with a little of your prepared cinnamon salt.

9) Gently press each pair together, and then turn each sandwich in a bowl of caster sugar until lightly coated.

10) Shake off any excess, and store in an airtight tub until needed. These biscuits will keep well for up to a week. *(But they won't).*

11) About 5 minutes before you wish to serve these, you should prepare your apples - don't be tempted to pre-prepare these, as caramel apples have a very short shelf life before they start to weep and become soggy. Make them fresh, eat them fresh.

12) Prepare your apple wedges by coring and slicing each apple into 8 wedges - then using kitchen paper, pat each slice as dry as possible. This will help the caramel to stick to the apple. (*Some people use cornflour for this purpose, but I prefer not to as it does deaden the flavour*).

13) If you have a ridged cast iron pan, now is an ideal time to use it. Otherwise, any heavy based pan will do. Pre-heat it until it is uncomfortable to hold your hand above the surface for more than a few seconds, then add the caster sugar and watch it caramelise.

14) As soon as the sugar starts to turn brown, place the prepared apples into the pan, and press them down on the ridges, ideally you are looking for an occasional scorched bar mark on the apples.

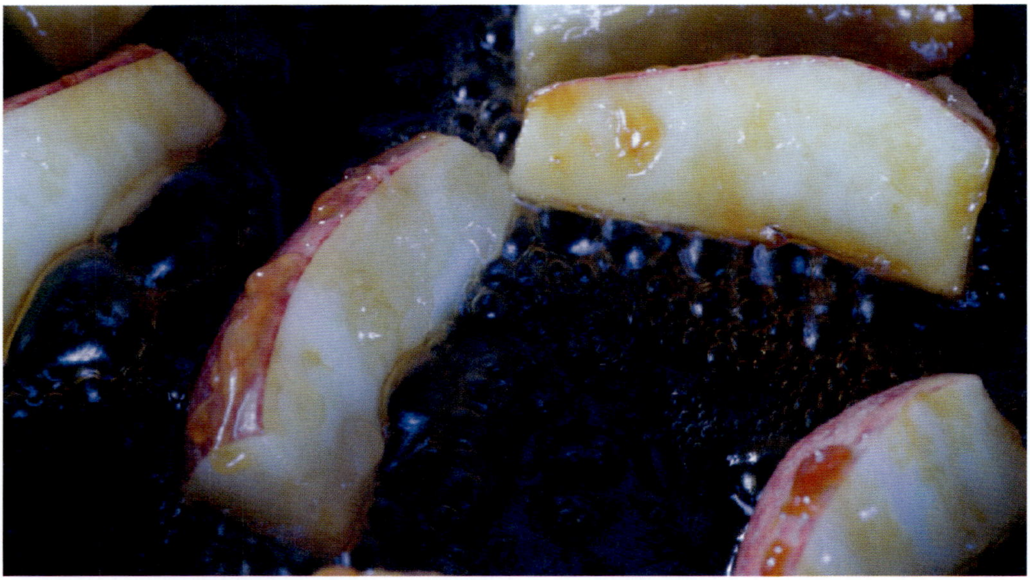

15) Turn the apples in the caramel, and remove them from the pan as soon as the caramel has reached your desired level of colouration. (*Beware of going too dark with this caramel, you are looking for a slight smoke flavour, rather than a bitter hit*).

16) Place the apples on your serving plate, and add a shortbread sandwich *(or two)* to the plate.

17) Sprinkle a little of the cinnamon salt over the caramel apples.

18) Enjoy.

chocolate chip cookies

makes about 36 cookies

This is a recipe I couldn't leave out. My son devours these, as do my customers, they have a great balance of chewy inside with crisp outer edges, and are absolutely packed with chocolate chips.

Do use a good quality chocolate chip (*I use bake-stable Callebaut*), or half the delight of this cookie will be lost.

Note that unlike most biscuits, in this case you should use strong flour and allow the gluten to develop, to ensure that you have a chewy rather than crumbly cookie.

ingredients:
250g unsalted butter
170g light brown sugar
170g granulated sugar
370g strong white flour
1 tsp baking powder
1 tsp fine salt
2 eggs, beaten
1 tsp vanilla extract
340g bake-stable dark chocolate chips
170g chopped cashew nuts

method:

1) Beat together the butter, brown and white sugars, until you have a creamy light mass. Add the beaten eggs and vanilla, and beat again until combined.

2) Mix in the flour, baking powder and salt into your batter, and beat well, to activate the gluten.

3) Add the chopped cashew nuts and chocolate chips, and stir well to distribute them into the dough.

4) Divide the mixture into three equal parts, and roll each into a small log about 30cm long. Chill for at least a couple of hours.

5) Cut each log into 12 equal pieces, and place on lined baking sheets, ensuring that you leave plenty of room between them, and stagger the rows, as they will spread when cooking.

6) Bake at 190°C until just done, about 10 minutes. The cookies should still be a bit soft in the middle, and just slightly brown at the edges.

7) Cool on a wire rack, they will firm up as they cool, but they are utterly delicious while still warm too.

8) When I make these, I usually prepare the three logs, then only cut and bake a single section. Sealed in cling film and wrapped in foil, the remaining cookies sections will keep for up to a week in your fridge, and can be baked quickly if you have guests, giving you fresh cookies to offer. A total treat.

9) They also work well if you cut them into individual cookies, then freeze them on an open tray. Once they are frozen, they can be bagged up in your freezer, and will bake from frozen in 15 minutes.

(I also find that baking these when they are needed stops me from eating them as a 'snack', and keeps them firmly in 'treat' territory where they belong.)

chocolate orange biscotti

makes about 20 - 40 biscotti depending upon the size chosen.

Biscotti are an Italian speciality, and an example of a traditional twice cooked biscuit.

They are made for dunking - into chocolate, coffee or sweet wine. Whatever takes your fancy. This is one situation where you must dunk, as they are otherwise unpleasantly hard to eat.

ingredients:
150g strong white flour
150g ground almonds
50g brute cocoa powder (*unsweetened*)
150g granulated sugar
100g chopped almonds
75g chopped candied orange peel
2 eggs, beaten
finely grated zest of 2 oranges
1 ½ tsp baking powder
½ tsp bicarbonate of soda
½ tsp fine salt

method:

1) Mix together the flour, almonds, cocoa powder, baking powder, bicarbonate of soda and salt. Set aside.

2) In your working bowl beat the eggs, orange zest and sugar, until the mixture is thick and lighter in colour.

3) Add the mixed dry ingredients to your batter, taking care not to over beat. Finally, stir in the candied orange and chopped almonds.

4) Turn the dough out onto an oiled work surface, it will be quite sticky.

5) Knead gently until smooth, then shape into an oval or rectangular loaf (*no more than 3 cm high*). The longer your loaf, the more biscotti it will yield, the wider your loaf, the larger each individual biscotti will be. Take your choice.

6) Bake at 175°C for approx. 30 minutes.

7) The loaf should be firm to the touch.

8) Place on a wire rack and allow to cool completely.

9) Once cool, and using a serrated knife, slice the loaf diagonally into slices 1cm thick. Place the biscotti, cut side down, on trays lined with baking paper.

10) Bake at 175°C for approx. 12 minutes, turning the biscotti over half way through the cooking time. They should be dry, but not over browned.

11) Allow to cool completely before storing.

12) They will keep in an airtight container for several weeks.

Maltese honey rings (qaghaq ta' l-ghasel)

This recipe makes 18 medium honey rings, or 54 small honey bars.

These were originally a Christmas treat but are now eaten throughout the year. I still tend to bake a large batch at Christmas as presents.

These were, as the name implies, originally made with Maltese honey. (*Actually they were made with the super sticky residue which was left over once the more liquid honey was extracted from the combs*). These days, they are usually made with treacle, but I prefer the flavour of a true honey ring.

One year I was making these in a rush before Christmas, and decided to just make bars, rather then circles - I got lots in the oven at once, and actually most people preferred them. While they may not be quite as traditional as the rings, they are easier to cook, store and eat.

Now I tend to make a few rings for nostalgia's sake, and make bars with the rest of the mix.

ingredients for filling:
500g of thyme honey
350g fine semolina
100g dark brown sugar
grated rind of 2 lemons, 2 oranges, and 4 clementines
the mixed citrus juice from your zested fruits made up to 400 ml with additional water if necessary
2 tbsp orange blossom water
3 tbsp cocoa powder
1 tsp cinnamon, 1 tsp cloves, 1tsp nutmeg, ½ tsp ground aniseed
ingredients for pastry:
500g plain flour
50g unsalted butter
1 egg
zest & juice of 1 orange + extra orange juice to bind the pastry

method:

Note: The filling needs to rest in the fridge overnight, so start preparing it the day before you intend baking these. Make the pastry the next day but do allow it to rest for at least 1 hour before filling and baking.

1) Place all the filling ingredients, other then the semolina, in a heavy based pot, and gently bring to the boil, stirring to ensure that the mixture is heated evenly.

2) Lower the heat to a gentle simmer, and in a fine stream, slowly add the semolina. Stir constantly, as you don't want lumps in the mixture.

3) Cook for around 10 minutes, stirring constantly, until the semolina is completely absorbed and has lost it's gritty texture. If it still tastes gritty, then you need to continue cooking for a few minutes more. You should end up with quite a soft mixture - don't worry, it will firm up in the fridge overnight.

4) To make the pastry, beat your egg with the zest and juice of 1 orange and set aside.

5) Rub the fat into your flour until your mixture resembles fine breadcrumbs - this is a very low fat pastry, so it won't take long. The function of the fat in this instance is just to mitigate the hardness of the pastry, and allow it some tenderness - (*don't be tempted to add more, as traditionally much of the appeal is the contrast between the crisp, crunchy pastry and the soft yielding interior*).

6) Now mix your pastry using the egg and orange mix, and use as much additional orange juice as necessary to produce a reasonably soft (*but not sticky*) pastry.

7) Cover in cling film, and rest the pastry for 1 hour at room temperature before using it.

8) Prepare your trays by lining them with baking paper, and dust your work surface generously with semolina. Keep some handy to add more if necessary. Also, prepare a bowl with some water and a pastry brush.

9) Weigh your filling mixture, and divide by 18 - (*should be approx. 75g, but will vary slightly from mix to mix*), once you know what weight of filling should be in each section, you can weigh it out as you go.

10) Do the same for your pastry - (*should be approx. 40g, but will vary depending upon how much liquid was used to bind the pastry*), you will want to keep the bulk of the pastry covered while you work with each individual piece.

11) Roll out your pastry to a rectangle approx. 8cm x 24cm.

12) Take your portion of filling, and place it down the centre of the rectangle, making a 'sausage' shape. Press down the edges to seal. The filling will expand as it cooks, so don't worry it if seems a little small.

13) If you are making rings, form the rectangle into a small ring and press the join firmly, tucking it under. If you are making bars, simply cut each of the filled rectangles into three even pieces (*approx. 8cm long*).

14) Transfer the ring or bars to your prepared tray, and with a very sharp knife, make some slashes in the top and ease these cuts open with your fingers to encourage the filling to expand outwards.

15) Repeat the process, and pre-heat your oven to 180°C while you are working. Once you have completed the preparation, bake for 20 minutes, until the pastry is lightly golden (*don't over bake, as the pastry will become so hard as to be inedible).*

16) Lift carefully from the tray and cool on a rack until completely cold. They will firm up as they cool.

kwarezimal (Maltese lenten almond cakes)

makes about 12 biscuits

These were originally baked during Lent, as they contain no fat or eggs, and were therefore allowed even if you were fasting. Now you can just eat them because they are lovely.

Malta has always been known for its honey, it is after all the basis of the name of the island, originally called Mellite (*sweet honey*) by the ancient Greeks and Romans.

Many Maltese sweets rely heavily upon what used to be a wonderful product, but authentic Malta honey is quite rare now and very expensive.

See the extra's section for a way to bump up the flavour of your honey.

ingredients:
200g blanched almonds
200g plain flour
250g caster sugar
½ tsp cinnamon
grated zest of 1 orange, 1 lemon & 1 tangerine
1 tbsp orange flower water
to finish:
the best honey you can find
chopped pistachio nuts

method:

1) Lightly roast the almonds, and chop coarsely by hand. You want to retain some texture so don't chop too much.
2) Mix with the flour, sugar, cinnamon, citrus zests and orange flower water.
3) Add just enough water to make a stiff dough.
4) Knead lightly until well amalgamated and divide your mixture into 12 portions.
5) Shape each portion of dough into an oval, approx. 1.5cm thick.
6) Place on a tray lined with baking parchment, and bake at 190°C for 15 to 20 minutes.
7) Carefully lift with a spatula, and place on a cooling rack.
8) While still hot, brush with the honey, and sprinkle and press on the chopped pistachio nuts.
9) Allow to cool completely before storing in an airtight container.

ricarelli

makes approx. 24 biscuits

Originating from Siena in Italy, and traditionally given as gifts at Christmas, these wonderful small biscuits are great with a strong coffee, or a small glass of sweet wine.

ingredients:
2 egg whites
250g ground almonds
250g sifted icing sugar
1 tsp baking powder
1 squeeze of lemon juice
grated rind of 1 orange or 1 lemon
seeds scraped from a vanilla pod.
to finish:
approx 100g sifted icing sugar

method:

1) Beat your egg whites until just foaming slightly - you're not trying to increase the volume, just make it easier to mix the biscuit.

2) Add the squeeze of lemon juice, grated orange or lemon rind and vanilla seeds then mix well.

3) Now beat in the sifted icing sugar, baking powder and ground almonds. Once you have a stiff (*albeit sticky*) mix, you're almost done.

4) Cover your bowl, or put it in an airtight tub, and leave in the fridge for at least 2 hours. As if by magic, the mix will have absorbed the excess moisture, and be much easier to handle.

5) Weigh out 25g pieces of the dough and roll them into a small ball in the palm of your hand. Then drop them into the icing sugar and mix them around to ensure they are well covered. When you pick the ball out, squeeze it firmly between thumb and forefinger of both hands, to produce a slightly squashed, indented shape.

6) Place on a baking tray, which has been lined with baking parchment. (*Previously these had to be baked on rice paper, as they are so sticky, but it's not necessary any more - if you love the taste and texture of rice paper, by all means buy some and use it instead*).

7) Bake at 170°C for approx 15 minutes, but do check them after 12. They should have risen slightly, and cracked, with delightful golden edges to the cracks. They will remain soft when warm, so should be gently left on a rack to cool until able to be handled.

8) The biscuits can keep for at least 2 weeks if kept in an airtight tub, but will undoubtedly disappear much sooner when the tub is opened.

Please note: don't discard the icing sugar which you used to coat the shaped biscuits. Sieve it and return to your tub for future use.

coconut kisses

makes approx. 24 biscuits

I often make these at the same time as the ricarelli, as they use up the egg yolks that are otherwise spare.

They can also shaped in the same way, and dusted with icing sugar, so the same bowlful may be used for both.

Once cooked, they are distinctly different and equally tasty.

ingredients:
250g unsweetened desiccated coconut
100g rice flour
250g icing sugar
½ tsp baking powder
1 whole egg & 2 egg yolks
1 tsp vanilla extract
to finish:
additional icing sugar for dusting

method:

1) Beat the egg, egg yolks and vanilla extract together until foamy.

2) Add the coconut, rice flour, baking powder and icing sugar, and beat until a firm (*albeit slightly sticky*) mass.

3) Cover the bowl, and place in the fridge to firm up for at least 1 hour.

4) Weigh out 25g pieces of the dough, and roll into a ball in your palms. (*I find it's easier to roll all the biscuits first, before coating them in icing sugar*).

5) Dip into a bowl of icing sugar, and squeeze with your fingers to give some indentations. (*These will not be as pronounced as the ricarelli, as the dough is softer*).

6) Bake on a lined tray at 170°C for 12 to 15 minutes, until spread slightly, lightly golden brown at the edges, and moderately firm.

7) Cool completely before removing from the tray & storing.

garibaldi biscuits

makes about 16 biscuits.

These are an old fashioned biscuit, but one of my favourites.

You can also cut back on the amount of butter and add more water to the dough to make a lower fat but still very good biscuit.

ingredients:
110g unsalted butter - cubed
110g caster sugar
250g plain flour
75g currants pinch of salt
1 small egg, separated
sufficient milk to bind the dough

method:

1) Put the flour, butter, salt and sugar into the bowl of your food processor, and blitz until worked to fine crumbs.

2) Add the yolk of your egg, and process again. The pastry should have formed into a ball around the blades. If absolutely necessary, you may add a little milk, but only a teaspoonful at a time.

the biscuit dough should be quite soft, but not sticky

3) Roll out your dough on a lightly floured work surface, and sprinkle your currants over half the area.

4) Fold the other half of your dough over the currants, and roll again to a depth of approx ½ cm.

5) Shape into a rectangle, and cut into 16 finger biscuits. (*It helps to use a large chefs knife, as it's easier to cut across the whole dough with a single motion*).

6) Place on a lined baking tray, and bake at 160°C for 10 minutes.

7) Remove from the oven, and brush with the reserved egg white. (*which should have been lightly beaten to make it easier to work with*).

8) Sprinkle with a little granulated sugar, and bake for a further 10 - 15 minutes until lightly golden brown at the edges.

9) Cool completely and store in an airtight jar - or just eat them!

Maltese sesame seed biscuits

makes approx. 20

These biscuits are also extremely popular in Malta.

Nearly every household used to be stocked with a bag or two of these when I was a child, and they are frequently served with a large cup of milky coffee for dunking.

ingredients:
225g plain flour
225g self-raising flour
½ tsp baking powder
250g butter
140g icing sugar
grated zest & juice of an orange
grated zest of a lemon
1 tsp toasted aniseed
1 egg - beaten
to finish:
milk and sesame seeds

method:

1) Put the flour, baking powder, butter and icing sugar in a bowl and mix either by hand, rubbing in, or using a food processor or mixer. Work until the mixture resembles fine breadcrumbs.

2) It is important to do this before adding any moisture, as you do not want to activate the gluten in your flour - rubbing fat into the mix coats the flour and helps to retard the development of gluten. So what is bad in bread terms is great in biscuit terms, as it gives you a tender and crumbly biscuit. (*If you wanted a chewy biscuit, you'd use strong flour and add moisture early*).

3) Mix in the orange and lemon zest, toasted aniseed, eggs and orange juice and form a dough.

4) I like to use an oiled surface for my biscuits, as adding extra flour at this stage could toughen your dough, so using a neutral oil such as sunflower, just lightly rub your work surface - use your hands, as you'll be handling the dough anyway.

5) Portion the dough into 50g pieces. Using your hands, roll the dough into a rope the shape and size of a long pencil, and form a figure of 8, or if you prefer, a circle. Press firmly where the edges meet, and continue until the dough is completely used.

6) Have a large shallow bowl handy, with just enough milk to cover the base, and another which is full of sesame seeds.

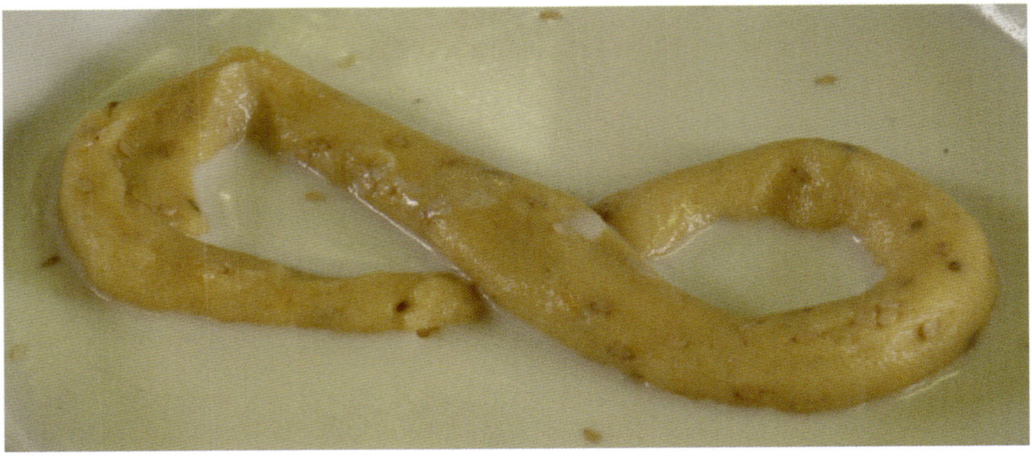

7) Dip the shaped biscuits in the milk, and then the sesame seed, to give a crunchy topping.

8) Place on a baking sheet lined with parchment, and bake in a 200°C oven until golden brown.

9) The biscuits might still be a bit soft after cooking. Its important to let them cool well as this process will make them crunchier. Do not store them while they are still hot, they need to be completely cold before storing in an airtight container.

don't be concerned about uneven biscuits - the variation in thickness will give you a variation in the crunch of your biscuit once it is baked.

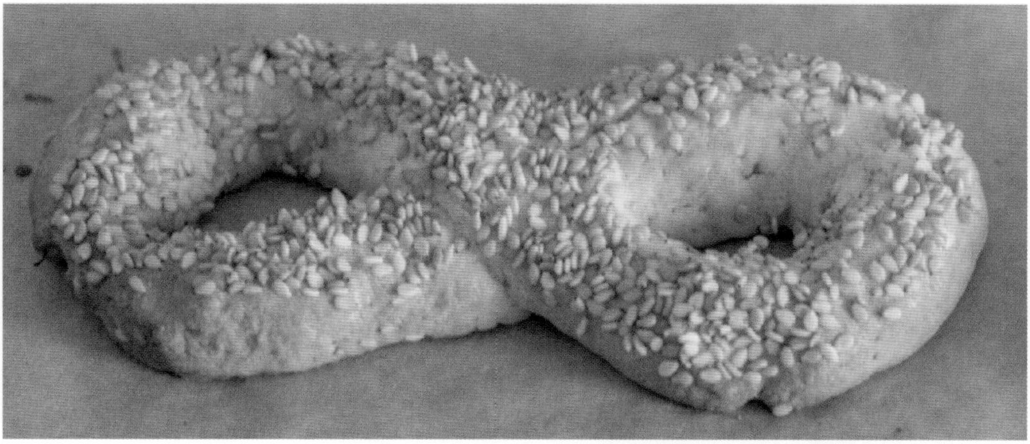

these biscuits are crisp enough to dunk, but tender enough to eat as they are.

my grandmother used to claim that the reason for the shape was to allow you to easily offer half of your biscuit to the person you were sharing a pot of tea with, true or not, sharing a biscuit with a friend can never be a bad thing surely.

small sweet things

Sometimes it's just fun to make them.

Yes, they can contain lots of sugar - but you don't have to eat many, and they make great gifts.

I have also found that some of these work well in desserts, adding a little crunch and colour. The honeycomb in particular is so easy, and so useful, that it's good to have some in the cupboard. (*If you can resist it*).

Caramels, pralines, these all add to your dishes, and it has lately become quite acceptable to use caramel in a savoury rather then just a sweet context - a Miso Chilli Caramel is a taste sensation.

Working with chocolate can be something that strikes fear into the heart of many cooks, but once you understand the basics, it's very rewarding.

You simply need to understand what is going on, and how you can deal with any problems. I hope that my section on working with chocolate will encourage you to give it a try.

When I first started working with chocolate I had some very frustrating experiences, and Ruth Hinks of Cocoablack gave very generously of her time and expertise to help me. It was many years ago, but I've never forgotten her kindness.

Practice makes perfect, don't be disheartened if it doesn't go to plan the first time you try it. Just try again.

tempering chocolate

Tempering chocolate is something that makes a huge difference when working with it. If you have ever used melted chocolate to coat something, and been disappointed with it's dull surface, lack of 'snap' and the fact that it melts on your fingers almost immediately upon being picked up, you've failed to temper your chocolate.

There are several different ways to achieve a properly tempered mix, and I will describe them here for you, but personally I use the Mycryo method. It is easy, quick, and Mycryo is a really useful product generally, so I would recommend that you seek some out and use that.

(I am indebted to Callebaut for their technical information on using their excellent chocolate).

how to melt chocolate:

Chocolate should be melted at a temperature between 40°C and 45°C. A double boiler should be used, to ensure that the chocolate does not come into direct contact with your heat source. This is the ideal temperature for tempering (*pre-crystallisation*) to begin.

what is tempering for:

The purpose of tempering chocolate is to pre-crystallise the cocoa butter in the chocolate, and the process is related to the working temperature of the chocolate used.

During tempering, the cocoa butter in the chocolate changes into a stable crystalline form. It ensures the hardness, shrinking force and gloss of the finished product after it has cooled.

how to temper chocolate:

Firstly, it is important to remember that the working temperature of dark chocolate is usually 32°C, while it is usually 30°C for white chocolate and milk chocolate.

As you can see from this fine distinction, you must have an accurate (*ideally digital*) thermometer for tempering chocolate, and care must be taken if success is to be achieved.

The three factors which are important during tempering are time, temperature and movement.

pre-crystallisation with callets:

Tempering is very easy if you add chocolate which has already been tempered to the melted chocolate, as the process is kick-started by the seeded chocolate. Callebaut callets are useful for this, as they are usually pre-tempered.

By adding some pre-crystallised chocolate to the melted chocolate, the crystallisation seeds itself, and spreads throughout your mix. The required quantity of callets depends upon the temperature of the melted chocolate and the callets.

When the melted chocolate reaches a temperature of approx. 40°C, you can add 15 to 20% callets at ambient temperature (*between 15°C and 20°C)*.

pre-crystallisation in the microwave

It is possible to temper small amounts of chocolate in a microwave. When working with larger quantities there can be a greater tendency for the chocolate to scorch, so this is best used for small quantities only.

Put your chocolate into a plastic or glass bowl, and melt at 800W to 1000W. Take the bowl out of the microwave every 15 to 20 seconds and stir well, to evenly distribute the temperature of the chocolate and ensure that it does not scorch.

Repeat this process until the chocolate has almost all melted, some small pieces of chocolate should still be visible.

Remove from the microwave and stir well, until all the pieces of chocolate have disappeared and a slightly thickened liquid has been obtained. Keep stirring, until the appropriate temperature for your chosen chocolate type has been achieved.

pre-crystallisation with Mycryo (*my preferred option*):

Bring a pan half filled with water to the boil, and turn down to a gentle simmer. Place over a metal or glass bowl which fits snugly, to give you a double boiler.

Add the chocolate to your bowl, and leave until you can see that the chocolate has started to melt, but some definition of the chocolate can still be seen.

Remove from the heat, and stir well. If necessary, return to the heat until all of the chocolate has melted. (*Check the temperature frequently to ensure that you do not go above 45°C which could compromise your chocolate flavour).*

Remove from the heat, and stirring well, add 5% Mycryo cocoa butter to your mix. This will increase the fluidity of your mix slightly, and help to ensure you have a good snap to your temper.

Use when you have achieved your desired temperature.

how to check pre-crystallisation:

To check pre-crystallisation, spread a tiny amount of chocolate on the tip of a knife or on a piece of paper. If the chocolate is properly tempered, it should harden evenly within 3 minutes at an ambient temperature between 18 and 20°C. If it does not, continue tempering.

if the chocolate becomes too thick:

After a time, the tempered chocolate may start to thicken rapidly. This is called over-crystallisation, and is caused by the sudden, rapid swelling of the cocoa butter crystals.

Over-crystallised chocolate has less shine, and it's shrinkage force is weak, making it very difficult to remove from moulds.

To remedy this, raise the temperature of the melted chocolate by adding more melted chocolate to your batch, or reheating your chocolate gently, either in a double boiler or in the microwave.

chocolate truffles

makes lots - but it's not worth making a small amount, they'll go in a flash

This is a basic truffle recipe, for a classic chocolate truffle.

It is coated in a crisp (*tempered chocolate)* shell, and dusted with brute (*unsweetened*) cocoa powder.

This is the overall method - once you have mastered this, try the suggested variations, and use other ganache fillings, before developing your own favourites.

ingredients for ganache center:
450g dark chocolate (*best quality available*)
250 ml double cream
1 tsp good quality vanilla extract
ingredients for chocolate shell:
300g dark or milk chocolate as desired
1 tsp Mycryo
to finish:
unsweetened cocoa powder (*quantity as required*)

method:

1) If you are not using callets, chop the chocolate finely, either by hand or in a food processor.

2) In a small pan bring the cream to the boil, remove from the heat, then add the vanilla extract and wait 20 seconds.

3) Pour the cream over the chopped chocolate, leave for 20 seconds, and then gently stir with a whisk until the mixture is blended.

4) Leave to cool for at least 1 hour, but do not refrigerate. If the truffle mixture is too firm to whip, set over a double boiler to warm the chocolate very slightly, then remove the bowl from the heat and whisk the mixture until smooth and creamy. (*You may skip this step, but your truffle centre will be much denser*).

5) Pipe out or scoop the mixture onto baking paper, keeping each portion fairly small as the truffle mix is very rich. (*I just use a pair of teaspoons to scoop out each centre*). Once this is done, refrigerate to harden for at least 1 hour.

6) When almost ready, prepare the coating - melt the chocolate over a double boiler, and temper - remember, the correct temperature to temper plain chocolate is 31°C/32°C, and for milk chocolate is 29°C/30°C.

7) Holding the truffle centre on a fork, dip the truffles into the coating mixture, and allow the excess to drip off. Give it a little shake to make sure as much as possible is removed.

8) Place the truffle on baking paper to allow the coating to dry. Once the coated truffle is dry, pop it into the dusting powder, and shake it in a sieve to ensure that only the finest coating of cocoa remains.

9) Set aside to harden, and repeat for the remaining truffles.

rum or brandy truffles

prepare in exactly the same way, but fold in 75ml of your chosen spirit before piping the truffle mixture.

cinnamon truffles

add 2-3 cinnamon sticks to the cream, and infuse for about 10 minutes, before removing, re-heating the cream, and proceeding as in the normal recipe.

tea truffles

add ¼ cup of your preferred leaf tea to the cream before boiling, allow to infuse for at least 1 hour, then strain out, and re-heat the cream before using as in the normal recipe.

peppermint truffles

add a few drops of peppermint oil to the chopped chocolate mix before melting in the cream.

'child friendly' truffles

use milk chocolate rather than dark, then roll them in a dusting powder mix of 25% cocoa powder, and 75% icing sugar.

marshmallow truffles

make a marshmallow mix as desired, take truffle mixture at the piping / shaping stage, and pipe onto your base marshmallow mix, topping over with additional marshmallow - allow to set, and cut if necessary.

orange truffles

add the zest of a couple of oranges to the cream, bring up to scalding point, and infuse for about 2 hours. Re-heat the cream, and proceed as in the normal recipe.

blackcurrant ganache

makes quite a lot

This may be used as a soft filling in a chocolate shell, or with the addition of an extra 100g chocolate, allowed to harden overnight and used as a cutting chocolate.

This is a great base for other chocolates, tarts, and makes a totally divine hot chocolate.

ingredients:
150g blackcurrant purée
40g sugar
75g whipping cream
500g dark chocolate (*or 550g for cutting chocolate*)
40g glucose or other invert sugar
25g unsalted butter
(***optional)*** 20g blackcurrant liqueur
to finish as a cut chocolate:
milk or plain tempered chocolate

method:

1) Boil purée and sugar for a few minutes, and bring the cream to scalding point. Add the cream to the purée, mix well, and immediately add to the chopped chocolate.

2) Add the liqueur and invert sugar, and stir until well amalgamated.

3) Now either pipe it into your chocolate shells, or pour into a lined form and allow to chill overnight to harden.

4) If using as a cut chocolate, cut into your desired shapes, and dip into tempered chocolate (*leaving one side un-dipped to allow it to rest on a wire rack*) allow to harden then dip the remaining side and leave to harden once again.

'lava' chocolate ganache

This is a classic filling for cut chocolates, easy to make and delicious.

ingredients:
300g whipping cream
50g glucose or other invert sugar
500g dark chocolate
100g butter
blade mace (*or ground mace*) to taste
grated zest of 2 lemons

method:

1) Bring the cream and mace to the boil - if using blade mace, allow to steep for ½ hour, strain out the mace, and return the infused cream to the boil.

2) Pour the infused boiling cream over your chopped chocolate, and add the invert sugar and grated lemon zest.

3) Leave for 30 seconds, then stir gently to amalgamate the mixture and bring the chocolate ganache together.

4) Allow to cool to approx. 30°C, before adding the soft butter and stirring well to ensure no lumps of butter remain.

5) Pour into a lined tray, and allow to harden overnight. (*Alternatively, you may pour into individual silicon moulds to achieve shapes which you may coat in tempered chocolate once hardened*).

6) You may now cut & coat your ganache as required.

peanut butter & milk chocolate ganache

This is an absolutely delicious filling for a truffle, but very rich.

A little goes a very long way, so when using it, take care to scoop out small portions.

ingredients:
450g peanut butter
115g milk chocolate
55g sugar
2 tsp sea salt
170g softened unsalted butter

method:

1) Melt the chocolate over a double boiler, and meanwhile put the peanut butter, sugar and salt into a food processor. Blend until well mixed, then add the slightly cooled melted chocolate and blend again.

2) Finally, add the soft butter, and blend until a smooth texture is achieved.

3) Place into an airtight tub and refrigerate until firm.

dairy free peanut butter & chocolate ganache

I developed this variation for those intolerant of dairy, who still love chocolate. Using olive oil with chocolate rather than cream works very well, but does give you a softer set to your finished ganache - using Mycryo with this helps to set your product when it is chilled.

The olive oil flavour sings with the dark chocolate, take care to use an olive oil with a full flavour for best effect.

ingredients:
450g peanut butter
150g dark chocolate
55g caster sugar
2 tsp sea salt
25g olive oil (*extra virgin - best you can find*)
125g Mycryo

method:

1) Melt the chocolate over a double boiler, and meanwhile put the peanut butter, sugar and salt into a food processor.

2) Blend until well mixed, then add the slightly cooled melted chocolate and blend again.

3) Finally, add the olive oil and Mycryo, and blend until a smooth texture is achieved.

4) Place into an airtight tub and refrigerate until firm.

5) If you wish to use this in a shaped form - pour directly into your moulds, and either set them in the fridge, or covered with cling film, in the freezer. Then continue to coat as normal.

honeycomb

makes a lot, but somehow, never quite enough

Unlike most commercial honeycomb (*which contain no honey*), this one does. So seek out a well flavoured honey to enhance the flavour of your sweet.

Do be aware however, that if you don't coat it with something it will become sticky and gooey within hours.

Commercial honeycomb is usually coated with a neutral fat for this reason. I prefer to vac pack mine if I'm not chocolate coating it.

However, why on earth wouldn't you chocolate coat it.

ingredients:
375g caster sugar
115g golden syrup
105g honey
125g water
15g bicarbonate of soda
1 tbsp salt
to finish:
milk or dark tempered chocolate

method:

1) Lay silicon paper *(or ideally a Silpat if you have one)* over a large wooden board, or marble slab. This will help to transfer the heat away from your honeycomb, and ensure that it stops cooking quickly and doesn't over brown.

2) Put the sugar, golden syrup, honey and water in a large saucepan and stir over medium heat until the sugar has dissolved.

3) Stop stirring, and bring to the boil - cook until the mixture reaches 145-150ºC.

4) Remove from the heat and add the bicarbonate of soda- whisk immediately to just combine, and pour the foaming mixture onto your prepared mat - it may well continue to expand.

5) Leave to cool, then break up and store in an airtight container, *(or vacuum pack)* if you are not coating it.

6) Otherwise, temper your chocolate following the instructions given.

7) Dip your honeycomb into the chocolate and allow to drain a little, then place on some silicon paper to dry. If necessary, turn and dip the other side. I like to use a couple of different types of chocolate to dip opposing sides of the honeycomb in.

8) Once completely dry, store in an airtight container at room temperature.

almond butter crunch

makes about 1 kg

This is utterly indulgent.

You must use a very heavy based pan for this recipe, ideally it should be a material such as cast iron, which will retain the heat.

If you use a light pan, the mix will not cook properly, and you will scorch the base while the top of your mix is still too cool.

Take the time to heat this slowly and throughly, and you will have an excellent result.

ingredients:
550g granulated sugar
240 ml water
115g glucose
115g salted butter
1 tsp vanilla extract
to finish:
500g tempered milk or plain chocolate
200g finely chopped toasted almonds

method:

1) Prepare a baking tray by oiling it lightly with butter, or use a silicon mat with a raised edge (*as you need to retain the mixture, which is fluid when hot*).

2) Warm the water in your heavy based pan over a low heat, adding the sugar and stirring until dissolved.

3) Add the glucose and bring the mixture to the boil quickly, stirring all the time.

4) Continue to boil and stir until the mixture reaches 143°C (*firm ball stage*), then remove from the heat and add the butter a piece at a time, whisking well between each addition.

5) Once all the butter is incorporated, return to the heat for 1 minute without stirring, then remove from the heat, add the vanilla, and pour into your prepared tin or mat and allow to cool a little.

6) When the crunch is almost cool, turn it out of your silicone mat or tray, and use a large sharp knife to mark it into squares, to make it easier to snap into portions once it is cold.

7) When completely cold, break into the marked pieces, and dip part of each piece first into the tempered chocolate, then into your finely chopped toasted almonds.

8) Allow to set on baking paper, and once firm, store in an airtight container.

9) Try really hard not to eat it all at once.

marshmallows

Home made marshmallows bear little resemblance to the commercial variety (*unless you've got them very wrong indeed*).

They should be light flavourful puffs, in the mouth for a moment, then melting away.

You can add inclusions, fruits, flavours - all sorts of things, but you have to abide by a few important rules. Experiment by all means, but be prepared for the occasional disappointment, as working with egg whites and gelatine both have their own limitations.

working with egg whites:

Always ensure that you never have any grease or oil on your bowl or whisk, or you will not achieve a good volume from your mix.

Try not to use a plastic bowl, as they tend to retain grease.

Use a stainless steel or copper bowl for the best volume of egg white.

Think about fat. Don't use flavours like lemon or orange zest until you have achieved your desired volume, the flavour is carried in fruit oil - if you do use it, be prepared to lose some of your volume. Don't forget, chocolate contains fat too!

Don't use cheap eggs, when the egg white is the star use the best ingredients possible.

Don't use old eggs, they won't achieve a good volume, and the finished product will have a shorter shelf life.

working with gelatine:

I always use leaf gelatine, using powdered gelatine can cause problems with lumps and poor distribution which simply don't happen with leaf. Make life easier for yourself, use the best product for the job.

When working with leaf gelatine, you should always 'bloom' it before use. This just involves soaking it in a cold liquid (*usually water*) for a minimum of 5 minutes. The gelatine will transform from a hard cellophane like product to a soft gel.

If you are not using the soaking liquid in your recipe, then always squeeze it out as well as possible, before melting the gel in your warm liquid.

Don't use raw kiwi fruit, pineapple, papaya or mango in your marshmallows, they all contain an enzyme which will impair the set of your gelatine.

Don't boil the gelatine - although you are adding it to a boiling syrup, by adding it with a quantity of cool liquid you are bringing down the temperature of the mix - therefore it is important that if you substitute the soaking water, your alternative liquid is also cool.

Boiling gelatine for a prolonged time will stop it setting.

vanilla marshmallows

ingredients for basic marshmallow recipe - makes lots

ingredients:

675g sugar

3 free range egg whites

25g glucose

350ml water

14 leaves gold gelatine (30g)

2 tsp vanilla extract

to finish - dusting powder:

50/50 mix of sifted icing sugar and cornflour - mix well and keep in a tub, make a decent quantity as you can re-use this each time you make marshmallows

method:

1) Start by preparing your gelatine. Count out your leaves, and measure out 150ml of cold water, into a working bowl.

2) Cut your gelatine to size, allowing it to soak in your working bowl. Try to ensure that the gelatine is completely covered by the cold water.

3) Set aside to bloom.

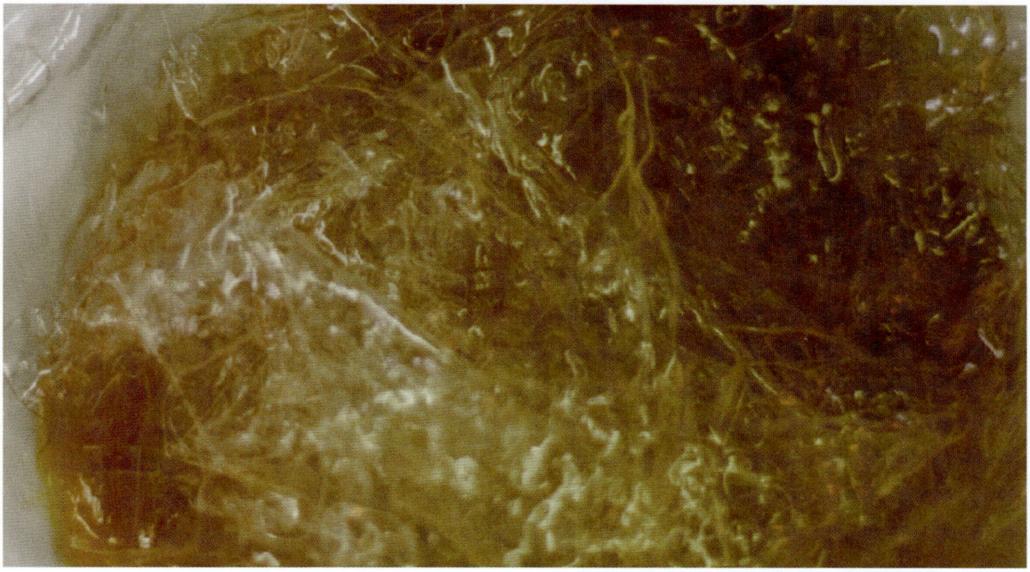

4) Separate your egg whiles, and place them into the bowl of a stand mixer, with a whisk attachment.

5) Place the remaining 200ml of water into a medium sized pan, and add your sugar and glucose.

6) Meanwhile, start to whisk your egg whites until they achieve a soft peak stage. Stop at this point.

7) Bring the pan containing your sugar mixture up to 125°C then remove it from the heat, and stir in the bloomed gelatine, and any liquid remaining in the bowl. Beware, the mixture will foam up - this is why a medium sized pan is specified, rather than a smaller one. Whisk gently until the gelatine mixture is dissolved into the syrup.

8) Start the stand mixer again, and very slowly pour in the hot sugar and gelatine mixture into your egg. Too quickly, and you will have scrambled egg whites - too slowly, and your mixture will start to grain and set. It's practice.

9) Once all the mixture is amalgamated, you may prepare your setting tray for the marshmallow. Choose a reasonably sized tray, but don't worry too much if it seems a little big, as you don't actually have to fill it.

10) Brush it with a little neutral oil (*sunflower is perfect*), then sift over a good layer of the marshmallow dusting powder specified above.

11) Once the marshmallow is fluffy and starting to hold it's shape, you may add any flavouring or colouring, which I prefer to hand fold in to minimise losing volume.

12) Scrape the mixture into your prepared tray, and if you wish, smooth out the top with a spatula. If you are going to make double decker marshmallows (*2 flavours*), then leave the top surface sticky, to allow the 2nd flavour to adhere well. Otherwise, sift more dusting powder over the top and leave to set.

13) You may set the marshmallow either in the fridge (*fairly quickly*), or at room temperature (*take a bit longer*). In either case, when the marshmallow is a little yielding to the touch, but springs back, then it is set.

14) Remove carefully from the tray, and place on a cutting board.

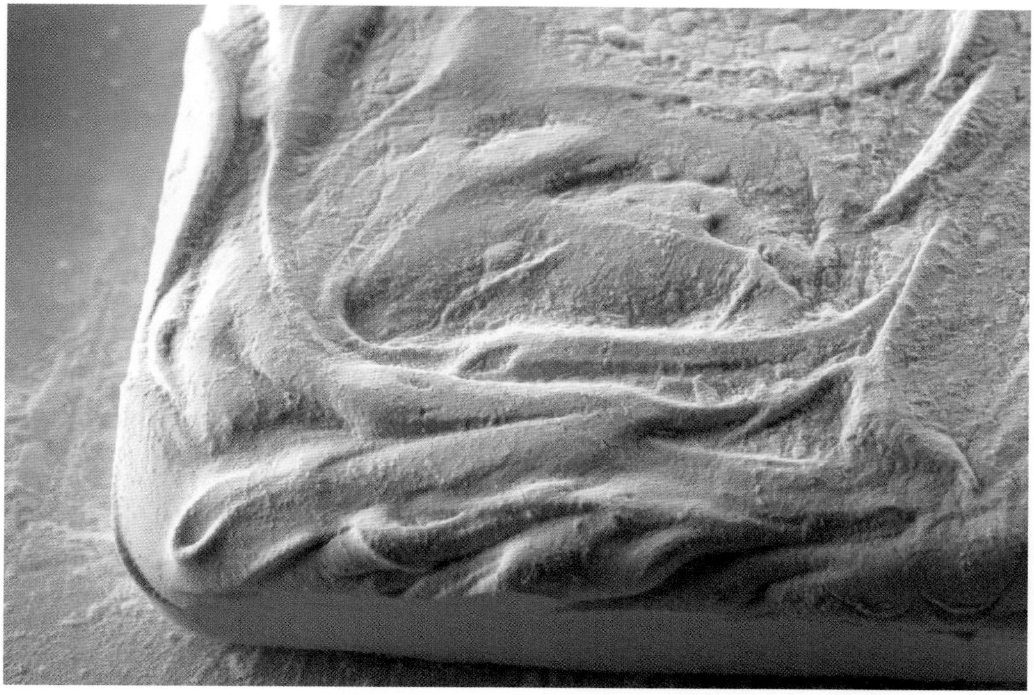

15) Cut your marshmallow mass into strips.

16) Now cut your strips into cubes, and put each cube in your dusting powder. Toss them around, and shake to remove excess powder.

17) Your marshmallows are now ready to serve, or may be placed into an airtight container for storage until required.

gin & lemon marshmallows

The alcohol in the gin impacts the set of this marshmallow slightly, giving a slightly denser product. Folding it in gently at the end of your mix rather than whisking it in will help to mitigate this though.

The flavour makes up for any slight difference in texture.

This is a real (*adult*) crowd pleaser.

ingredients:
1 batch basic marshmallow recipe
100 ml Ophir Gin
finely grated zest of 2 lemons.

method:

1) Follow the basic recipe instructions, but once the gelatine has bloomed in cold water, squeeze out as much moisture as possible.

2) Mix the marshmallow as normal, and once you have achieved the desired volume, fold in the finely grated lemon zest.

3) Finally, add the gin to your mix, and gently fold it in.

4) Allow the marshmallow to set, and portion as normal.

mint choc marshmallows

ingredients:
1 batch basic marshmallow recipe
fresh mint purée to taste (*see extra's section*)
100g brute cocoa powder *(for dusting)*

method:
1) Follow the basic recipe instructions.
2) Mix the marshmallow as normal, and once you have achieved the desired volume, fold in the fresh mint purée.

3) If you wish, instead of using a 50/50 dusting powder mix, you may use some brute cocoa powder instead. It tastes great, but does leave you with fingers to lick!

blackcurrant marshmallows

Marshmallows made with fresh fruit purée tend to be a little more sticky, and have a slightly shorter life, but they are packed with flavour.

ingredients:
1 batch basic marshmallow recipe
150 ml blackcurrant purée
finely grated zest of 1 orange.

method:

1) Follow the basic recipe instructions, but once the gelatine has bloomed in cold water, squeeze out as much moisture as possible, and add the blackcurrant purée to your bowl.

2) Mix the marshmallow as normal, and only once you have achieved the desired volume, fold in the finely grated orange zest.

rose marshmallows

ingredients:
1 batch basic marshmallow recipe
rose water (*or rose oil*) to taste
pink gel food colour

method:

1) Follow the basic recipe instructions, and once you have achieved the desired volume, and the marshmallow is almost cool, add rose flower water to taste.

2) Don't overdo it, you want to achieve a 'Turkish Delight' type of flavour, not soap.

3) Add a little food colour - but only use gel colours, as liquid colours will impact your set.

4) When adding the rose colour, I prefer to only lightly fold it in to give a swirl effect, but you may whisk it in if you want a consistent colour.

blackcurrant 'pâte de fruit'

makes approx. 1 kg of sweets

'Pâte de fruit' are wonderful intense sweets, halfway between a set jam and a firm gel.

Authentic French style recipes use only pectin, to give a yielding set which melts in the mouth.

They only difficulty with using pectin is that if you refrigerate it, it does tend to give a damp product, which can clump together when stored. One way around that is to store it unsugared, and only cut and sugar just before serving, to give a crisp contrast of granular sugar against soft centre. But the best way is to keep it out of the fridge.

Some alternative recipes use gelatine, which works and gives a moderate set, and you can also use gellan, a really useful seaweed based product which will give you a firm set, but for truly authentic 'pâte de fruit' you should use pectin, for a moderately firm but yielding set.

(*Do not be tempted to use liquid pectin instead - it work differently. See the information on pectin use at the end of the book.*)

ingredients

500ml pure blackcurrant juice (*or sieved purée*)
500g caster sugar + additional 50g caster sugar
100g glucose
2 tbsp apple pectin powder
to finish:
granulated sugar

method:

1) Line a tray that will hold 1 litre of product with cling film, and set aside. (*This makes it easier to remove from the tray later*).

2) Combine the blackcurrant juice, 500g sugar and glucose in a large pan (*it will bubble up as it boils*), and bring to a simmer over a medium heat.

3) Whisk well to dissolve the sugar, then as any foam rises to the top skim off with a fine skimmer.

4) Continue to simmer with a low heat for approx 10 minutes, until the liquid is clear.

5) In a moderate sized bowl, mix the remaining 50g caster sugar with the apple pectin (*do this well, as if the pectin is not mixed with the sugar, it will cause lumps in your mix*).

6) Pour half the hot sugar and juice mix into your pectin mixture, and whisk well, to eliminate any lumps.

7) When well mixed, return this mix to the rest of the mixture in your pan, and continue to whisk while you bring the pan back to a simmer.

8) Cook, whisking all the time, until your mixture has thickened and reached a temperature of 105°C.

9) Remove from the heat and immediately scrape into your prepared lined tray, smoothing the top with an offset spatula if necessary.

10) Allow to cool to room temperature for at least 1 hour, or more, until completely set. (*If your room is too warm, you will need to set it in a refrigerator, but in that instance, ensure that you cover the exposed surface with clingfilm, pressing it down onto the surface. This will help to avoid having moisture forming on the cling film and dripping down onto your product.*)

11) Once set, cut into small cubes, and roll in granulated sugar to coat.

12) Store at room temperature in an airtight container.

Do not refrigerate uncovered. If you do, you will cause the gel to weep, and make it so moist that it will clump up as soon as you roll it in sugar, melting the sugar, and giving you a sticky mess.

Be patient. Wait until they set at room temperature. They're worth it.

savour *or* US savor

noun

1. **the quality in a substance that is perceived by the sense of taste or smell**
2. **a specific taste or smell - the savour of lime**
3. **a slight but distinctive quality or trace**
4. **the power to excite interest - the savour of wit has been lost**
5. **archaic - reputation**

verb

6. (*intransitive* ; often followed by *of*) **to possess the taste or smell (of)**
7. (*intransitive* ; often followed by *of*) **to have a suggestion (of)**
8. (transitive) **to give a taste to; season**
9. (transitive) **to taste or smell, especially appreciatively**
10. (transitive) **to relish or enjoy**

Reference: Collins English Dictionary

extras; great tasty bits & pieces

These will help to lift your cooking (*and your spirits*).

As this whole book is effectively all about flavour, layering it into broths, surprising your tastebuds, and adding textures to your dishes, it seems only fair to include some of my standby mixes, which I reach for when tasting and balancing whatever I cook.

I've also included a preliminary bit of information about seaweed.

I am lucky enough to live in a part of the world which has excellent seaweed, readily available in areas of excellent water quality. It's a lot of fun to gather, and even better to use such a wonderful vegetable.

While not all of you will be so lucky, it is easy to buy dried seaweed in many stores, and this may very easily be re-constituted and used, wherever fresh seaweed might be useful.

Finally, there are a few additional recipes that didn't really fit into the other sections, but I wanted to share.

seaweed

While not everyone will have the opportunity to harvest their own fresh seaweed, for those of you who can, here is some basic information to help you on your way.

1) Only ever harvest seaweed from areas where the water is of excellent quality.

2) Never harvest more than you need.

3) Don't worry about type of seaweed too much - there is only one type of seaweed that can poison you, and it grows in extremely deep water, so you won't be wading out to pick some.

4) Do be aware, seaweed has purgative properties. A little is a great flavour boost, but too much will make you rather miserable. Don't bulk out your recipe with seaweed, use it as a flavour or texture enhancement.

5) Adding seaweed to your soup or stew will add both flavour and aid in thickening your broth. You may choose whether to chop the seaweed into small pieces, to retain it in your recipe, or leave it in a large piece, and remove it before serving.

6) Many seaweeds are delicious if deep fried, lightly boiled, or tossed in some flavoured butter.

7) If using kelp, don't use the heavy stem anchor, but instead use the blade.

8) While you may of course dry your seaweed, as has been traditionally done for centuries, I personally have started to cut my seaweed into suitable sizes, and freeze them in individual bags, to be ready to add to my stocks. Much easier, much faster, no mess.

kelp may be boiled, fried or shredded finely and added to a fresh salad

gutweed must be washed well, as it's tubules can contain sand, but is absolutely delicious in soups, or deep fried.

when foraging for seaweed, don't forget the humble limpet - it's a great addition to your fish stock, and the flesh may also be minced and added to dumpling fillings to great effect - tap sharply with a pebble to dislodge from it's mooring, and pop into a lidded pot with fresh seawater until you get it home.

dulse can range in colour from mid brown to deep red, and may be eaten fresh, dried, ground into a powder as an alternative to salt, or deep fried. it is rich in both iron & iodine

one of many types of wrack which are abundant around the coast. this is a fairly coarse seaweed, which I use more for flavour, than as a finished product, as it can be rather fibrous.

samphire

Marsh samphire is a sea vegetable that can be abundant around the coast, growing in tidal flats or marshy shallows. It is crisp and crunchy, and has a distinctive salty pop in your mouth.

Be aware that in some areas this is a protected plant, and you are advised to buy your samphire if you are not sure, rather than pick some which may damage your local ecology.

I add it to salads, or lightly steam it, but sometimes you can have a glut of samphire, and in that case, I love to pickle it.

pickled samphire

makes 1 kilner jar full of pickle

I love to buy samphire if I see it available, but often find that I have some left over at the end of a few days - there's a limit to how much of this I can eat, however much I love it, so a pickle is a good way to go.

This is a very basic pickle, as I don't want to alter the taste of the samphire, just preserve it.

ingredients:
500ml white vinegar
150 caster sugar
500g samphire

method:

1) Clean and spin dry your samphire
2) Sterilise a 1 litre kilner jar, and pack the samphire into it.
3) Bring your vinegar and sugar to the boil.
4) Pour the boiling liquid into your kilner jar, and tap to ensure that no air bubbles are trapped among the samphire.
5) Seal the jar, and leave on the counter until cool.
6) Store for up to 3 months, but use sooner rather than later.

Whaligoe spice mix

This mix adds warmth and spiced complexity, without heat.

It has a particular affinity with tomato, and I use this in my spiced lamb mix, my Maltese tomato sauce, and many other dishes.

Great to keep to one side and dip into.

While you can of course use entirely ground ingredients for this mix, it tastes much better if you toast some whole spices first.

ingredients:
100g coriander seed
100g grated nutmeg
50g cinnamon
50g ground cardamom
25g cloves
25g blade mace

method:

1) Lightly toast the coriander, cloves, blade mace and cinnamon in a dry pan, until their fragrance is released.

2) Allow to cool, then grind to a fine powder.

3) Grate the nutmeg, and mix it in together with the ground cardamon.

4) Mix well, and store in an airtight tub, or if you have one, vacuum pack in small batches.

advieh (Persian spice mix)

you can scale this up to make as much as you need

ingredients:

2 tbsp dried rose petals
2 tbsp ground cinnamon
2 tbsp ground cardamom
1 tbsp ground cumin

method:

1) Mix together, and store any excess in an air tight tub.

Whaligoe pepper mix

I mix up a batch of this every so often - keep it in an airtight tub, and just grind some as you need it, so it's at peak flavour.

ingredients:
100g Tellicherry peppercorns
50g rose bay berries
50g coriander seed
10g fennel seed
20g cumin seed

method:

1) Toast the whole seeds in a dry pan until fragrant.

2) Mix well and store the bulk of your mix in an airtight container.

3) Fill a good grinder with the remainder, and use when seasoning.

lemon salt

makes approx 150g

ingredients:

5 lemons

125g Maldon Salt

method:

1) Using a potato peeler, remove the zest from your lemons, and reserve the lemons for other uses.

2) Dehydrate the lemon zest, either in a dehydrator or in a very low oven, until they are completely dry.

3) Put 75g of the Maldon Salt, and the dehydrated zest in a food processor, and blitz until they resemble a fine powder.

4) Now mix that throughly with the remaining salt, which gives you a pleasing mixture of flavour and texture.

5) Store in an airtight tub.

thyme infused honey

This is a great way of bumping up the flavour of your honey.

ingredients:
approx. 3 jars of clear honey
60g fresh thyme
10g cracked (*not ground*) tellicherry peppercorns

method:

1) Place your jars of honey in a pan of hot water, to allow them to thin and make it easier to scrape all of the honey from the jars.

2) Pour all the honey into a large heavy based pan, together with the fresh thyme and cracked peppercorns.

3) Very gently, bring the honey up to the boil, then switch off the heat and allow it to infuse until cool.

4) Re-warm the honey mixture, again bring it to the boil, and again switch off and allow to infuse until cool.

5) Bring to the boil for a third time, and strain through a muslin cloth to capture all of the debris.

6) Pour back into the original jars, and seal while still hot - label carefully so you know it's been 'bumped'.

7) Use whenever you want to add some more complex honey flavours, rather than just sweetness.

infusing the thyme several times in your honey will intensify the flavour
pack into sterilised jars once drained, and use as desired

buttermilk bath

I often use this when making fried chicken, it's also a great coating for sweet potato strips, as it's a great way of adding another layer of flavour to your ingredient.

Feel free to add whatever additional flavouring ingredients you wish.

ingredients:
1 litre buttermilk (*scale up to make sufficient to submerge your ingredients*)
3 crushed cloves of garlic
4 tsp fine sea salt
1 tsp ground black pepper

method:

1) Combine ingredients, and submerge your chosen ingredients (*poultry works particularly well with this marinade*).

2) Refrigerate for at least 4 hours or overnight.

3) If you are intending to flour and bread your poultry (*or whatever you are using*), you may just shake off the excess from your pieces, and go ahead with the process.

4) If you are not, then rinse off the buttermilk brine, dry your poultry (*or other ingredients*) and continue with your recipe.

citrus & peppercorn dry brine

The differential between a dry rub, and a dry brine, is the presence of salt. This is necessary for it's curing properties, therefore to make a true brine, you must use salt.

Otherwise you are just making a rub. Still nice, but not a brine.

This is excellent used with poultry, but is also useful with some vegetables, if you wish to make a salt cured pickle.

ingredients:
2 tbsp black peppercorns
1 tbsp pink peppercorns
2 tsp white peppercorns
2 tsp coriander seeds
3 bay leaves (*ground in a spice grinder*)
120g Maldon salt
2 tbsp light brown sugar zest from 4 lemons
zest from 2 oranges.

method:

1) In a dry pan, toast the peppercorns until fragrant.

2) Allow to cool for a few minutes, then crush coarsely.

3) Combine the other ingredients, and apply to your poultry.

4) For dry brining, just a few hours of contact will make a difference.

5) Rinse off from your bird before patting dry, and continue with your chosen recipe.

tangy soy dipping sauce

ingredients:

100 ml light soy sauce
2 ½ tbsp rice vinegar
¼ tsp sugar
3 tsp chilli oil
1 tbsp grated ginger
1 tsp crushed garlic

method:

1) Combine all the ingredients except the ginger and garlic, and stir to dissolve the vinegar.

2) Taste, and adjust the flavours to suit your palate.

3) Just before serving, add the grated ginger and crushed garlic, and stir well to combine.

hot chilli & garlic sauce

This chilli & garlic sauce is simplicity itself, but allows you to create a sauce (*or 2 or 3*) with the specific level of heat that you prefer.

ingredients:
300g fresh chillies - your preferred type
10 cloves of garlic
2 tsp salt
2 tbsp honey
2 tbsp white vinegar

method:

1) Place all the ingredients in the bowl of your food processor and blitz to a coarse texture.

2) Taste, and adjust with extra salt, honey or vinegar.

3) Either refrigerate as it is, or if you want a mellower sauce, bring to a simmer at a medium heat and simmer for 5 minutes before allowing to cool.

4) Whichever you prefer, the raw or cooked version, it should last for up to 6 months in a fridge.

spiced chilli vinegar syrup

makes approx. 2 litres.

This is a great addition to many sauces, and makes a superb dressing over a tomato salad. It does make quite a lot, but you will find good homes for it I'm sure, and it keeps for years.

Be sure to make this on a fine day, as you will want to have the windows open - boiling vinegar is quite pungent.

ingredients:
3.5 kg granulated sugar
2.5 litres malt vinegar
550g shallots
50g cinnamon quills
35g habanero chillies
15g star anise
15g juniper berries
20g black peppercorns
10g cloves
3 tbsp salt.

method:

1) Mix all the ingredients together and bring the mixture to the boil in a large pan.

2) Simmer gently for 2 – 4 hours, stirring occasionally, until the quantity of liquid is reduced by half.

3) Strain out the flavouring ingredients & bottle while warm.

spiced lemon vinegar syrup

makes approx. 2 litres.

This works very well drizzled over fried fish.

If you are making the spiced chilli syrup, I suggest making this at the same time

ingredients:
3.5 kg white sugar
2.5 litres malt vinegar
5 whole lemons (*sliced*)
50g blade mace
25g coriander seed
4 tbsp salt.

method:

1) Mix all the ingredients together and bring the mixture to the boil in a large pan.

2) Simmer gently for 2 – 4 hours, stirring occasionally, until the quantity of liquid is reduced by half.

3) Strain out the flavouring ingredients and bottle while warm.

chestnut & chocolate soup (imbuljuta)

makes enough for 12 (or will keep well bottled or frozen as a treat)

This is a very rich winter soup, and when I was a child in Malta it would be served very early Christmas Morning after your return from Midnight Mass, in quite small bowls.

When we lived in London, my nanna used to make this on cold winter days, as a treat for us upon our return from school. The smell as you came in the door was divine.

variation: I sometimes make this as a dessert, rather then a sweet soup. Simply add sufficient dark chocolate callets to your mix in the last 10 minutes of cooking time, to make a thick sauce, and add a splash of Cointreau or dark rum.

Serve with ice cream for a delicious and different dessert.

ingredients:
500g good quality dried chestnuts - soaked overnight
50g brute cacao powder
150g caster sugar - or if you prefer - thyme honey
(**optional**) 500ml red wine, port or marsala
½ tsp ground cloves
½ tsp ground cinnamon or 1 tsp of Whaligoe spice mix
the peel from 4 tangerines
(stripped of their excess pith and finely sliced into shreds)
to finish:
whipped cream

method:

1) Strain the soaking water of your chestnuts into a clean pan. Pick over your soaked dried chestnuts, and if any skins remain, remove them. Any chestnuts which appear discoloured should also be discarded.

2) If using it, add the wine to your pan, then add sufficient water to cover your chestnuts to a depth of 10cm. ***If you are planning on using this as a dessert, that should be sufficient liquid. As a sweet soup, add double that amount of water.***

3) Cook the chestnuts until tender (*to speed this up, you may use a pressure cooker if you have one*). Add the remaining ingredients, and cook for another 30 minutes, stirring frequently.

4) The liquid should be the consistency of single cream, if necessary, cook longer to reduce and thicken the liquid.

5) Serve hot, with a generous dollop of whipped cream.

almond paste

makes approx 900g

This is often used when you want to add a layer of almond to a cake, without the additional sweetness of marzipan.

However, unlike marzipan, it does not have a very long shelf life, so it must be used within a few days.

ingredients:
285g blanched almonds
285g icing sugar
approx 300 ml simple sugar syrup (*see extras section)*

method:

1) Place the almonds in the bowl of a food processor, and blitz until fine.
2) Add the icing sugar, and blitz again until fine and well mixed.
3) Slowly, through the feeder tube while the processor is running, add just sufficient sugar syrup to make a stiff paste. How much you use will depend upon the dryness of the almonds.
4) Once you have achieved a stiff paste, it is ready to use.

marzipan

makes just under 2 kg of marzipan

Unlike the almond paste recipe, marzipan will keep well (*as long as appropriately packaged*) for several weeks (*or even months*).

It is considerably sweeter than the almond paste, but still less sweet than most commercial marzipan. (*Which when you see the amount of sugar involved is a scary fact*).

ingredients:
approx. 900g almond paste (*1 batch of almond paste*)
approx. 900g sifted icing sugar (*equal weight of almond paste*)
120g glucose or invert sugar

method:

1) In a stainless mixing bowl slowly mix the glucose or invert sugar with your almond paste. (*This is hard work by hand, so I usually find a stand mixer is the best tool for the job).*

2) Once this is well combined, slowly add the sifted icing sugar until you achieve a fairly firm but still malleable dough. (*If you mix the paste quickly, you will warm it, and this will mean that extra sugar will be absorbed, making it over sweet*).

3) Wrap your marzipan in plastic, or vacuum pack if possible, and store in a cool place, or the refrigerator.

lemon curd (non-traditional)

This is a cross between a lemon curd and a lemon custard. I prefer it, as I can find a traditional lemon curd a little slimy sometimes. This works brilliantly as a tart filling.

ingredients:
4 unwaxed lemons, zest & juice
200g caster sugar
100g unsalted butter
3 eggs + 3 additional egg yolks

method:

1) Put the eggs, egg yolks and 100g of caster sugar in a mixer, and whisk until thick and creamy.

2) Zest the lemons, and put the zest, juice, cubed butter and remaining sugar into a pan (*make sure there is plenty of room to add the creamed eggs later*).

3) Heat the pan until the butter and sugar are melted, whisking as required. **Do not boil the mixture**.

4) Spoon in the creamed eggs, mixing carefully with each addition, and gently continue to heat (*while whisking*) until the mixture has achieved a temperature of 80°C, and the eggs are clearly stable and cooked.

5) Place into a storage container, and to avoid a skin forming either dust with icing sugar, or place some cling film directly on the surface of the mixture.

6) Will keep in the fridge for up to 2 weeks.

7) Stir well before use.

mint purée

This is a very simple purée, which is a great way to use up any leftover fresh mint. You can keep it in the fridge for a week or so, alternatively, you may freeze it in ice cube bags and use it whatever you need some.

The spirit is there for it's keeping properties - very little is used.

You may replace the spirit with vinegar or sugar, however, it will change the taste of the purée. I prefer to use a little spirit, as it allows you to then use the purée for either sweet or savoury applications.

Adding vinegar tends to limit it's use to mint sauce.

ingredients:
as much mint as you have available
granulated sugar
neutral spirit (*such as vodka*)

method

1) Strip the mint leaves from their stalks, and discard the stalks.

2) Using a mortar and pestle, add the mint leaves to the bowl and sprinkle with some granulated sugar (*this is used to help give you traction, so don't overdo it).*

3) Grind the leaves to a smooth paste, and add just sufficient vodka (*or other spirit*) to give you a loose paste.

4) Scrape out of your mortar, and store in an airtight tub in the fridge, or freeze in ice cube bags for future use.

lemon custard (dairy free)

Mycryo is a fantastic ingredient, it is deodorised granulated pure cocoa butter, has a high melting point, is brilliant for frying food, and also acts as a stabiliser in mixtures where butter is not used, but an element of 'fat' is wanted for it's mouthfeel.

Seek it out, (*find it online*) it's worth having in your store cupboard.

ingredients:
4 unwaxed lemons, zest & juice
200g caster sugar
100g Mycryo
25ml extra virgin olive oil
3 eggs + 3 additional egg yolks

method:

1) Put the eggs, egg yolks and 100g of caster sugar in a mixer, and whisk until thick and creamy.

2) Zest the lemons, and put the zest, juice, olive oil and remaining sugar into a pan (*make sure there is plenty of room to add the creamed eggs later*).

3) Heat the pan until the sugar has melted, whisking as required. **Do not boil the mixture**.

4) Spoon in the creamed eggs, mixing carefully with each addition, and gently continue to heat (*while whisking*) until the mixture has achieved a temperature of 80°C, and the eggs are clearly stable and cooked.

5) Sprinkle in the Mycryo, and whisk well to incorporate it.

6) Place into a storage container, and to avoid a skin forming either dust with icing sugar, or place some cling film directly on the surface of the mixture.

7) Will keep in the fridge for up to 2 weeks.

simple sugar syrup

Simple syrup is very useful, it will keep for ages if made correctly, and can be used to moisten cakes, thicken chocolate and sweeten your drinks.

I've put together a simple lemon version here.

You can of course add your own spices to suit your palate.

Please do use the invert sugar element, as otherwise you will find that the syrup will crystallise within a very short space of time. While it can be quite beautiful to watch, it's a pain to clean out of your bottle.

simple lemon syrup ingredients:
2 litres water
1.5 kg granulated sugar
650g glucose or light corn syrup
peeled zest of 1 lemon

method:

1) Place all ingredients in a heavy based pan, and bring to the boil - simmer for only 1 minute, then allow to cool.

2) Once cool, strain out the lemon peel, and store in an airtight bottle.

Whaligoe spiced sugar syrup

This syrup is based on a traditional gomme syrup.

I've been making variations on this since my early twenties, as I was rather geeky about cocktails then. (*probably still a bit geeky about most things now as it happens*).

It's all about the mouthfeel, it really does make a silky and delicious drink. It also tends to be quite 'slippery', so a light hand is needed when adding it, which means that you add less sugar to your drink.

A good thing all around in my book, (*which this is of course*).

It does need to be started 2 days before you need it though.

ingredients:
1 litre water
1.5 kg granulated sugar
500g glucose
330g pure gum arabic
peeled zest of 1 lemon
2 sticks of cinnamon
10g blade mace
1 tsp black peppercorns
2 cm length of peeled ginger
1 tsp allspice berries
1 whole nutmeg - broken into pieces
½ tsp cloves

method:

1) Place your gum arabic crystals (*or powder*) into an airtight tub, and cover with 330g of water.

2) Stir well, and cover.

3) Set aside for up to 48 hours for the gum arabic to dissolve.

4) Meanwhile, place the remaining 770g of water in a large heavy based pan, and add the glucose and granulated sugar.

5) Gently bring to the simmer, then add the lemon zest, cinnamon, mace, peppercorns, peeled ginger, allspice berries, nutmeg and cloves.

6) Simmer very gently for 25 minutes, then remove from the heat and allow the syrup to cool with the spices still within it.

7) Set the mixture aside, covered, at room temperature until your gum arabic mixture is dissolved. (*This may well take the full 48 hours - if the gum arabic has not all dissolved after 48 hours, you may use it anyway. It will just require a bit more whisking*).

8) Bring the sugar and spice mixture up to a gentle simmer, then strain out all the spices to achieve a clear liquid.

9) Whisk in the gum arabic mixture, and simmer gently for 5 minutes until you have achieved a thick clear syrup. If there is any white foam forming on the top, whisk it in and continue to simmer for a few more minutes. If necessary, you may skim the foam off.

10) Pour into a jar - if made correctly, this should keep for several months - you may refrigerate it if you wish, but it will also keep well at ambient temperatures.

enriched almond orzata

makes approx. 1 litre

All around Malta you will find kiosks on street corners, offering refreshing drinks in the heat of the day.

One of the typical drinks is an almond orzata, with optional additional lemon juice for a less sweet product. This is a drink that is widely available across the island as a concentrate, but not necessarily elsewhere.

While French or Italian orgreat can be found more easily, it has a different flavour profile.

This recipe is inspired by the flavour of the Maltese version, but is richer and more complex. It contains rum for both flavour and preservative properties. Try this recipe out for something different. Makes a great cocktail, teamed with some gomme syrup and a good slug of white rum.

(*if you can get hold of bitter almonds, use them, otherwise, use sweet almonds, and add the optional bitters*)

ingredients:
250g ground almonds
250g granulated sugar
3 x 5cm lengths of cinnamon stick
10 cloves
1 vanilla pod, split
peeled zest of one large lemon
1 tbsp orange flower water
½ tsp salt
400g evaporated milk
600ml water
optional: if using sweet almonds, add a large dash of Angostura Bitters
to finish:
100ml white rum

method:

1) Place all the ingredients other than the rum in a heavy based pan.

2) Bring to the boil, and simmer for 5 minutes, stirring well.

3) Allow to cool, and remove the spices. *(If you have thought ahead and placed the cloves in a mesh bag, well done, I didn't as you can see from the picture - picking out individual cloves is no fun).*

4) Once the mixture is cool, blend well until smooth and whisk in the rum. You may leave out the rum, but the concentrate will have a shorter life. You may add more liquid (*rum or water)* to achieve a thinner consistency if you wish, but remember this is a concentrate and will be diluted further before use.

5) Chill well, and store in the fridge until needed.

6) Use a sparing amount with still or sparkling water for a refreshing drink, or use it as the base for a cocktail.

a bottle of enriched orzata - ready for use…

sazerac

I am indebted to Marshall Hyde (*another great glass person*), for buying me my first sazerac while at a GAS (*Glass Art Society*) conference in Portland, Oregon.

The start of a slippery slope I'm afraid.

This is the official cocktail of New Orleans, and I've only tweaked it a very little bit, as I prefer a curl of orange peel rather than lemon, and a splash of gomme for the luscious mouthfeel.

ingredients:
50ml good rye whiskey
absinthe (*or if not available, use pastis*)
3 dashes Peychaud's bitters
2 dashes Angostura bitters
1 sugar cube (*or a splash of my spiced gomme syrup*)
1 seriously chilled crystal tumbler
curl of orange or lemon zest

method:

1) In a mixing glass, muddle the two bitters and your sugar cube, or splash of gomme syrup if you are using that.

2) Add your rye and fill with ice. Stir well and leave for a moment.

3) Rinse your chilled glass with a little absinthe, and strain in the rye mixture.

4) Garnish with a curl of orange peel (*or lemon peel for purists*).

5) Drink.

some favourite suppliers

Glasstorm - www.glasstorm.com

Nicky and Brodie of Glasstorm were generous enough to supply me with many beautiful vessels to display my food.

If you have a need (*or desire*) for beautiful glassware to enhance your table and your life, you can't do better than them.

Northshore Pottery - www.northshorepottery.co.uk

Jenny at Northshore Pottery also supplied me with great dishes, which added to the appeal of many recipes.

Lumberdecor - www.lumberdecor.co.uk

Jamie made me some lovely walnut spatulas, and rolling pins that are a joy to use - don't underestimate the pleasure in using a rolling pin that is perfect for the job.

Cocoa Black - www.cocoablack.com

Ruth Hinks is a UK World Chocolate Master, and thoroughly good person. She runs excellent chocolate classes and can supply you with Silpat products and Callebaut cooking chocolate. Not to mention her own wonderful hand made chocolates.

Karen Davies Glass - www.karendaviesglass.com

Some of my glass pieces have crept into the background - or foreground of some of the photographs in this book. Take a look to see a parallel obsession to food.

John McMaster - www.johnmcmaster.com

My favourite photographer (*conveniently*) based in Scotland.

indices

'GF' = Gluten Free, 'Veg' = Vegetarian, 'Vegan' = Vegan
'x' = recipe qualifies as is, or 'xx' = recipe could qualify with minimal changes

small plates section	page:	GF	veg	vegan
baba ganoush (aubergine purée)	108	x	x	xx
barley & grape salad	112		x	x
beef khoresh	184	x		
black olive tapenade	103	x	x	x
braised octopus in red wine	158	x		
caramelised padron chillies	130	x	x	x
cauliflower 'couscous'	116	x	x	x
charred broccoli	128	x	x	x
chicken (or rabbit) stew	174	x		
clementine scallop ceviche	146	x		
coconut & chilli potato cakes	118	x	x	x
crispy pork belly	188	x		
dried Maltese cheese (ġbejniet moxxa)	96	x	x	
dukkah or duqua	106	x	x	x
fresh Maltese cheese (ġbejniet fresca)	92	x	x	
fried chicken wings	176	x		
giardiniera salad (pickled vegetables)	110	x	x	x
Glasstorm's seafood platter	150			
green olive tapenade	102	x	x	x
grilled aubergine with ginger & honey	126	x	x	xx
haggis stuffed mushrooms with whisky sauce	180	xx		

sauces section	page:	GF	veg	vegan
rich tomato sauce	328	x	x	x
salmon roe & fruity tomato sauce	340	xx		
wild garlic sauce	336	x	x	x

pastry section	page:	GF	veg	vegan
feta pastries with honey	357			
flan pastry	351		x	
Maltese lampuki pie	370			
Maltese pastizzi	358		x	
pâte sablée	352		x	
pea filling for pastizzi	360		x	x
potato & red onion samosa filling	355		x	
rich short pastry	348		x	
ricotta qassatat	356		x	
rough puff pastry	349		x	
samosa pastry	354		x	
sour cream pastry	350		x	

sweet things section	page:	GF	veg	vegan
banana cake (from the Maldives)	388		x	
buttermilk panna cotta	386	x		
cardamom meringue	377	x	x	
chocolate & chestnut cake	394	x	x	
chocolate chip, walnut & orange meringue	377	x	x	

sweet things section	page:	GF	veg	vegan
chocolate fondant	380	xx	x	
chocolate meringue	377	x	x	
chocolate, cherry & almond cake	398	x	x	
churros with chocolate	390		x	
glazed egg custard or crème brûlée	384	x	x	
hazelnut & banana cake	393	x	x	
imqaret	404		x	
Marti Negri's thyme honey mousse with hazelnut daquoise	408		x	
meringues	374	x	x	
Middle Eastern orange & almond cake	396	x	x	
nutty noodle meringue	378		x	
prinjolata - a Maltese celebration cake	424		x	
raspberry meringue	377	x	x	
ricotta kannoli	400		x	
rose meringue	377	x	x	
salted honeycomb meringue	377	x	x	
thor cake	422	x	x	x
vanilla meringue	378	x	x	

biscuits, crackers & oatcakes section	page:	GF	veg	vegan
chocolate chip cookies	456		x	
chocolate orange biscotti	458	xx	x	
coconut kisses	468	x	x	
flaky parmesan biscuits	444		x	
garibaldi biscuits	470		x	
Whaligoe oatcakes	438	x	x	x
kwarezimal (Maltese lenten almond cakes)	464		x	x
Maltese galletti	442		x	x
Maltese honey rings (qaghaq ta' l-ghasel)	460		x	
Maltese sesame seed biscuits	474		x	
parmesan melba toast	441		x	
ricarelli	466	x	x	
rye & sesame seed crackers	443		x	x
Scottish oatcakes	440		x	x
Scottish shortbread	446		x	
Steve Klein's millionaire shortbread sandwich	450		x	

small sweet things section	page:	GF	veg	vegan
almond butter crunch	494	x	x	
blackcurrant 'pâte de fruit'	510	x	x	x
blackcurrant ganache	488	x	x	
blackcurrant marshmallows	508	x		
child friendly truffles	487	x	x	
chocolate truffles	486	x	x	
cinnamon truffles	487	x	x	
dairy free peanut butter & chocolate ganache	491	x	x	x
gin & lemon marshmallows	505	x		
honeycomb	492	x	x	x
lava chocolate ganache	489	x	x	
marshmallow truffles	487	x		
marshmallows	496	x		
mint choc marshmallows	506	x		
orange truffles	487	x	x	
peanut butter & milk chocolate ganache	490	x	x	
peppermint truffles	487	x	x	
rose marshmallows	509	x		
rum or brandy truffles	487	x	x	
tea truffles	487	x	x	
tempering chocolate	480	x	x	x
vanilla marshmallows	498	x		

extras section	page:	GF	veg	vegan
advieh (Persian spice mix)	522	x	x	x
almond paste	536	x	x	x
buttermilk bath	528	x	x	
chestnut & chocolate soup (imbuljuta)	534	x	x	x
citrus & peppercorn dry brine	529	x	x	x
enriched almond orzata	546	x	x	
hot chilli & garlic sauce	531	x	x	x
lemon curd (non-traditional)	538	x	x	
lemon custard (dairy free)	540	x	x	x
lemon salt	524	x	x	x
marzipan	537	x	x	x
mint purée	539	x	x	x
pickled samphire	520	x	x	x
sazerac	565	x	x	x
seaweed	516	x	x	x
simple sugar syrup	542	x	x	x
spiced chilli vinegar syrup	532	x	x	x
spiced lemon vinegar syrup	533	x	x	x
tangy soy dipping sauce	530	x	x	x
thyme infused honey	526	x	x	
Whaligoe pepper mix	523	x	x	x
Whaligoe spice mix	521	x	x	x
Whaligoe spiced sugar syrup	544	x	x	x